Separation Anxiety and the Dread of Abandonment in Adult Males

SEPARATION ANXIETY
AND THE
DREAD OF ABANDONMENT
IN ADULT MALES

GWENDOLYN STEVENS
AND
SHELDON GARDNER

Westport, Connecticut
London

Library of Congress Cataloging-in-Publication Data

Stevens, Gwendolyn.
    Separation anxiety and the dread of abandonment in adult males /
Gwendolyn Stevens and Sheldon Gardner.
        p.   cm.
    Contents: Includes bibliographical references and index.
    ISBN 0–275–94609–6 (alk. paper)
    1. Men—Psychology. 2. Loss (Psychology) 3. Separation anxiety.
4. Divorced men—Psychology. 5. Divorce—Psychological aspects.
I. Gardner, Sheldon. II. Title.
BF692.5.S77   1994
616.8′223—dc20   93–37884

British Library Cataloguing in Publication Data is available.

Library of Congress Catalog Card Number: 93–37884
ISBN: 0–275–94609–6

First published in 1994

Praeger Publishers, 88 Post Road West, Westport, CT 06881
An imprint of Greenwood Publishing Group, Inc.

Printed in the United States of America

∞™

The paper used in this book complies with the
Permanent Paper Standard issued by the National
Information Standards Organization (Z39.48–1984).

10 9 8 7 6 5 4 3 2 1

The god to whom little boys say their prayers
has a face very much like their mother's.

—Sir James M. Barrie

Contents

Preface

Although books dealing with the psychology of men have recently become popular, this work actually was conceived more than twenty years ago, when the senior author divorced her husband and noticed his apparent psychological deterioration. Subsequently, other return-to-college women who have divorced their husbands have reported similar destructive behaviors.

The financial problems and feelings of loss suffered by divorcing women have long been obvious, and we women have therefore elicited sympathy and received welcome support from our sisters. But hardly anyone seemed to notice or care that divorcing men were exhibiting even worse distress. The men we were divorcing were frequently depressed, hostile, abusive, and unable to function competently, or suffering from various combinations of these. Mental health workers acknowledged the plight of men who were forced into a separation from their wife or significant other, but, until recently, finding literature on male psychology in general and the vulnerabilities of males in particular was almost impossible.

We know that some feminists argue against discussing any male trauma because they hold males responsible for general discrimination and harassment of women. However, we believe that while particular males are often real threats to the lives of women and that the patriarchal culture discriminates against women, men are every bit as much victims of our history as *homo sapiens* and our Euro-centered culture.

The new trend to understand male psychology is both necessary and long overdue. The decision that Sheldon Gardner and I made to limit the focus of this book to gender differences in separation/attachment phenomena reflects the original intention to explain why men do not usually cope well when "abandonment" is imminent. We found that most publishers were not yet ready to accept a sympathetic, albeit well-documented, treatment of American males—one which emphasized that they are victims of their biology, their maladaptive social expectations, and their success in dominating and intimidating women. Good evidence of this lack of sympathy came from the numerous editors who rejected the prospectus for this work merely because it suggested that men suffer trauma in divorce.

We are especially grateful, therefore, for the courage and foresight of our editor, Paul Macirowski, who didn't even hesitate in suggesting that the work go forward. Others we would like to thank include the numerous individuals with whom we have discussed the issues at presentations to both professional organizations and civic groups. We have appreciated their candid comments about our theory.

We would also like to thank Patricia Daragan, Director of the U.S. Coast Guard Academy (USCGA) Library, and her staff, particularly Jean Hayek, the interlibrary loan technician, who were always willing to find the "one more" source for this work. Our thanks also go to Lieutenant-Commander Anne Flammang, Associate Professor of English and Director of the Cadet Writing and Reading Center at the U.S. Coast Guard Academy, for reading an early version of the work; and Frank Tito, Instructional Support Facilitator, USCGA, for his help in constructing the tables.

Finally, we would like to thank Jay Williams and Nina Neimark, Production Editors at Praeger, and the copy editor, proofreader, typesetters, and all other individuals who were involved in the production of this work for their thoughtful attention to detail.

Separation Anxiety and the Dread of Abandonment in Adult Males

1

Babes and Pashas

You experience the masculine dream, as seductive as it is absurd, of being coddled by women like a baby and at the same time commanding them like a pasha. (cited in Miller, 1981, p. 89)

Men are socially conditioned simultaneously to deny their innate attachment needs and to assert their domination over the women to whom they are intimately related. Individualism and power are highly valued in the United States. They are characteristics bestowed upon males as part of their birthright and imposed upon them as goals for psychological development. Real men do not eat quiche. The competent man needs help from no one. The successful man dominates. The powerful man is a loner.

Selection for membership in the preferred gender is based on "biological" factors, not merely anatomical or on the possession of a penis. The biological definition of sex includes muscle mass, aggression, and activity level. Those biological differences that underlie socially determined gender roles are to a degree congruent with the dominant pasha image, but the social definitions, values, and goals ignore the crucial fact that females, especially young females, are constitutionally superior to males and, during the formative years, mature faster than males.

Much of this book deals with gender differences that most researchers have chosen to minimize, as does society in general. The greater muscle mass, aggression, and dominance of young male infants and boys, which would indeed qualify many males for the pasha role in the realization of the "masculine dream," are attributes that researchers usually notice. These physical attributes are, however, of limited utility in enhancing attachment to a mothering person and thus obtaining a security base that encourages curiosity and autonomy-striving. The constitutional weakness of males makes them more helpless as infants (and thus more in need of "coddling" by women), and their maturational delays, particularly in cognitive development, impede their development of an adequate self-identity and, paradoxically, their individuation and the development of most idealized "masculine" traits.

AUTONOMY AND ATTACHMENT

> The shock of realization of his separateness, of the alienness of the world, comes to every child. Although the experience of isolation brought about by the dissolution of the original unity is the primary source of anxiety, it cannot be considered pathogenic in itself. In fact, this isolation represents an opportunity to become human; it requires the child to re-relate himself to the world by experiencing the two basic human trends, mastery and love. (Angyal, 1965, p. 74)

Separation from security and nurturance providers is inevitable and necessary for the establishment of a mature personality, as is the ability to recover from the feeling of loss that is associated with autonomy-striving. As we shall see, there is reason to believe that affirmation of separateness, in a process Margaret Mahler (1968) called "individuation," may be innate and imperative of both genders, although individuation may be easier and earlier for females (Lewis, Brooks-Gunn, & Jaskir, 1985; Olesker, 1990). There is reason to believe that the distress and anxiety that are consequences of loss and isolation are also innate (Bowlby, 1973).

In direct contradiction to the constitutional differences between the sexes and the earlier development of cognitive skills, social forces—as reflected, for example, in traditional child-rearing practices—have defined autonomy as "masculine" (Spieler, 1986). This focus—of making males independent and self-sufficient—is so prevalent and powerful that boys who are conscious of their dependency needs suffer low self-esteem (Kagan & Moss, 1962). The distinctions inherent in gender roles, although reflecting the relatively greater aggressiveness of male infants (Freud, 1925), are "unnatural" in the sense that they (1) ignore or distort the more important, enduring sex differences in constitution and maturity; and (2) create impediments to individuation by making innate homonomy needs problematic for men.

There is considerable evidence that a child does not develop his or her self-identity adequately, and will not complete the individuation process, when emotional support is lacking or there is personality incompatibility between mother and child. Separation anxiety, or what has been described as a distress reaction, may be the result of early experiences of separation from an attachment object,[1] for example, and later repetitions of separation and loss often interfere with resolution of independence-dependence conflicts in sensitized individuals—more often males. The theory of the Umbilicus Complex, which will be described later in this book, suggests that socialization practices and androcentric values not only make individuation differentially more problematic for all males, but also, for some males, create a susceptibility to breakdown in the face of what they perceive to be anticipated abandonment. Because the behavior of such men sometimes includes violent acts toward women, the extreme cases are dramatic and are sensationalized in the press.

THEORETICAL ASSUMPTIONS OF THE UMBILICUS COMPLEX

Fairly early in the history of psychoanalysis, Carl Jung contributed the idea that certain unconscious motives and memories of infantile experiences are integrated into a focused, complicated theme, which he named a "complex." Freud adopted this idea in the formulation of his most famous concept, the Oedipal Complex. Years before the emergence of "sexual" feelings toward an opposite-sexed parent, however, infantile bonding and attachment experiences and (probably unconscious) need states become focused in a developmental theme we call the *Umbilicus Complex*. The separation and attachment theme might include conflicted drives, trauma, molding influences on self-identity, and anxiety elicitation. When a major component of the Umbilicus Complex is an exaggerated, irrational fear that the absent parent will never return and that the loss of nurturance will be permanent, the individual suffers a *dread of abandonment*. When the most prominent, persistent anxiety that complicates the Umbilicus Complex emerges later, after object constancy has been established, the relatively less severe signaling, rather than crippling, affect that accompanies nurturant loss is called *separation anxiety*.

The theoretical assumptions that underlie the Umbilicus Complex are as follows:

1. Psychobiological mechanisms underlie the trend toward autonomy of all humans (perhaps all animals) as well as that of homonomy—the need to obtain security by attachment to important persons.

2. Beginning with the earliest differentiation from mother, individuation is a life-long process, one which becomes a focus of personality development at various critical periods of life.

3. Social-experiential factors generally distort the smooth functioning of biological processes. In the specific case of separation/individuation, child-rearing practices that influence mothers to (a) push away a two-year-old boy and (b) encourage exploration and competence outside the home while (c) rejecting the boy's need to remain attached to mother will disturb the autonomy-homonomy balance.

4. A person is vulnerable to later emotional stress when there is a disturbance (objective or psychologically "real") of the mother-child relationship within the first two years of life. This disturbance results in the person's developing a morbid dread of abandonment.

5. Personality characteristics of children are as likely to produce problems in early individuation as is the pathology of mothers (or any primary caretaker) or the failure of a "temperament fit" between the two. Males are more likely to develop the dread of abandonment than females because of relative retardation in development and because of pressure for earlier separation from mother and what she represents.

6. Males are doubly vulnerable because of their inability to adequately deal with stress. Males are most likely to show adjustment problems when faced with insecurity.

7. There are situations that evoke the dread of abandonment. These life events need not be inherently traumatic or occur at critical periods of individuation. When these events arise in the life of a particularly vulnerable man, however, pathological responses are likely to appear. An unwanted divorce initiated by a wife (sixty-six percent of all current divorces are wife initiated) is among the most prominent situations that evoke this dread.

SEPARATION ANXIETY IN ADULTS

Separation, or even the prospect of being separated from a security provider, can lead to severe emotional reactions. Although often ignored in books on mental hygiene, separation anxiety is more likely to stimulate dysfunctional behavior than other sources of stress. Separation anxiety is very important in the psychological development of the individual because it first appears when an individual is very young and re-occurs at other times when separation is actual or threatened. The dysfunctional behavior associated with this anxiety can persist long enough to have ruinous consequences for a person, and the irrational fears associated with being abandoned are difficult to deal with.

There are three primary situations in which adults may involuntarily be separated from a loved one: death, divorce, and relocation. How an individual copes with loss in these situations is determined by his or her psychological makeup, which is the result of psychobiological factors and accumulated life experiences.

Relocation is deliberate and often under the control of the person doing the abandoning. The most common relocation is when a family member decides to move for purposes of career advancement. The person who decides to relocate has control, and this control is almost always recognized by other family members. For example, even in the military when one is reassigned, an individual could—and some have—refused to be transferred. In relocation, the anger is more rational, even though it is often displaced onto the agent effecting the separation, such as the head of the company or the commanding officer.

Mitigating the severity of the reaction to this form of separation and contributing to shorter-term upset is the factor that the separation is usually only temporary. For example, there are many modern couples whose occupations determine that they live miles apart. Their marriages probably survive only because each spouse recognizes the temporary nature of the decision.

Death is inevitable and is usually involuntary. Modern researchers, particularly Elisabeth Kubler-Ross (1969), have described a grieving process that follows a regular pattern and is successful for persons in good mental health prior to the loss. In normal persons, the anger one feels toward the deceased is short-lived, partly because one's rationality prevails and the separation is not perceived as a voluntary act of hostile rejection. In addition, the survivor is the recipient of "pity": condolence is bestowed upon those who suffer the death of a loved one.

However, in the research of Holmes and Rahe (1967) and Vaillant (1977), the death of a spouse received the highest rating of any trauma facing adult males.[2] Widowers have a very high suicide and death rate. Divorce is second in terms of a stress provoking trauma.

The current literature on the trauma of *divorce* focuses mostly on wives and children. We believe that the separation trauma that men experience has been underemphasized—symbolic punishment because men have traditionally, and somewhat inaccurately, been portrayed as the initiator of divorce, with concern for women and children by the mental health professions in the forefront. We suggest that the plight of men who experience an unwanted divorce is only secondarily a result of current social factors that have liberated their wives and mothers, and provides them no avenue of emotional support. Research consistently demonstrates that men—more than women—need marriage for stability and often for survival; divorce appears to destabilize men, even when they initiate the process.

Marriage provides more than companionship and connectedness, although these are extremely important to gregarious animals, who cannot survive and develop without social relationships. Marriage is an integral part of our society. It provides the only highly sanctioned vehicle for gratification of our most basic needs. In traditional marriages, wives make meals, offer love, and provide a stable, secure home base for married men—they provide a sanctuary, a "castle" where men can feel in control.[3] As the only socially acceptable context for adults to meet their security needs, marriage effectively allows a male to be adult and independent without yielding the impulse to have a secure position of dependence and security with a nurturing female.

Marriage alleviates primitive separation anxiety in men by providing stability and security while encouraging them to "act like men."

There is no better guarantor of long life, health, and happiness for men than a wife well socialized to perform the "duties of a wife," willing to devote her life to taking care of him, providing, even enforcing, the regularity and security of a well-ordered home. (Bernard, 1972, p. 10)

ALBERT EDELSTEIN: A PASHA FACES DIVORCE

Albert Edelstein,[4] the older of two sons of a dual-career couple, had not come to the attention of mental health professionals until he was forty, two years after he was divorced. A reasonably successful trial attorney, he admitted himself to the psychiatric unit of a general hospital; his unsuccessful attempts to effect a reconciliation with his ex-wife had finally led to thoughts of suicide.

Edelstein, who is a charming and clever man with a sense of humor tinged with sarcasm, described himself as an "accident" that happened to older parents who were too busy to care for him personally and thus hired a series of nannies. It was in his relationships with these caretakers, he believes, that his persisting style of relating to others developed. Fantasizing that nannies were his personal slaves, he became manipulative and devious, according to his self-evaluation, and excessively preoccupied with dominating others and gaining whatever he wanted when he wanted it.

He graduated from a prestigious college in Massachusetts and a top law school. Popular with fellow students, often a leader, Edelstein impressed others as being fiercely independent, somewhat callous, ambitious, energetic to the point of hyperactivity, and too much of a con artist to be trusted. He met Andrea in law school and they married shortly after they both passed the bar exam. He described his conquest of Andrea as "perhaps the greatest selling job of my life," since she was even more determined to succeed professionally and was not interested in establishing a home with children.

In terms of income, Andrea, who was a corporate lawyer with a large New England firm, was clearly more successful than her husband, but Albert established a spectacular career as a defense lawyer in Boston. The two were not competitive with each other, and neither money nor envy nor infidelity ruined the marriage. Strong-willed and totally dedicated to her career, Albert's wife had no time (or inclination) to devote to meeting his needs. "She was not a bad cook," he recalled, "she just didn't cook." Andrea, meanwhile, became increasingly unhappy with Albert's "demanding, infantile behavior" and spent as little time in their apartment as she could.

Clearly the marriage had different meanings for each of them. Although the marriage was no more satisfactory to Albert than to his wife, he believed that it was permanent. "I realize the conflict was mainly in my head," he observed. "I wanted a companion whom I could respect and trust, but I also wanted someone to care about me, put me first. If Andrea had babied me, I don't think I would have respected her."

Andrea's intentions were made clear to Albert when he was served with papers. "I was stunned," he reported, and he is resentful that he had no opportunity to influence this decision or her plan to join a Midwestern firm as soon as the divorce was final. "I was never consulted, we never discussed it, and it couldn't have happened at a worse time for me. She abandoned me when I most needed her," Albert lamented. His widowed mother died just before the divorce was finalized, and he was also involved in an important murder trial. He remains convinced that, if he had had more time, he would have been able to convince Andrea to remain married to him.

Once gregarious and an extroverted life-of-the-party, Albert became reclusive and seemed to suffer despair. He drank too much and neglected his appearance and his practice. When Andrea moved to St. Louis, he quit the firm of which he was a member and has not practiced law again. He was a pitiful figure and, in his ex-wife's eyes, trying to obtain her pity was Albert's obsession for two years. He badgered her, argued, and cajoled, usually on the phone, but sometimes at her residence. Looking derelict, unshaven and unkempt, Albert would show up unexpectedly and plead with her to return to Boston. If she would not, he suggested, he would end his life. While he never made a suicide attempt, there were a number of arrests for driving while intoxicated (and driving when his license was suspended) and progressively serious auto accidents. The psychologist who examined him in the emergency room believed that a fatal accident was more probable than Albert's deliberately taking his life, and it was for this reason that he talked Albert into admitting himself into the hospital.

We were not able to follow up Edelstein's progress directly, since he moved back to New England after he abruptly terminated his therapy, but a rather lengthy newspaper article featuring him appeared some years later. His story appears to have a happy ending: Albert married a nurse who had three children from a previous marriage, relocated to California, and established and administers an institute there that provides legal and psychological support services to divorcing men.

Some research evidence would suggest that Albert should have had less difficulty in coping with his new status than he actually did. Milardo (1987), for example, reported that divorced men are better able to establish a "social network" through their occupation than divorced women.[5] There is also some evidence that divorced men receive considerable social support generally (McKenry & Price, 1990). In the case of Albert, the opposite was true. Although he was an emotionally dependent man, at first he found no one interested in offering sympathy or support.

Albert has some notable positive attributes. He is, for example, highly intelligent and had graduated from outstanding academic institutions. He had obtained special training in a profession that, if not universally admired, enables an individual to attain worldly prestige. He was able to persist, with a high degree of effectiveness, in the same firm for several years. Albert is not merely a manipulative man with a strong need to dominate; he had channeled these attributes—the ability to influence others and his strong competitive drive—into professionally useful skills. One might argue that even his faults—his abrasive aggressiveness, hostility, and apparently showy self-confidence—were assets in his chosen profession. As an attorney, Albert cultivated a number of dubious social traits and integrated them effectively into his occupational identity, if not successfully into his social life.

Albert's desire to control nurturance providers, which led to inflexible, driven, insatiable behavior, resembles what Alice Miller (1981) calls the "masculine dream." His babe-pasha pattern was revitalized when abandonment was threatened. Flaws in his character were the result of early experiences that provided none of the coping skills that allow many men to deal with divorce (Hunt & Hunt, 1977; Johnson, 1977; McKenry & Price, 1990). Albert seems to have been overwhelmed by secret fears and a revitalization of infantile hostile dependency needs.

One can see in Albert's case that the struggle with independence-dependence conflict, which made his initial attempt at coping with divorce almost self-ruining, and the fact that it featured aggression and dominance, was a primitive theme compulsively repeated. The dynamic replicates the prototypical experiences described by Sigmund Freud (1920) in *Beyond the Pleasure Principle* and explained further by Marie Jahoda (1977) and Jacques Lacan (1968). Freud's earliest example of "repetition compulsion," that in the play of infants is a reproduction of mother's absence in a manner enabling the helpless infant to feel a sense of control, is revealed in a distorted, exaggerated form in almost all Albert's relationships with nurturance providers.

His wife-initiated divorce was a serious blow to Edelstein's self-esteem. A "real" man can satisfy his mate while remaining independent and competent in his occupation. There was a special threat to self-perception in this case, however, since Edelstein had life-long success in manipulating and controlling others, and Andrea (and his own parents) could be neither controlled nor manipulated. Edelstein blamed his postdivorce distress solely on his strong, conflicted dependency needs, which caused him to be anxious when alone and prevented him from coping with his wife's leaving.[6] In this, notes Goldberg (1976), he is not unlike the typical male of modern America, since the core conflict involving the need for security versus the socially reinforced need for independence is endemic to and yet a threat to the survival of all men in this society.

SUMMARY

Everyone dreads the potential loss of a person to whom one is attached. Throughout life, separation experiences normally elicit anxiety, with the anticipation of being deprived of what the dependency gratifer had provided. For some individuals, however, anxiety over separation in adulthood revitalizes "old" unconscious conflicts, which probably had their origin in infantile fantasies that caregivers might abandon them.

Unfortunately, the psychological makeup of some individuals makes it impossible for them to adjust normally to anticipated, or real, loss. The fear that they will be abandoned makes them "sick."

That males are more vulnerable both psychologically and physiologically, are more prone to stress-related illness, and suffer from a long list of sex-linked disabilities and disorders is well documented. Complicating their physiological problems is the fact that males, in this culture, are separated from their mothers—their first dependency gratifiers—sooner and more completely than are their sisters. Maturing later than females throughout childhood, males are less capable of successfully effecting individuation. This combination predisposes men to separation anxiety and increases the probability that particularly vulnerable men will suffer the dread of abandonment.

We are not suggesting that all men are susceptible to psychological disintegration when faced with potential abandonment. We only suggest that some men who have had particular experiences in their childhood have a higher probability of overreacting, of becoming "sick," when faced with separation and loss. The development of this unique weakness results from deviations in the usual process of individuation that begins at birth.

NOTES

1. It is traditional to call a child's primary caretaker (and earliest attachment "object") "the mother," even though the biological mother may not be the one who actually plays this role.

2. On the Holmes and Rahe scale, marital separation is listed third, as a stress producer, and a change in job is listed as seventeenth.

3. While we would like to think that the traditional marriage—one where the wife contributes more to nurturance than the male—is in decline, research dealing with dual-career couples suggests that women are still providing more of the "house-wife" duties (Cowan, 1992; Ferree, 1987; Hochschild, 1989; Nyquist, Spence, & Helmrich, 1985).

4. Identifying details for all the case studies have, of course, been disguised. For this first case the authors were provided a unique opportunity since one of them was the inpatient therapist and the other a therapist in the community clinic where Albert received outpatient treatment. A few years later, two newspaper articles provided additional information.

5. In the research described by Milardo (1987) and McKenry and Price (1990), men are more likely to effect a normal adjustment to divorce than what is reported by Briscoe, Smith, Robbins, Marten, & Gaskin (1973), Reissman & Gerstel (1985), and a score of earlier studies. A large percentage of divorced men become seriously depressed and suffer some sort of personality disorientation.

6. In the majority of cases, people who suffer separation anxiety and the dread of abandonment are not, prior to the situation, recognizably neurotic or disturbed in any sense. These are normal, average individuals who, when subjected to an involuntary separation situation, find they cannot cope.

2

Homonomy and Autonomy

Persons of all ages and occupations must deal with the Attachment/Separateness polarity. If we become too separate, our contact with the world is lost and our capacity for survival jeopardized. If we become too attached to the environment, we endanger our capacity for self-renewal, growth and creative effort. Although a balance of attachment and separateness must be found at every age, it will necessarily change from one era of the life cycle to the next. (Levinson et al., 1979, p. 240)

Various theories of child development emphasize different elements. For example, psychoanalysis suggests that intrapsychic forces early in development are most important, whereas behaviorism focuses on extrinsic reinforcement and punishment from the environment. Common to all theories of child development, however, is the notion that satisfying the needs for both dependence and independence is central to positive psychological development. Described as "polar opposites" because they motivate behaviors that are essentially opposite in intention,[1] these life-long psychobiological (genetic) mechanisms—autonomy (independence) and homonomy (dependence)—are present at birth in all animals including humans, and enter into every incident that affects the process of personality integration (maturity). These two determining tendencies have been observed in the prototypical movements of the neonate (Allport, 1937; Pratt, 1934) and continue to interact at every "stage" in the life cycle.

Although both separation (autonomy) and attachment (homonomy) impel behavior about equally in early childhood development, the socialization practice for males common in the United States consistently encourages independence motives while concurrently suppressing or inhibiting dependence motives. This gender-specific socialization emphasis leads to behavioral and psychological attitudes that are significantly different in men and women. Furthermore, by exaggerating and denying the constitutional differences between women and men, traditional socialization exacerbates the male's natural biological vulnerabilities, making men succeptible to a whole host of syndromes and diseases later in life.

MATERNAL BEHAVIOR

It may be nature's most dramatic irony that the human infant is dependent, unable to cope or survive physically, far longer than the young of any other species, while the human adult is possessed of the greatest discretion to gratify the infant's needs or not. Maternal behavior in other animals is considered "instinctive," or more or less under the control of "innate releasers." The observed diversity in human maternal behavior,[2] including the choice to ignore the survival needs of one's offspring in extreme cases, however, points to a most complicated situation.[3] Social forces and learning experiences in humans, less controlled by a "natural" social group, dominate and sometimes distort the natural or biological basis of nurturance.[4]

Psychobiological mechanisms,[5] which is how we refer to "universal patterns . . . which are the result of genetically controlled biological tendencies" (Ford & Beach, 1951, p. 3), govern or determine human behavior and consequently influence child-rearing behaviors. However, humans have evolved the ability to override these controlling mechanisms. Human parents can be irresponsible or harmful, or follow fads and expert advice that violate natural imperatives (Montagu, 1974a). We can also abrogate our responsibilities in favor of substitute caregivers.[6]

Infants are not yet able to be influenced by social and environmental forces; they are more readily, at least at first, controlled by their psychobiological mechanisms. Their personality does, however, influence parental interaction (Bell & Harper, 1977)—for example, an individual infant's need for autonomy and homonomy will elicit differential behavior from parents. To the degree to which there is an emotional and psychological mesh between parents and children, there will be smooth parental-child interaction (Adler, 1927; Hartup, 1963).

The history of child-rearing philosophy (Clausen & Williams, 1963; Young, 1990) is replete with an amazing variety of changes in the conception of the nature of infants. In the United States, for example, there has been a general shift from a perception of the child as inherently evil—the Calvinist orientation, which implored parents to "break the child's will," which held sway throughout the nineteenth century—to the conception of the child as inherently innocent, deserving of gentle treatment and love-oriented discipline techniques. Wolfenstein's (1951) analysis of advice given in *Infant Care Bulletin* from 1914 through 1951 suggested, similarly, that, as American culture moved increasingly to value "fun and play" for adults, rigidity, scheduling, and harshness in child-rearing philosophy has decreased accordingly. Since the 1920s and 1930s, which were the peak of regimentation in proposed child-rearing practices (Escalona, 1949; Stendler, 1950; Vincent, 1951), possibly as a result of Watsonian assurance of the efficacy of parental behavior in shaping infinitely moldable infants (Clausen & Williams, 1963), demand feeding and scheduling when the child is "ready" have increasingly been proposed by experts.

Although more idealistic writers have advocated child-rearing practices that are "natural" (Montagu, 1974a), the influence of social forces and fads is so pervasive that one cannot hope to determine what natural child-rearing might entail. In fact, a case could be made that intervention, or perhaps interference, in the mother-child relationship by "informed" others is itself "natural."

NEONATAL VULNERABILITY

> The biological unity, the symbiotic relationship, maintained by mother and conceptus throughout pregnancy does not cease at birth but becomes—indeed, is naturally designed to become—even more intensive and interoperative after birth than during uterogestation.
>
> When mother and child most need each other, they are too often separated from each other, the one isolated in her room, the other banished to a crib in the nursery. . . . The separation begins from the moment of birth, so profound has our misunderstanding of the needs of human beings grown. (Montagu, 1974a, pp. 32–33)

Humans come into the world helpless and only partially formed. The customary term to describe the condition of the neonate, neoteny,[7] connotes more than that he or she lacks the capacities of adults to attain unaided locomotion, forage for food, or protect him or herself from danger. When the neonate becomes separated from the umbilicus and suffers parturition at a normal birth, she or he is at least four months "premature" (Montagu, 1974a).[8]

Human maturation is slow, and the infant's development outside of the womb begins in an only partially completed state. The early separation from mother results in consequences later in development—some positive, some negative. The most obvious positive benefit is that extrautero development allows the neonate to interact with a far more stimulating environment and the possibilities for change through learning are infinitely greater. The womb is a safe and undemanding place, but is a sterile environment with a limited variety of stimuli; it is only mildly adequate for biological maturation. The external environment offers better support and encouragement for physical growth as well.

The helplessness of the neonate increases the contact between itself and its caregivers. There are benefits in the form of opportunities to practice motoric functions and all sorts of learning. Dependence upon a selected few nurturance providers assures that the full range of social forces and cultural values, as introjects of the parenting person, will be part and parcel of environmental influence from the moment of birth. As Thomas and Chess (1980) remind us, the human animal is a social animal and a communicating animal.

Human existence is social from the moment of birth on. The neonate could not survive without the immediate, active, and continuous involvement of other human beings. . . . At the same time, the biological endowment of the newborn infant makes this social involvement a mutually interactive and reciprocally influential process from the beginning. (Thomas & Chess, 1980, p. 40)

The inevitable dependence that results from neoteny encourages the development of social motives and presents the prototypical experiences that are manifested in the psychobiological process called *homonomy*.

The down side of neoteny is a result of these same conditions. The neonate is invariably dependent upon one or more adults for satisfaction of needs that, in the human colony, caregivers are allowed to ignore. In extreme cases, neglectful parental care can lead to "failure to thrive," and children may die when the parent-designates do not provide sufficient care or protection. Generally, parental figures who cannot or will not provide adequate maternal care have been labeled pathological. What is often ignored, however, is the impact that a totally helpless infant may have on adults: the infant's dependence may itself place an overwhelming burden on persons who are otherwise psychologically normal (Hartup, 1963). One way an individual may deal with the overwhelming nature of child care is to retreat from the parenting process.

The neonate requires constant, consistent nurturing during the several months of "exterogestation";[9] it has even been suggested that human infants would benefit physically and psychologically if mothers carried them for several months in a pouch like a marsupial. Direct research on the most important aspects of the bonding process is not only impossible but, more importantly, unethical and immoral. Therefore, we are left with naturalistic observation, which confirms the helplessness of infants and the universal need for nurturance; the extrapolation from research on animals, especially those for whom imprinting makes bonding almost immediate and automatic (Lorenz, 1952); and anecdotal reports of neglected or abandoned children.

In the prescientific era there was considerable interest in the study of feral children, who, having been found abandoned by adult caregivers, were thought to have been reared by animals in the wild (Singh & Zingg, 1942). Almost nothing is known of the early experiences of such children, who, despite the belief of the earnest nonscientists who discovered them, were probably abandoned shortly before discovery because they had some mental or developmental anomaly (Dennis, 1941). Skeptics suggest that it is not possible for a human to develop human characteristics or survive for long periods without the care of human adults, and the few children who have been the recipients of severe maltreatment coroborate this notion.[10]

DIFFERENTIATION

That at birth, and for the first few weeks, the partially formed neonate is weak in perceptual ability, lacks control of motoric functions, and responds to stress in a highly diffuse, generalized way is well accepted. Observations by William James, as early as 1890, support this general conclusion and suggest that the initial stage of autonomy involves differentiation—development from the general to the specific. "The baby, assailed by eyes, ears, nose, skin, and entrails at once, feels it all as one great blooming, buzzing confusion" (James, 1890, p. 488).

For various self-theorists, sociologists, social psychologists, and psychoanalysts, the starting point for the development of personality is the primitive act of autonomy involved in the discrimination of what is "me" from what is "not-me."[11] Further evidence comes from observing the highly generalized *adient* (toward a stimulus) and *abient* (away from a stimulus) movements that appear early in the repertoire of infants and suggest that differentiation has begun. It is generally concluded that attachment—literally in utero and figuratively in the emotional and conative life of young infants—is obvious. However because of our society's bias for autonomy, the emphasis is usually put on the acts of separation, with the state of homonomy becoming a backdrop for progressive individuation.[12]

Both biological and psychological separation is inevitable and necessary for the survival and growth of animals, human and nonhuman. There has been speculation about how traumatic or unpleasant the first separation is and when it occurs. Sandor Ferenczi (1950) and Otto Rank (1924),[13] for example, early psychoanalytic thinkers, presented fairly resilient, poetic views of the predifferentiated state, and both indicated that the act of birth was extremely traumatic and unpleasant. Although Rank's theory of "birth trauma," with the consequent desire to "return to the womb" (which may be a dramatic representation of the trend toward homonomy),[14] was once famous and has become ensconced in the apperceptive mass of the lay public, it has long been refuted by scientists on the grounds that the cognitive processes attributed to the neonate are neurologically impossible (Hurlock, 1964). The feeling of helplessness and total passivity, inherently unpleasant but the prototypical experience of anxiety, which was a crucial aspect of Rank's contribution, implies the existence of a primitive dread soon after the infant is able to make differentiations between what is "me" and "not-me." Freud and his followers, although rejecting Rank's birth-trauma theory,[15] nevertheless accepted the potent "signaling" effect of events that re-evoke anxiety when they recreate the experience of helplessness of the infant, albeit without the conscious awareness of the individual (Freud, 1926).

Ferenczi's imaginative analysis of birth, which begins with a "description" of the (unconscious) thoughts and feelings of the fetus, who lives "as a parasite of the mother's body [and] all its needs for protection, warmth, and nourishment are assured by the mother" (Ferenczi, 1950, p. 218) , suffered a somewhat different fate. Although the description of what birth feels like is very similar to that offered by Rank, few outsiders to psychoanalysis became aware of Ferenczi's ideas and he was not well-known to the public.[16] The primary importance of Ferenczi's work on early neonatal differentiation, which he called "renunciation of magical-hallucinatory omnipotence," was his influence on other psychologists.[17] Margaret Mahler, for example, who was a student of Ferenczi, has included his ideas in her own, more verifiable theory of differentiation.

Regardless of how the differentiation is precipitated or whether the child "knows," in a truly cognitive sense, that it has been ejected from its first home, the gradual awareness of the child's separate nature is anxiety producing. Problems, as a result of the differentiation phase, abound in psychoanalytic literature and run the gamut from mild to serious—from minor separation anxiety to severe forms of gender identity problems (Greenson, 1968).

DEPENDENCE AND INDEPENDENCE

Psychology has described the close relationship between an infant and its caregiver as a symbiotic one and, because of limited information from the infant, has traditionally overemphasized the benefits to the parenting person. The passive "receptive" mode of the infant to its personal environment leads to impressions that the child receives pleasure when its wants are satisfied. It is likely, however, that any disruption in the dependency-gratification process—for example, the mother's absence when biological drives are heightened (the child is hungry or wet)—provides the origin of the dread of abandonment. Later, as the child matures cognitively and can recognize that an absent mother generally returns, the child's sense of expectation provides the source of separation anxiety (Settlage, 1971).

The Holistic Perspective

> In the first orientation [autonomy] he is struggling for centrality in his world, trying to mold and organize objects and events, to bring them under his own control. In the second orientation [homonomy] he seems rather to strive to surrender himself and to become an organic part of something that he conceives as greater than himself. (Angyal, 1965, p. 15)

Fifty years ago Andras Angyal (1941) presented a "holistic" theory of personality development that emphasized the interplay of two basic processes or orientations.[18] Angyal suggested that dependence and independence are not "developmental tasks" that come to predominate at a particular time in the life of a person, but are continuing, sometimes conflicting developmental forces. This tug-of-war begins with the almost complete helplessness of the neonate and continues throughout life; resolution is a function of early experiences, psychobiological characteristics, and emotional support.

According to Angyal (1941, 1951, 1965), the trend toward autonomy is the psychobiological push to become more independent, separate, and self-sufficient. Assertiveness, aggression, and self-determination are manifestations of this tendency. Susan Spieler (1986) has asserted that autonomy has become the distorted goal of self-development in male-dominated psychoanalytic theories.[19] Like Angyal, Spieler suggests that an integration of separation and attachment needs is necessary for mental health. Spieler's highly original observation that autonomy is "masculine" and preferred in this society—as well as in psychoanalysis—over homonomy is important; this preference partly explains why the symptoms of the Umbilicus Complex have historically been overlooked or ignored.

Homonomy, Angyal's second developmental concept, refers to the tendency to attach oneself to others, to find comfort, security, and emotional warmth in the company of others. Dependency as well as loyalty, intimacy, and working toward group goals require "yielding" (Angyal, 1951), surrendering one's autonomy. Spieler would, as would others, describe these as "feminine" aspects of the personality. In 1979, Daniel Levinson and his associates (1979, pp. 239–240) presented evidence that both autonomy and homonomy appear as life-long forces in men. What they call the "attachment/separateness polarity" is defined slightly differently from the concepts of Angyal and Spieler. Levinson's group takes a more Hegelian approach to their "synthesis," but their research clearly shows that there are periodic crises in the life process of men—for example, the "mid-life crisis," where the conflicts are clearly between autonomy and homonomy.

Although Levinson's research efforts began as an extension of Margaret Mahler's pioneering efforts relative to individuation of young children (Mahler, 1963, 1968; Mahler, Pine, & Bergman, 1975), it is clear from Levinson's life histories that autonomy-striving generally dominates homonomy needs in the motivation of normal adult males in this society. Whereas young boys cannot achieve successful separation without the comforting, sheltering "anchor" of homonomy gratification (Mahler, 1968), healthy, adult males usually only dimly acknowledge their continuous need for security. As we shall see, boys—even those for whom individuation is only mildly problematic—will achieve mental health and success more often if they marry. On the other hand, males who are saddled with a life-long dread of abandonment because of very early traumatic experiences, who suffer serious problems in individuation, who are not able to resolve a fully developed Umbilicus Complex, and who do not remain happily married become vulnerable to breakdown during "crises" involving separation.

Object Relations Theorists

A branch of the psychoanalytic movement, which began to make influential contributions during the 1950s, object relations or self-psychology concentrates on the damage to the sense of self and the lack of psychic structure integration that results from disruptions and frustrations relative to a basic need for connectedness.

Defining *object* as "the residue of the individual's relations with people upon whom he was dependent for the satisfactions of primitive needs in infancy and during early stages of maturation," Herbert Phillipson (1955, p. 7) indicates that early self-development is a function of frustration. No infant can continue in the "state of perfect, nonfrustrated security" (St. Clair, 1986, p. 57). The child struggles with rejection from parenting figures, primarily mother, at the same time that it struggles with the autonomy-homonomy conflict. Dysfunctional resolution results with the child's having an almost idealized perspective of the parent, which leads to distortions in other relationships: the individual is emotionally needy while acting as if she or he were emotionally distant.

W.R.D. Fairbairn (1941) presents a three-stage developmental theory that emphasizes the transition from "infantile dependence" to "mature relations." The emotional end state is an adult who experiences both giving and receiving, independence from others and dependence on others. In contrast, when development has been arrested, in the transitional period (stage 2), for example, the individual feels infantile dependency needs but wishes to reject them.

Donald Winnicott (1960) has offered the term "good-enough mother" to describe the parent who provides for and adjusts to the needs of the infant in a manner that encourages positive emotional development. According to Winnicott, the good-enough mother helps the child traverse the difficult path between homonomy and autonomy so that the child can develop the "true-self." The true-self can react wholly and genuinely in relationships, whereas the false-self lives compliantly, always hoping for positive and nurturing relationships when none exist. Winnicott also presents a three-stage perspective of development, one which addresses the conflict between homonomy and autonomy: Absolute Dependence, Relative Dependence, and Toward Independence (Winnicott, 1963).

The task of this period for the infant is to increase its awareness of separateness of the self and the other, which coincides with the origin of a sense of self, of true object relationships, and of awareness of the reality of the outside world (Mahler, Pine, & Bergman, 1975, p. 48).

Narcissistic personalities—those who have difficulty with autonomy-homonomy—experience objects as "self-objects" instead of maintaining a realistic psychological separateness from them (Kohut, 1971). While it is natural for the infant to experience self-objects—those objects who have not yet been recognized as part of the "not-me"—if development has progressed positively, the child learns to rely on his or her inner resources for gratification.

Healthy narcissism is expressed in adult function, such as creativity, humor, or empathy. Parents who lack empathic responses to their children's needs, who fail to provide a bridge between the security of the parent-child relationship and the real world, or who fail to give children the appropriate level of appreciation, can create narcissistic personalities. The individual who becomes "stuck" at the infantile narcissistic stage suffers in relationships, is boring or listless, or develops maladaptive behaviors such as promiscuous sex or gambling.

The Behaviorist Position

Often, at first glance, the object relations and holistic perspective seem quite different from the behavioristic. However, when it comes to the problem of dependence-independence in childhood development, there is a great deal of similarity in spite of the different language. Dependence is defined by behaviors whose goals are to receive satisfaction from contact with others, and independence is defined as self-reliant and self-assertive behavior (Hartup, 1963). In the language of behaviorism the infant learns how to elicit helping behavior from others. Mothers often note that they can tell the differences in an infant's cries, for example, and to the degree that these behaviors work—that is, they are followed by favorable responses by others—they will be reinforced and will continue in the child's behavior repertoire. Because it is "natural" for parents to respond to the cries of their infants, it is not difficult for the child to elicit helping behaviors. The more often the mother is present when primary needs are reduced—the child is fed, changed, and so on—she develops properties of a secondary reinforcer and thus, she, herself, can be used later by the child as a substitute reinforcer.

Robert Sears, Eleanor Maccoby, and Harry Levin (1957) have suggested that a problem with dependence emerges only after the mother has occasionally disappointed the child or punished dependency behaviors: "Dependency acquires motivational properties as a result of a conflict induced by the mother's nonreward or punishment" (Hartup, 1963, p. 347). Interestingly, the more the child denies dependency, the more the child increases his or her attempts to obtain dependency satisfaction. Sears et al. (1957), for example, report that as severity of weaning increases so do dependency behaviors and also does a failure of mothers to respond nurturantly. Interestingly, overprotection, which leads to frustration of autonomy needs, also has been found to be related to increased levels of dependency (Marshall, 1961).

SUMMARY

The two developmental processes that influence the life cycle—autonomy or "self-government" and homonomy or "government from outside" (Angyal, 1941)—are manifested early in the psychology of the neonate. The developmental processes are almost certainly psycho-biological mechanisms, which means that they are inevitable and universal, but like most constitutional components of humans, they are highly influenced by social forces, particularly by individual variations in mother-child interactions and prescribed child-rearing practices.

While it is clear that the issue of autonomy-homonomy is a critical element of human development, it is also clear that certain events in one's lifetime can threaten the balance. Experiences of loss, commonly through death or divorce, that elicit counteractive homonomy needs and the demand for intimacy in love relations that elicits autonomy-flight reactions (Chodorow, 1978) are but two examples. Child-rearing practices that overcompensate and ignore the gender-specific psychobiological weak-nesses and relatively delayed maturation of males produce adults who are more likely to have difficulty in dealing with loss as well as intimacy and are frequently reported to have serious defects in self-identity (Goldberg, 1976).

In general, reasonably successful resolution of autonomy-homonomy conflict facilitates the smooth, progressive, on-going development of self-identity (Erikson, 1950, 1968). A reasonable balance between depend-ency needs and independence striving contributes to the establishment of a self-image that is constant, integrated, and accurate (what we refer to as having "self-insight"), reduces confusion and insecurity, and leaves a person feeling competent and loved. On the other hand, unsuccessful, unsatisfying, anxiety-evoking experiences during autonomy-homonomy crises, such as divorce for most men, can distort the maintenance of an adequate self-identity. Self-image can be threatened and competent, coping behavior can collapse during a crisis if there has been a history of abnormal experiences involving separation and/or loss. This is particularly true if a significant number of such experiences occurred during infancy.

The dread of abandonment most likely has as its source unpleasant experiences of separation from a primary caregiver during the period when cognitive differentiation of self from environment was incomplete. Some theorists have suggested that the emotional concomitant of infantile dread is a result of a revitalization of the trauma of birth, but this is implausible because of the lack of neurological maturation at birth. The so-called psychological birth of the child (Mahler et al., 1975) occurs when self-differentiation is completed, but the dread of abandonment arises during the "autistic" phase "before object constancy has been achieved" (Settlage, 1971, p. 147).

NOTES

1. Beller (1955) and Heathers (1955), among others, have suggested that independence and dependence are not opposites but separate, overlapping concepts.

2. Physiologists are not ready to assert that genetic "prepotencies" have been eradicated in humans through evolution. Lang, Rice, and Sternbach (1972, p. 627), for example, state that there should be (and are) remnants of releaser mechanisms in emotional responses "if the hypothesis of phylogenetic continuity is to be maintained."

3. While there have been notable experimental studies with animal subjects where the maternal behavior has been manipulated to the deleterious effect of the infant, maternal behavior of wild animals is less varied, with only minor aberations having been noted (Strum, 1987; van Lawick-Goodall, 1971).

4. Maternal behavior is found in all human societies (Ford & Beach, 1951; Murdock, 1975; Whiting & Child, 1953), but its apparent absence in some humans has led to doubts concerning a "maternal instinct."

5. The concept of "instinct" has, even for animals lower on the phylogenetic scale than humans, been replaced by the concept of "species-specific behavior," which takes into account learning (Harlow, 1962; Lorenz, 1952; Tinbergen, 1951). This term is similar to "open" instincts—those genetic predispositions that are relatively complex and highly influenced by learning (Tinbergen, 1951).

6. By this we do not mean that employing child care or babysitters is necessarily an abrogation of parental responsibilities. We mean, rather, a lack of caring, abandonment, or general irresponsibility regarding child care. See Scarr and Eisenberg (1993) for a review of child-care research.

7. Neoteny has at least three meanings in zoology. One of the earliest uses of the term was that of Killman, who discovered that the larvae of *Ambystoma* (the Mexican newt) had gonads and could fertilize other larvae (Hickman, 1970). Pedogenesis was important to nineteenth-century evolutionists because it provided a mechanism for the emergence of new species. Observed "similarities" between the ape fetus and adult humans led to the theory that humans may be a "neotenous form of a primitive apelike ancestor," a view still held by "many evolutionists" (Hickman, 1970, p. 798).

8. The usual explanation of why birth occurs or must occur before gestation is completed is that evolution of the human brain capacity has led to increases in the size of the head of fetuses while, at the same time, the female pelvic outlet has decreased in size.

9. Actually, Montagu suggests that exterogestation should be nine months long. This is based on a hunch reflecting primitive survival. He is careful to note that few human activities, performed independently, are possible for several years after birth.

10. Montagu (1961) and Fromkin et al. (1974) provide two very different perspectives on feral children. The now classic case of chronic child maltreatment that supports the importance of a nurturant parent-child interaction is the case of Genie, who, after thirteen and one-half years of neglect and confinement in an attic, was severely developmentally delayed in several areas—for example, interpersonal and language skills (Curtiss, 1977).

11. It is logical to suppose (but unknowable) that the first differentiation in self-development involves progressive repudiation of aspects of the environment from one's sense of self.

12. As Campbell (1988, p. 69) has noted, the emphasis on self assertion and independence is a Western concept and diametrically opposed to human values in Eastern cultures, where "meaning and fulfillment [come by] his subjugation through identification with . . . social archetypes, and his . . . quelling . . . of every impulse to an individual life."

13. Publication dates, as they appear in cited references, refer to the most accessible U.S. editions and are often historically misleading. Ferenczi's paper, "Stages in the Development of the Sense of Reality," for example, was written between 1908 and 1914. Rank's work on birth trauma was a product of the mid-1920s.

14. Lederer (1968) notes that a return to the womb, as desirable, is a possible interpretation of several myths. For example, it has been suggested that Oedipus' eye gouging and cave dwelling were symbolic returns to the womb state (Mullahy, 1948).

15. Initially Freud liked the birth-trauma theory, even though the concept replaced the Oedipus Complex as the cause of neurosis. It has been suggested that Rank's theory was rejected by psychoanalysis because it was a product of pure speculation rather than clinical observation (Lieberman, 1983).

16. The similarities are not surprising since Rank and Ferenczi were friends and worked together. Since Ferenczi's paper anticipates Rank's book by more than fifteen years, the Hungarian can only have influenced his much younger colleague. It is interesting that each man was, in turn, Freud's "favorite" and later incurred their mentor's wrath (actually the principal reason for the rejection of Ferenczi and Rank were innovations each made to psychoanalytic treatment). Interestingly, the psychoanalytic "inner circle" eventually insisted that both Rank and Ferenczi had become insane.

17. Ferenczi also had a profound influence on Melanie Klein, who was another of his students and became an important theorist, like Mahler specializing in the psychological development of very young children (for a brief biography of Klein, the reader is referred to Stevens and Gardner [1982]). The Budapest-Vienna psychoanalytic tie was very strong between the two world wars (Gardner & Stevens, 1992).

18. Angyal, who worked for several years as a psychiatrist at the state hospital in Worcester, Massachusetts, was the least known of the "organismic" theorists (Hall & Lindzey, 1957). Like other like-minded theorists, most prominently Kurt Goldstein and K. S. Lashley, Angyal's background was in neurophysiology. He called his orientation "holistic" to establish his relationship with the Gestalt psychology movement, which opposed the more molecular behaviorism and emphasized the integration of individuals and experiences and functions into unanalyzable "wholes."

19. A relational paradigm for male development is in the process of being created (Bergman, 1990).

3

The Biological Roots of Gender Differences

The general traits of human nature appear limited and idiosyncratic when placed against the great backdrop of all other living species. Additional evidence suggests that the more stereotyped forms of human behavior are mammalian and even more specifically primate in character, as predicted on the basis of general evolutionary theory. . . . These facts are in accord with the hypothesis that human social behavior rests on a genetic foundation. (Wilson, 1982, p. 33)

Every known society assures that the life experiences of its male members will be different from those of its females. Although there are slight variations generally in how a given society may deal with such issues as division of labor or gender roles, almost all social groups prescribe certain behaviors, labeled "masculine" or "feminine," which are based on real or mythical biological differences between the genders.

Scientific investigation reveals that many of the cherished beliefs about gender differences that are part of our society's tradition are highly influenced by societal expectations and differential treatment of boys and girls. But not all gender differences can be attributed to socialization practices and learning. Males and females differ in their chromosomal makeup and show neonatal differences, which, as in the case of temperament traits, may have a persisting influence on personality development.

Not all psychologists take the position that the generally observed and important gender differences have a physiological or genetic basis, even though evolutionary psychology, as represented by Barkow, Cosmides, and Tooby (1992), has been gaining support. Social psychologists, including almost all feminists, tend to take an environmentalist position and argue that the major source of notable gender differences is a result of socialization practices. The social-forces approach does, of course, recognize some differences between the genders. For example,

there are very few clear-cut differences between males and females. Males, compared to females, tend to be more physically vulnerable, aggressive, and sexually active, to excel in visual-spatial and quantitative skills after age 8, and to dominate communications. Females, compared to males, tend to mature faster, to have cyclic hormonal production, to have less localized brain functions, to excel in verbal skills after age 11, to be more interested in people after adolescence, and to be capable of multiple orgasms. (Basow, 1980, p. 96)

Environmentalists suggest, however, that these are relatively unimportant.

A general evaluation of the data that support the difference position, a predominantly biological perspective, leads one to conclude that, in most respects, it is the males of our species, not the females, who are the "weaker" sex. These real biological differences assure that men in our society will have problems during the individuation stage of development. In particular, males who suffer from unrealistic socialization demands for early and complete autonomy will mature with a confused sense of identity and greater separation anxiety.

Many of the typical "male" behavior patterns that occur between four and seven years of age are inevitable and relatively independent of environmental influence: they result spontaneously and predictably from the young boy's attempt to acquire and exhibit the aspects of masculinity that he has used to define his gender. If the male child experiences a discontinuity between his existing attributes and those he must acquire to confirm his masculinity, it is likely that he will strive to exhibit "appropriate," if not exaggerated, masculine behavior, and that his choices will be consistent with the adult male attributes of size, strength, and physical prowess. (Ullian, 1981, pp. 498–499)

THE NATIVIST POSITION

The debate about whether one's genetic constitution or one's environment has a greater effect on cognitive processes and personality development has a long history in psychology.[1] While parents observe unique characteristics in their child from the time of birth, sometimes perceiving personality traits in the infant that influence how the parents react and interact with the child for years afterward, most American psychologists have emphasized the environmentalist perspective. The latter position emphasizes the role of learning and the sociocultural context in shaping human personality.

Currently, however, with increasing evidence of biological influences on personality development, from research as part of the twin studies conducted at Minnesota (Bouchard, Lykken, & McGue, 1990) and the more complete picture of the influence of genetic inheritance on behavior presented in the Human Genome Project (Shapiro, 1991), for example, it is difficult to maintain the strict tabula rasa view of development. Although discussion of the relative influence of genetic and social experience (or learning) determinants persists, there has been a sort of negotiated settlement to the effect that the "constitution of the individual sets the limits within which all subsequent environmental events act" (Beck & Rosenblith, 1973, p. 36).

The once common assumption that human development is "controlled" by biology—a position which had more or less been displaced in this country with the rise of behaviorism in the 1920s—has enjoyed a resurgence of popularity in the form of sociobiology (Wilson, 1982). This approach explains relatively complicated social phenomena, including such "human" traits as altruism, as a function of species-specific determinants (the new name for "instincts").

Related more specifically to human behavior and cognitive development, the relatively new evolutionary psychology applies Darwinian principles to explain how aspects of "human nature" have (or once had) adaptation value: "the available evidence strongly supports [the] view of a single, universal panhuman design, stemming from our long-enduring existence as hunter-gatherers" (Barkow, Cosmides, and Tooby, 1992, p. 5). In this context, Barkow, Cosmides, and Tooby present the major premises of this nativist school:

1. "there is a universal human nature, but this universality exists primarily at the level of evolved psychological mechanisms, not of expressed cultural behavior";
2. "these evolved psychological mechanisms are adaptations, constructed by natural selection over evolutionary time"; and
3. "the evolved structure of the human mind is adapted to the way of life of Pleistocene hunter-gatherers, and not necessarily to our modern circumstances."

There has been similar interest in psychoanalytic literature. Looking for constitutional differences in the separation-individuation processes, for example, Fries and Woolf report:

One of the significant factors observed in the neonates was the sensorimotor response to stimuli. The response is characteristic of the infant's mode of adaptation to independent life. It was noted that trauma of birth or illness could modify the intensity of the response temporarily, but that the typical response persisted nevertheless. From all the findings before and at birth, it seemed reasonable to conjecture that the neonate's response was due to a combination of genetic endowment, intrauterine experiences, and the birth process. (1971, p. 275)

SEX AND GENDER DIFFERENCES

The investigation of sex or gender differences[2] has always been controversial and politically charged,[3] yet almost from psychology's birth as a separate discipline in 1879, investigations or polemic articles arguing the differences between men and women have been published. The earliest papers raised questions not only about the methodology used in the study of sex differences but also about the often-obvious relationship between the researcher's social expectation of men and women and the results of the scientific investigation.[4]

In 1896, for example, Joseph Jastrow wrote a paper defending the "variability hypothesis," which suggested that men's greater attainment of eminence was due to the greater variability of traits, particularly intellectual ability, as distributed in the population (Jastrow, 1896). This Darwinian notion suggested that traits in females had a narrower range— that women are more like each other in their mediocrity. It is interesting that Jastrow's paper appeared in the same issue of the periodical that carried an article by Mary Whitton Calkins, who was the first woman to be elected president of the American Psychological Association. In fact, Jastrow was writing in rebuttal to Calkins, whose thesis was that gender differences in achievement were primarily due to social training and opportunity (Calkins, 1896). One is reminded, since the claim of sex differences in variability was not founded on systematic observation (later research, in fact, proved that the opposite was true: women's traits actually show greater variability),[5] of Helen Thompson Woolley's ascerbic assessment of nineteenth-century research on sex differences:

There is perhaps no field aspiring to be scientific where flagrant personal bias, logic martyred in the cause of supporting a prejudice, unfounded assertions, and even sentimental rot and drivel, have run riot to such an extent as here. (Woolley, 1910, p. 340)

The most notable collection of research findings on sex and gender differences is Havelock Ellis's (1930) *Man and Woman*, an extensive collection of information that was updated and issued in six editions between 1894 and 1930. The lack of a seventh edition may reflect an apparent decline of interest in the area between 1930 and 1966, when *The Development of Sex Differences*, edited by Eleanor Maccoby, was published.[6] In 1974 Eleanor Maccoby and Carol Nagy Jacklin presented a two-volume work, *The Psychology of Sex Differences*,[7] which is comprehensive and is used as a benchmark, particularly by individuals who stress "no differences" between the sexes. Most contemporary researchers either assume that the two genders would perform identically if only the world were fair or they control for the variable of sex as "noise" (McGuinnes, 1987). In addition, there are a number of individuals who protest the continued investigation of human sex differences, especially research results from animal studies that are generalized to humans (Tavris, 1992; Tobach & Rosoff, 1978).

There is a significant amount of research supporting the notion that biological differences (outside of obvious reproductive function) between the sexes exist, that these differences have significant influence on the subsequent physical and psychological development of humans, and, as a consequence, have an influence on human social interaction.[8] Additionally, we believe, as do many other investigators in the area of individual differences, that the data from animal studies are useful, particularly in support of data collected on humans.[9] For example, after a survey of gender stereotypes in thirty societies, Williams and Best concluded that gender differences are actual and will persist despite social changes. They presented the following:

We . . . reject a unisex position in which one attempts to minimize or deny all differences between men and women maintaining that such behavioral differences are artifactual in nature and evil in consequence. There is too much biology, sociobiology and history involved to make the unisex position a comfortable one for the women and men of tomorrow. (1982, p. 308)

The Biology of Gender

Mammals are prototypically female until the sixth week of fetal development, when, if the new organism has an XY chromosome pair, androgens—often referred to as the male sex hormone,[10]—are produced and, if all goes well, a male body begins to differentiate from the basic female form. That is, the vas deferens, seminal vesicles, ejaculatory duct, testes, and penis begin to develop. Sometimes, however, there are problems and a "normal" gendered child is not produced (Hoyenga & Hoyenga, 1979; Money & Ehrhardt, 1972).

One type of complication is the birth of a child with some chromosomal anomaly that may include the presence of extra gender chromosomes— for example, XXY, XXXY, or XYYY—or the lack of androgen production or tissues insensitive to androgen production, or the sex-inverted female (a male with an XX chromosome pair) (Polani, 1972). The XXY or XXXY individual, who suffers from Klinefelter's syndrome (also referred to as a pseudohermaphrodite), often has physical characteristics that appear slightly "feminine," is usually sterile, and has gender identity and social or emotional problems more frequently than genetically normal males. Such XXY males are, for example, often found in the population of psychiatric patients. On the other hand, the XYY male, at one time believed more likely to be a criminal than a genetically normal male, is often described as "displaying 'exaggeratedly male' characteristics" (Hoyenga & Hoyenga, 1979, p. 36). A person with androgen insensitivity syndrome, while born with an XY chromosome pair, does not differentiate into a male and, in fact, is born phenotypically female. These genetic males are reared to be and develop to look like normal females, however they cannot reproduce (Barfield, 1976; Brisco, 1978; Hoyenga & Hoyenga, 1979).[11]

Other complications surrounding the biology of gender involve the incidence of particular disorders or diseases that are more prevalent in the male—sex-linked or sex-influenced traits.[12] A sex-linked characteristic is distributed by the X chromosome; therefore, males are more likely to display sex-linked traits because they only have one X.[13] It has been suggested that there are over 243 sex-linked conditions carried by a recessive gene on the X chromosome and, when paired with the Y of the male, find expression. Some of these conditions include albinism of the eyes, congenital baldness, maldevelopment of the sweat glands, congenital cleft of the iris, color blindness, day blindness, defective hair follicles, defective iris, defective tooth enamel, double eyelashes, skin cysts, glaucoma of the juvenile type, hemophilia, scalelike skin, enlargement of the cornea of the eyeball, diminution of the cornea of the eye, stricture of the bicuspid valve of the heart, myopia, night blindness, nystagmus, optic atrophy, peroneal atrophy, retinal detachment, thrombasthenia, a patch of white hair in the occipital region, a form of muscular dystrophy, Duchenne pseudohypertrophic muscular dystrophy, some metabolic disorders, and one type of diabetes (Burns, 1976; Hoyenga & Hoyenga, 1979; Montagu, 1957; Shapiro, 1991).

Sex-influenced traits are traits influenced by genes located on the autosomes and are equally inherited by both sexes.[14] However, expression of the characteristic is determined by the sex of the bearer. Male pattern baldness is an example of this type of genetic trait; the gene for pattern baldness is dominant in males and is expressed in the environment of the male sex hormone. A female who carries a sex-influenced-trait gene needs two dominant genes, one from each parent, to display a sex-influenced characteristic (Burns, 1976).

Problems can also develop as a function of the Y chromosome itself. The Y chromosome is very small (only 1.8 microns long) (Brisco, 1978; Hall, 1985; Ounsted & Taylor, 1972) and in addition to its carrying the sex determination and fertility factor, has been suggested to also carry Holandric genes for traits that only find expression in males (Burns, 1976; Shapiro, 1991). Four physical conditions are suspected to be functions of Holandric genes: ichthyosis hystrix gravior (barklike skin), hypertrichosis (dense hairy growth on the ears), keratoma dissipatum (painful hard lesions of the hands and feet), and webbing between the second and third toes (Montagu, 1957).[15]

The X, on the other hand, is much larger (4.5 to 5.5 microns long) and is a more active chromosome: it carries all the requisite information for development. Interestingly, mammals can be born and live without a Y chromosome—Turner's syndrome women and sex-inverted males,[16] for example—but there is no record of individuals living without an X (Carter, 1972; Hall, 1985; Nicholson, 1984; Ounsted & Taylor, 1972).

The Vulnerability of Males

Along with these disabilities or conditions, males are physiologically more vulnerable than females to all types of illness and degenerative diseases. An indication of the inherent weakness of the male constitution is that, while 50 percent of sperm carry the X chromosome and 50 percent carry the Y, approximately 170 males are conceived for every 100 females and males are more likely to be spontaneously aborted (at birth there are approximately 106 males for every 100 females) (Department of Health and Human Services, 1982; Montagu, 1959; Ounsted, 1972; Taylor & Ounsted, 1972).[17] Fetal death rates are about 50 percent higher for males, within the first month the male death rate exceeds females by about 40 percent, and for the entire first year the male death rate is 33 percent higher than females (Frankenhaeuser, 1991; Markides, 1990; Montagu, 1959; Oakley, 1972; Ounsted, 1972; Waldron, 1991).

The difference between male and female mortality is consistent throughout life and has often been explained as a function of lifestyle and work habits. However, the mortality rates noted above for infants can hardly be seen as a function of different lifestyles! From the beginning it would appear, therefore, that being male requires more effort and is fraught with more danger than being female (Hall, 1985; Montagu, 1957; Ounsted & Taylor, 1972; Rudolf & Hochberg, 1990; Tobach & Rosoff, 1978).

Problems in Infancy and Childhood

As we mentioned earlier, considerable evidence suggests that more males are conceived than are carried to term, but, as Taylor & Ounsted (1972) note, because there is an excess of males in all abortions, miscarriages, and stillbirths, the ratio is almost even at birth. Unfortunately, probably because of the slower maturational development of males, not only intrauterinely but also after birth, males are more exposed to potential environmental risks. Thus risk level puts male infants at a higher incidence rate for almost all childhood disorders and congenital and genetic defects.

In the area of biological disorders, males suffer more birth defects than do females, 37 percent more males die in infancy, and boys are more often afflicted by all major diseases during childhood (Nolen-Hoeksema, 1990; Table 3.1).

Table 3.1.
Sex Ratios for Physical and Emotional Disorders of Childhood

DISORDER	SEX-RATIO (Males to females)
Cerebral Palsy	150-100
Seizure Disorders	122-100
Epilepsies of Childhood	140-100
Infantile Spasms	210-100
Infantile Autism	400-100
Reading Disorders	400-100
Child Psychiatry Referrals	200-100
Respiratory Problems	133-100
Sub-acute Sclerosing Leucoencephalitis	220-100
Perth's Bone Disease	400-100
Adolescent Epilepsy	140-100

For example, Taylor & Ounsted (1972 report that males are over-represented in the population of the mentally retarded, especially at the less serious levels and of those with cerebral palsy (the sex ratio is 150:100), seizure disorders (122:100), epilepsies of childhood (140:100), infantile spasms (210:100), and perinatal brain damage. They suggest that males' susceptibility to these disorders in particular is due to their slower maturation, which in turn results in specific immaturity of the cerebral hemisphere, especially the left temporal lobe.

Although controversial, the suggestion of left-hemisphere problems in males has been repeatedly reported. In addition, Buffery and Gray (1972) suggest, based on a review of relevant studies, that the brains of males are more lateralized than those of females. Because speech is most often specific to the left hemisphere, the greater lateralization might account for the overrepresentation of little boys in the population of children with speech and reading problems (Alvis, Dodson, Pusakulich, 1990; Kertesz, Polk, Black, & Howell, 1990).

DeLisi, Dauphinais, and Hauser (1989), investigating the higher prevalence of schizophrenia among males and their lowered positive treatment outcomes, agree with both Geschwind and Behan (1982) and Flor-Henry (1985) that the relationship of lateralization, or failure to lateralize, is responsible for the problems that males suffer in greater numbers than females. Using more up-to-date technology—for example, CT (computerized tomography) and MRI (magnetic resonance imaging), Flaum and Andreasen (1990) and Habib et al. (1991) report confirmation that males with either schizophrenia or aphasia are more likely to have CT scans that reveal abnormalities, especially in the left hemisphere. Covering a wide range of topics, other researchers have also found support for the hypothesis of male left-hemisphere difference—for example, Drake, Hannay, and Gam (1990) in their study of alcoholics; Notman and Nadelson (1991) in their study of language disorders, where it was reported that males have a higher incidence of developmental dyslexia, developmental aphasia, and infantile autism; and Joseph (1990) in his investigation of the development of tardive dyskinesia in schizophrenics, where he found incidence rates to be nonrandom—a greater number of males develop tardive dyskinesia.

McEwen (1991), as do others, suggests that these problems are the result of testosterone influencing brain development in the fetus or infant (for humans, "fetal" androgen secretion lasts from birth through the first two years of life [p. 36]). Because of testosterone production and also the slower maturational process for males, the resulting modifications of circuitry and/or structure lead to the development of a greater number of brain malfunctions.

One of the earliest differences between the sexes is the faster maturation rate shown by females, perhaps as early as the seventh week of embryonic life. After five months of pregnancy, females are two weeks ahead of males; at birth, they are four weeks ahead. Females complete most processes earlier, including the acquisition of skills as walking, talking, and bladder and bowel control. They also attain the peaks of certain characteristics sooner, including puberty and full physiological maturity. (Barfield, 1976, p. 67)

Recently, in an investigation of children with nonorganic failure to thrive disorder, in both rural Israel and Rhode Island, Rudolf and Hochberg (1990) report an overwhelmingly greater number of boys with this problem. These authors suggest that socialization cannot be responsible for this observation, as boys are more valued children in both Arab and American cultures. Rudolf and Hochberg further note that in cases of diet restriction, girls are better able to "catch up" than are boys, confirming the notion that boys in general are less hardy organisms.

Other examples of the suggested constitutional weakness of males include their higher number of both physical and mental disorders of all types. For example, prior to teen years, males show more of almost every type of psychopathology, adjustment reactions, antisocial disorders, anxiety disorders, gender-identity disorders, learning disorders, psychotic disorders, and affective disorders, including depression (Eme, 1979).

Problems in Adults

While the popular reports of depression statistics usually focus on the number of women, since women do exceed men in depression from about mid-adolescence to middle age, males far outnumber females prior to adolescence and after middle age in the incidence of depression and depression-related behavior, such as alcoholism and suicide (Baum & Grunberg, 1991; Drake, Hannay, & Gam, 1990; Frankenhaeuser, 1991; Gjerde & Block, 1991; Green & Bell, 1987; Lester, 1990; Mueller, 1983; Nolen-Hoeksema, 1990; Pickens et al., 1991; Pritchard, 1990; Radloff, 1975; Ratliff-Crain & Baum, 1990).

Among the reasons why males may be more susceptible to depression and a number of other disorders are their greater reactivity to stress situations (Frankenhaeuser, 1991) and their lack of beneficial social relationships (Revenson & Majerovity 1990), especially social relationships outside of a marriage situation (Ratliff-Crain & Baum, 1990). The disruption of a close personal relationship, as in marriage, is more stressful for men, which, in turn, not only may lead to depression and/or suicide, but their decreased ability to deal with stress weakens the males' immune system and makes them more susceptible to various illnesses.

Mention suicide and most people will note the great number of women who are rescued from attempted suicide. However, men far outnumber women in successful suicides, and this differential has been suggested to be related, to some degree, to male socialization, which encourages men to ignore psychological pain. It has been suggested further that the higher incidence of alcoholism among males is a "cover-up" symptom of adult depression, as acting out behavior is often considered evidence of depression for male teenagers (Nolen-Hoeksema, 1990).

In 1982 the suicide rate per 100,000 males between the ages of twenty-five to sixty-four was 25.9 percent, whereas the rate for the same age females was only 9.2 percent. From ages sixty-five to seventy-four, the suicide rate for males increased to 33 percent and for women decreased to 7.4 percent. Between seventy-five and eighty-four, the suicide rate for males continued to rise to 48.5 percent and the rate for females continued to decline to 6.1 percent. At ages eighty-five and above, the suicide rate for men rose to 53.9 percent and continued to decline for females to 3.9 percent (Nolen-Hoeksema, 1990).

In adulthood, males continue to suffer from the more fatal illnesses whereas females have a preponderance of the less life-threatening disorders such as all of the autoimmune disorders (Table 3.2).[18] It has been found that healthy women carry higher concentrations of immunoglobulins, and even as small children females are at an advantage against disease. Specifically, five immunoglobulin-deficiency diseases, including total agammaglobulinemia (the inability to produce antibodies), occur solely in males. Lower concentrations of immunoglobulin in males is suggested to account for the higher incidence rate in males of all types of infections, including osteomyelitis, respiratory infections such as pneumonia and bronchitis, gastroenteritis, poliomyelitis, and mononucleosis. Because of immune incompetence, males are more prone to harbor, and provide a good home for, living pathogens (Hall, 1985).

Stress-Related Disorders

Besides being more susceptible than women to all of the fatal diseases, especially cardiovascular system diseases, where they lead women two to one, men also appear to be more vulnerable to the ravages of smoking and alcohol (Drake, Hannay, & Gam, 1990; Ratliff-Crain & Baum, 1990).[19] In dealing with stress, men and women also appear to differ, not only in what they perceive to be stressful and in their physiological reactions to stress, but also in the methods used to combat stress. In situations where the individual perceives her- or himself to be in control of her or his own

Table 3.2
Sexual Differences in Susceptibility to Disease

DISEASE	PREPONDERANCE IN MALES
Acoustic Trauma	Almost exclusively
Acute Pancreatitis	Large majority
Addison's Disease	More often
Amoebic Dysentery	15-1
Alcoholism	6-1
Angina Pectoris	5-1
Arteriosclerosis	2.5-1
Bronchial Asthma	More often
Brucellosis	More often
Cancer, Buccal Cavity	2-1
Cancer, Gastrointestinal Tract	3-1
Cancer, Head of Pancreas	4.5-1
Cancer, Respiratory Tract	8-1
Cancer, Skin	3-1
Cerebral Hemorrhage	Greatly
Cerebrospinal Meningitis	Slight
Childhood Schizophrenia	3-1
Chronic Glomerular Nephritis	2-1
Cirrhosis of Liver	3-1
Coronary Insufficiency	30-1
Coronary Sclerosis	25-1
Diabetes *	More often
Duodenal Ulcer	7-1
Erb's Dystrophy	More often
Gastric Ulcer	6-1
Gout	49-1
Harelip	2-1
Harelip with Cleft Palate	More often
Heart Disease	2-1
Hemophilia	100%
Hepatitis	More often
Hernia	4-1
Hodgkin's Disease	2-1
Hysteria **	2-1
Korsakoff's Psychosis	2-1
Leukemia	2-1
Meningitis	More often
Mental Deficiencies	2-1
Muscular Dystrophy	Almost Exclusively
Myocardial Degeneration	2-1
Paralysis Agitans	Greatly
Pericarditis	2-1
Pigmentary Cirrhosis	20-1
Pineal Tumors	3-1

*According to Waldron (1976) diabetes is slightly more common in females.
**Refers to stress-induced hysteria; otherwise, hysteria is diagnosed more often in females.

Table 3.2 (*continued*)

DISEASE	PREPONDERANCE IN MALES
Pleurisy	3-1
Pneumonia	3-1
Poliomyelitis	Slight
Progressive Muscular Paralysis	More often
Pseudohermaphroditism	10-1
Pylortic Stenosis, Congenital	5-1
Q Fever	More often
Sciatica	Greatly
Scurvy	Greatly
Syringomyelia	2.3-1
Tabes	10-1
Thromboangitis Obliterans	96-1
Tuberculosis	2-1
Tularemia	More often
	PREPONDERANCE IN FEMALES
Acromegaly	More often
Arthritis Deformans	4.4-1
Carcinoma of Genitalia	3-1
Carcinoma of Gall Bladder	10-1
Cataract	More often
Chlorosis (Anemia)	100%
Chorea	3-1
Chronic Mitral Endocarditis	2-1
Cleft Palate	3-1
Combined Sclerosis	More often
Diptheria	Slight
Gall Stones	4-1
Goiter, Exophthalmic	6-1 or 8-1
Hemorrhoids	Considerable
Hyperthyroidism	10-1
Influenza	2-1
Migraine	6-1
Multiple Sclerosis	More often
Myxedema	6-1
Obesity	Considerable
Osteomalacia	9-1
Pellagra	Slight
Purpura Haemorrhagica	4 or 5-1
Raynaud's Disease	1.5-1
Rheumatoid Arthritis	3-1
Rheumatic Fever	Considerable
Tonsilitis	Slight
Varicose Veins	Considerable
Whooping Cough	2-1

Source: Hoyenga & Hoyenga, 1979, p. 375.

Table 3.3

Categories from DSM III-R in Which Males Have Greater Incidence Rates

CONDITION	PREPONDERANCE IN MALES
Mental Retardation	1.5-1
Pervasive Developmental Disorder	2-1 or 5-1
Autism	3-1 or 4-1
Specific Developmental Disorders	2 to 4 times greater
ADHD	6 to 9 times in clinic settings; 3-1 in community
Oppositional Defiant Disorder	More often in prepuberty
Gender Identity Problems	More often in clinic
Transsexualism	8-1
Gender Identity - non-Transsexual	More often
Tourettes Disorder	3-1
Transient Tic	3-1
Functional Encopresis	More often
Functional Enuresis	More often
Stuttering	3-1
Multi Infarct Dementia	More often
Alcohol Hallucinations	4-1
Inhalent Induced Organic Mental Deficiency	More often
Psychoactive Substance Abusive Disorder	More often
Nicotine Dependence	More often in adulthood
Social Phobia	More often
Obsessive Compulsive Disorder	More often
Paraphillias	More often
Sexual Masochism	20-1
Klein-Lewin Syndrome	More often
Sleep Terror Disorder	More often
Sleepwalking	More often
Factitious Disorder with Physical Symptoms	More often
Factitious Disorder with Psychological Symptoms	More often
Intermittent Explosive Disorder	More often
Pathological Gambling	More often
Pyromania	More often
Paranoid Personality Disorder	More often
Antisocial Personality Disorder	More often
Obsessive Compulsive Personality Disorder	More often
Sadistic Personality Disorder	More often

life, women handle stress, both physically and emotionally, more success-fully than do men (Frankenhaeuser, 1991; Nolen-Hoeksema, 1990; Ratliff-Crain & Baum, 1990).

Although it is possible that the disease and/or accident rate of males is related to their lifestyle—men are more often risk takers—it is also possible that, particularly in terms of childhood diseases and accidents, the difference in incidence rates may be a function of differing maturational level. While the data are meager, since men and women usually find themselves in different social settings, what evidence there is suggests that the susceptibility difference is more likely to be genetic than environmental. For example, women have not suffered the same as men as they have entered the workforce, and in a study of women and men in a religious cloister, men still faired less well than women in terms of contracting degenerative diseases (Madigan, 1957).[20]

Women are healthier than men—if by health one means the capacity to deal with germs and illness. . . . Death from almost all causes are more frequent in males at all ages. . . . The evidence is clear: from the constitutional standpoint woman is the stronger sex. (Montagu, 1957)

Currently we understand that the ability to handle stress is the key to guarding against contracting disease or developing an emotional disorder. Because of the weaker physiology of males, they are not as well equipped to handle stress as are women (Garai & Scheinfeld, 1968; Hoyenga & Hoyenga, 1979; Potts, 1970). Table 3.3 displays those psychiatric diseases listed in DSM III-R for which males have a higher incidence rate.

TEMPERAMENT

With roots in the Hippocrates-Galen humoral theory, the concept of temperament has been used to describe "dispositions that are almost unchanged from infancy throughout life," which are "saturated with a constant emotional quality, with a peculiar pattern of mood, alterness, intensity, or tonus" (Allport, 1937, p. 53). Emphasizing that temperamental differences are a function of physiological, possibly genetic determinants, J. P. Guilford (1959, p. 407), who was primarily interested in measuring differences, makes a more pedestrian distinction between types of personality traits: "Aptitudes pertain to *how well* the person performs. Temperament traits have to do with the *manner* in which his actions occur. Neither aptitudes nor temperament traits have much to do directly with *what* a person does; this is primarily a matter of motivational traits."

It has been Guilford's definition of temperament, along with his interactionist position—an emphasis on the response of caregivers and others to predominantly biological differences in children—that has influenced subsequent research on temperament trait differences (Thomas & Chess, 1977). Noteworthy because of their careful, formalized observation techniques, which meet Guilford's objection to much of the sloppy and casual trait measures of earlier researchers, Alexander Thomas, Stella Chess, and Herbert Birch have been in the forefront of the modern interest in investigating relatively enduring individual differences in temperament. Initially these researchers were interested in dispelling a too-exclusive emphasis upon environmental factors in child development.

Using a longitudinal design, Thomas, Chess, and Birch (1968, 1970) analyzed data from 231 children in New York City and identified nine aspects of temperament, which fit into three major categories or "types" that are apparent at birth and which clearly separate individual children: activity level, regularity, approach-withdrawal, adaptability, level of sensory threshold, positive-negative mood, intensity of response, distractibility, and persistence and attention.

The first category, which these authors named "easy children," describe those characterized by "positive . . . mode, regularity in bodily function, a low or moderate intensity of reaction, adaptability, and a positive approach to, rather than withdrawal from, new situations." The second, called "difficult children," are "irregular in bodily functions, are usually intense in their reactions, tend to withdraw in the face of new stimuli, are slow to adapt to change in the environment and are generally negative in mood." The third type was displayed by children labeled "slow to warm up," who have a "low activity level, tend to withdraw on their first exposure to first stimuli, are slow to adapt, are somewhat negative in mood and respond to situations with a low intensity of reaction."

Thomas, Chess, and Birch's (Thomas, Chess, & Birch, 1968; Thomas & Chess, 1977) research led to the suggestion that the individual temperament traits of a child interact with the individual temperament traits of the mother, setting up a situation for conflict or not. For example, if one is "slow to warm"—an indication of an individual's unease in making new acquaintances—but one's mother is gregarious, then undue stress may be placed on the child to be more outgoing.

It is our hypothesis that the personality is shaped by the constant interplay of temperament and environment. . . . What is important is the interaction between the two—between the child's own characteristics and his environment. If the two influences are harmonized, one can expect healthy development of the child; if they are dissonant, behavioral problems are almost sure to ensue. (Thomas, Chess, & Birch, 1970, pp. 2, 7)

The results of their research, however, do not provide impressive evidence of the endurance of early temperament differences—behavioral evidence showing the effect of shaping by social experiences, for example—nor clear sex differences. Concerning the latter, their work shows the same general tendencies, as reported elsewhere, for boys to be motorically more active and girls to be more complacent and calm, but the differences are usually not statistically significant (Thomas & Chess, 1977).

BIOLOGICAL MATURATION AND SOCIAL INTERACTION

While in the following chapters we discuss the socialization of the child, there are some relevant issues—for example, the interplay of biology and social situations—that need to be included in the discussion of biological differences between genders. Although reported differences between the genders typically stem from observations of adults who themselves have been socialized to expect different behaviors from boys and girls, an impressively large number of studies indicate that from birth on little boys and little girls are different and that this difference is at least in part biological. For example, male infants are noted to be more active and aggressive than female infants (Barrett, 1979; Houser, 1979; Pedersen & Bell, 1970; Rubin, Provenzano, & Luria, 1974).[21] Boys have also been suggested to be more fearful of strangers (Bronson, 1971) and more adventurous (Jersild & Holmes, 1935).

At birth boys exceed females in weight by 5 percent and height by about 2 percent (Hutt, 1972). Males have a higher basal metabolism rate, higher oxygen consumption, greater vital capacity, and a lower resting heart rate than girls. They have a higher caloric need than girls and their need for potassium also seems to be greater. Males in general, at all ages, have more muscle mass than females; even in young children, boys' grip strength is greater than girls'.

However, males' speed of growth lags nearly two years behind girls', their bone ossification is completed eight to twenty-seven months later than girls, and their physiological maturity is achieved as late as two and one-half years after girls' physiological maturity. It has been estimated that at birth a girl is equal to a boy at about four to six weeks after birth (Biller & Borstelmann, 1967; Cossette, Malcuit, & Pomerleau, 1991; Earls & Jung, 1988). The faster maturation of girls leads not only to a lessening potential for disorders, as discussed in the previous section, but also to an increase in social interaction with parents and/or caregivers.

The motor activity and perceptual patterns of boys are notably different from that of girls. Male infant activity primarily consists of startles while female infant activity includes rhythmic mouthing, smiles, and sucks. Female infants also are reported to have lower tactual and pain thresholds, visual acuity superior to males (although this superiority diminishes throughout adulthood with females, including other female primates' having worse vision than males), and better auditory discrimination and localization. Whereas males tend to look at visual patterns longer than female infants, female infants are better able to discriminate between various visual patterns at an earlier age (Baker, 1987; Cohen & Levy, 1986; Hutt, 1972).

Directly after birth newborns are thrust into a social situation where their caretaking is strongly affected by the temperament of the infant (Notman & Nadelson, 1991). Female infants, because of their increased calmness and readiness to settle down, their greater auditory responsiveness and sensitivity to tactile experiences, and their earlier face discrimination, are more ready to bond with the mother or another caregiver (Cossette, Malcuit, & Pomerleau, 1991; Neubauer & Neubauer, 1990; Olesker, 1984; Reinisch, Rosenblum, Rubin, & Schulsinger, 1991). These early interactions, in turn, set the child up for later ease in the development of identity and in dealing with feelings of abandonment.

Whether or not parents respond differentially to particular gendered children is hotly debated within psychology. Maccoby and Jacklin (1974) report that they found no evidence of differential treatment in the fifteen years of research they reviewed. However, others, including sociologists, anthropologists, and clinical psychologists, have maintained that gender is a stimulus to which adults respond differentially (Benedict, 1938; Mead, 1935, 1949). Different cultures and different socioeconomic classes (Whiting & Edwards, 1988) also have different expectations concerning gender-appropriate behaviors that the adults in the culture selectively reinforce. Because children need to "fit into" their culture, and the gender role one plays has been considered essential to fit in, gender-role socialization is probably the most important aspect of child-rearing as it prepares children to function as adults.

Neubauer & Neubauer (1990) suggest that "ability to engage one's environment appears to be predisposed"—that is, they suggest that individuals' particular temperamental characteristics determine how they interact with others within their environment and, subsequently, how others respond. For example, it is suggested that boys who have been reported to have a higher motility of behavior, especially large muscle behavior, elicit more vigorous play from their parents. Parental reinforcement of vigorous play may, in turn, encourage boys to fulfill the stereotype of being obstreperous (Cossette, Malcuit, & Pomerleau, 1991; Notman & Nadelson, 1991; Reinisch, Rosenblum, Rubin, & Schulsinger, 1991).

Taken together, the information on sex differences in behavior suggests that three statements might summarize the responsible factors: first is the familiar "You are what you eat," to which could be added, "You are what you secrete," and "You are whom you meet." (Barfield, 1976, p. 108)

A ubiquitous belief in our culture is that men should be aggressive, independent, objective, dominant, active, competitive, logical, worldly, direct, and self-confident. Paired with these "positive" characteristics there is also a set of "negative" characteristics, such as being blunt, rough, not aware of the feelings of others, not emotional, and having no need for security. All of these traits would suggest a person who has an independent attitude and who participates in external, goal-directed activities. To encourage little boys to grow up to meet these objectives, parents encourage differential behavior for boys and girls: little boys are socialized to become proficient at out-of-door activities, insensitive to the emotional needs of others and themselves, obstreperous, and convinced of their own invincibility.

Human and nonhuman primate mothers have been seen to treat their male and female children differentially. For example, human mothers touch their daughters more than they touch their sons (Goldberg & Lewis, 1969). This behavior leads, at thirteen months, to girls who touch and socially interact with their mothers more than do boys.[22] Studies of primates indicate that males wean themselves earlier than do females and that males have a greater number of aversive behaviors directed at their mothers and that mothers respond accordingly; they are more likely to rebuff a male offspring than a female offspring (McGuinnes, 1985). Primate mothers are also more likely to punish, reject, or withdraw from male infants (Mitchell, 1981); among nonhuman primates, mothers tend to favor their daughters (Fagan, 1972, cited in McGuinnes, 1985).[23]

A biosocial hypothesis has recently been offered as a valid and useful explanatory concept for the gender differences we observe. For example, that girls reach milestones of development that foster social interaction (Reinisch, Rosenblum, Rubin, & Schulsinger, 1991)[24] is a function of a biological process. This biological process, in turn, allows them to consistently show positive social behavior, empathize with strangers, be more interested in social events, and be more upset at having to leave their mothers (Goldberg & Lewis, 1969). These behaviors, in turn, encourage a more stable bond between mother and daughter than exists between mother and son.

The male infant (and child) is a more vulnerable biological organism. The rejection by mother, therefore, in the cause of either a biological predisposition against males (as may be suggested in the behavior of primate mothers) or as a means by which she may begin the arduous task of appropriate gender-role socialization, appears to put the male infant or child in a double-risk-factor situation. Not only is he biologically vulnerable but psychologically he misses out on the human connection that could lead to greater psychological stability.

Boys seem to be more permanently affected than girls by the emotional climate of infancy (Bayley, 1969, cited in Mitchell, 1981). Research suggests that between the ages of thirteen months and thirty-six months boys are especially vulnerable (Mitchell, 1981). For example, boys suffer from childhood schizophrenia eight to ten times more than girls do (Mitchell, 1981), boys are three times more often referred to children's clinics for head-banging than are girls, and male suicides at all ages except young adults in industrialized countries (Lester, 1990; Pritchard, 1990) outnumber females by three or four to one.

Marital disorder and maternal absence also appear to affect little boys more than little girls (Earls & Jung, 1988; Mott, 1991). Earls and Jung report that marital discord and maternal depression were related to depression for boys at two, but that there was no obvious influence of girls. Gender differences in problem behavior emerge by age two, and boys have more persisting problems and a higher incidence of problems by age eight (ratio of 2:1) (Richman, Stevenson, & Graham, 1982; Stevenson, Richman, & Graham, 1986). Mott (1991) found that boys are more sensitive to child care and that they are handicapped more than girls by mother absences. In attempting to explain what is responsible for these differences, Lewis, Feiring, McGuffog, and Jaskir (1984) suggest that the development of psychopathology is a function of a vulnerable organism who fails to develop a strong mother-child attachment. Unfortunately, in our culture and species it is boys who are biologically vulnerable and who are not encouraged to develop and maintain strong interpersonal relationships, especially with their mother.

IMPLICATIONS FOR SEPARATION ANXIETY

There are several ways in which the constitutional weakness of males and the relatively slower maturational rate of boys affect the reaction to separation and loss. Most social scientists who have concerned themselves with the issue of observed gender differences in regard to separation, including the catastrophic effects of widowhood and divorce on men, have taken an exclusively environmental position. Clearly child-rearing practices and differential expectations in relation to autonomy and masculinity, which are products of the social matrix, are important influences on personality development. Many writers, in particular Ullian (1981), however, have pointed to a subtle pathogenic element in the typical social learning experiences of males: society exacts greater demands for autonomy, unrelatedness, individual strength, and resourcefulness as goals for development of males than of females, despite the fact that males are less biologically equipped to meet these demands.

During peak development of autonomy-striving—the stage Mahler calls separation-individuation—the male child is not biologically mature enough to deal with the loss of emotional support. The association between separation and abandonment, which is the source of subsequent panic in the lifetime experiences of some individuals, with differential vulnerability in males, is thus, a function of cognitive and sensorimotor biological immaturity as much as it is a function of anxiety-ridden social experiences during toddlerhood and thereafter.

LAURENCE WITKOWSKI: INJURED PASHA

To his superstitious mother Larry's congenital heart disorder, anomalous pulmonary venous return, was caused by her insatiable craving for borscht while pregnant. Her consequent guilt feelings, combined with the fact that he was so much smaller as a neonate than were his two brothers and one sister, led to a great deal of worry and pampering. Mrs. Witkowski, who worked in the same gun factory as her husband and several other relatives, left her job to devote herself to Larry's care. For the first several weeks after he left the Yale–New Haven Hospital, family legend has it, the worried mother got not a minute's sleep; she was constantly focused on listening to his breathing, in dread that she would hear his last gasp.

The Witkowskis lived in a large Slavic community in Bridgeport, Connecticut, not far from the gun factory. To the boys in the neighborhood, sports—baseball and football—were the most important things—more important than academic achievement, more important than popular music, and much more important than girls. Larry's mother did not allow him to participate in sports, despite the physician's assurance that Larry's disability was minor. The boy spent much of his time on the sidelines watching; he felt like an outsider. Since he was not allowed to engage in brawls either, he might have gotten the reputation of a "sissy," were it not for his growing up to be huge and muscular.

By adolescence, he had become a gentle giant, blond and good-looking, quiet and unassuming, but lacking in self-confidence. He felt less competent than his age-mates; he didn't know how to hit a baseball or throw a football. He did not feel like an invalid, but his mother, now with his sister as her ally, constantly treated him as an invalid. They tended to his every need and he grew to be quite incompetent around the house; Larry did not, for example, know how to replace a light bulb. After graduating from high school, he acquired a job at the factory, a steady girlfriend, Dottie, whose family owned the local bakery, and a strong liking for alcohol.

Larry was uncomfortable in strange social situations and the neighborhood bar, frequented by people he had known all his life, became a second home to him. Most evenings he would drink to oblivion and his friends, accompanied always by Dottie, would make sure he arrived home safe and sound. Once, however, at the bar Larry did something uncharacteristic for him, and this action completely changed the course of his life. A friend of his had the temerity to make a sexual remark to Dottie, who was short and slight—something having to do with the mechanics of sexual coupling with such a disparity in stature. Larry became enraged and threw several punches. He then broke a beer bottle and slashed the other man's face.

Larry, who had never been in trouble with the law, received a suspended sentence and five years' probation. It was through the efforts of his probation officer that Larry was admitted into a training program at the nuclear power plant and the man's encouragement helped Larry become a high-paid electronic technician at the plant.

Larry and Dottie were married. Their parents loaned them the money for a down payment on a house in a fashionable suburb. But, despite the fact that they had known each other since they were small children, Larry and Dottie were incompatible and the marriage was in trouble from the onset. She had also been the youngest child and, although she had worked in her father's shop since she was twelve, she had not been required to perform any household tasks. Larry's tyrannical demands startled her and she did not know how to deal with his constant orders, his impatience, his refusal to do anything around the house (Dottie even mowed the grass), and his heavy drinking.

Dottie was not a rebellious or willful person. There were very few occasions when she did not do exactly what Larry demanded, but she began to feel that she was being treated as a slave. When she finally got up the nerve to complain, she made the mistake of doing so when Larry was drinking whiskey. He attacked her and the bruises were so obvious that she was ashamed to leave the house for three days. It was shortly after this incident that Larry began to suffer chest pains.

Larry's physician did not believe that his distress had a physical basis; all the test findings were negative. A few days later, Larry passed out at work and was briefly hospitalized. Apparently, even the slightest stress would lead to intense pain and shortness of breath, which he reduced by heavy drinking. At times, before he reached the stage of unconsciousness, Larry would precipitate an argument with his wife and beat her with his fists.

Dottie tolerated this treatment for several months before she told her family. They told her to leave "the screwball" immediately. By the time she returned to retrieve her clothes and personal belongings, Larry had committed himself to an alcohol rehabilitation center. Dottie returned to Bridgeport after the divorce was finalized, and again works in the bakery.

Larry shares the house in the suburb with two recovering alcoholics he met at the center. Convinced that he cannot handle the stress of his job at the nuclear plant, he works, when he feels healthy enough, for one of his housemates. He expresses no remorse for his treatment of Dottie. He is, in fact, even more furious with her than when they lived together. She abandoned him, he says, when he was suffering a severe mental disorder; her refusal to recognize his illness contributed to his "breakdown." Ostensibly conscientious about the A.A. program, Larry still drinks on weekends. Since leaving the rehabilitation center, Larry has come to the attention of authorities only once: at a bar in a neighboring city he was involved in a noisy brawl that resulted in an injury to a barmaid, whose face was slashed by a bottle. Although accused, Larry was not held because of lack of evidence.

The case of Larry Witkowski demonstrates the complicated, interactive relationship between biological and social factors. Born with a relatively minor, fairly common congenital disorder, Larry was pampered as an infant and discouraged from developing a sense of autonomy or of competence primarily because of his mother's excessive concern over his cardiac condition.

There are indications that even without his mother's persistent over-protection and restrictive attendance, Larry might have developed feelings of inadequacy and frustration-evoked violence, two of the strong tendencies in his character structure. He internalized a concern about his health and established a self-perception of a helpless, physically handicapped and imperilled boy and man. Whether his injured sense of identity was the cause or the effect of problems during normal autonomy-striving, Larry's social milieu expected—or rather, demanded—that a male be highly autonomous and possess certain physical skills, especially athletic skills. Because of his somatic overconcern and self-perception, which were aided and abetted by the persisting ministrations of the females of his family, Larry failed to practice those things that contribute to adult manhood in his community. What he did practice—and sought to re-experience in his relationship with women—were the pasha traits adaptive in his infancy:

he learned to be dependent upon women and to use his apparent weakness and helplessness in order to manipulate and control them.[25]

As is true of neurotic personality traits generally, those associated with dependent personalities reveal insatiability and inflexibility. What made Larry a unique babe-pasha was that in addition he did not develop the ability to delay gratification or to tolerate even the slightest frustration of his dependency needs. His rage toward Dottie and the barmaid victim, arguably mother "substitutes" because of their role, was a result, not because they refused to serve him, but because they did not serve him quickly enough.

The maturation of biological and psychological potentialities requires practice. Even in the case of boys who receive "normal" pampering during infancy, the separation experience that Mahler describes so eloquently of boys around two years of age is conflicted and problematic because of the socially directed discontinuity. Voluntarily separating from the mother's presence succeeds only after a period of practice; most boys achieve success if there is a proper balance between the positive valence of exciting, risky adventures "out there" and the safe anchoring of a mother who is available if needed. For Larry, who had internalized a perception of himself as biologically inadequate and had learned traits that were maladaptive for autonomy, "out there" was full of dangers.

Larry literally had not learned how to be a man. His life experiences, particularly those of his early childhood, had prepared him to be a "cardiac" patient or an alcoholic.

NOTES

1. The area of psychology that deals with differences among persons is called differential psychology (Anastasi, 1958; Tyler, 1965).

2. *Gender difference* is the term traditionally used when the focus is on social behavior, such as occupational choice or manners, whereas, *sex difference* is the term most often used when the focus is on differences that are more directly related to biology. We shall use the term *sex difference* in this chapter when we discuss physiological differences between men and women and the term *gender difference* to refer to behavior influenced by environmental factors such as socialization.

3. There is a long-standing controversy, for example, regarding possible racial differences in intelligence. Associated with the nature side, specifically in the case of "inherited" inferiority of African Americans, are Garrett (1971) and Jensen (1980). After more than 100 years, the inflamatory debate persists. Prominent proponents of the nurture position, which sees the observed differences in test scores due to unequal learning opportunities are Scarr and Weinberg (1976) and Hirsch (1975).

4. Modern psychologists generally repudiate the nineteenth-century theories of sex differences in cognitive ability; the older notions were almost always based on pseudo-

scientific observations, such as that women's brains were smaller. Among the many works discussing sex differences and cognitive ability are Shields (1975) and Tavris (1992). Montagu (1940) has noted that antifeminist and racial prejudice share similar motivations, and he speculated that their incidence may be inversely related—that is, when women obtain equal rights, racial prejudice increases, and vice versa.

5. As early as 1914, Leta Stetter Hollingworth found no experimental evidence to support the Darwinian notion of variability. Her explanations of the differences in achievement and mental deficiency were environmental (Hollingworth, 1914).

6. Attesting to the popularity of investigating sex and gender differences, Ellis's work lasted for six editions (1894 to 1930), and during that time several laboratories around the world were devoted to the investigation of sex and gender differences (McGuinnes, 1987).

7. This work covers only fifteen years of research and not all of that research was specifically developed to investigate sex and gender differences. Maccoby and Jacklin's work has been criticized for the limited scope of research presented. The review ignores clinical data and underrepresents psychodynamic theories. Experimental studies cannot do justice to the complexity and subtlety of socialization effects; Bloom-Feshbach and Bloom-Feshbach (1987), for example, discuss the limitations of all behavioral research to provide a clear and thorough understanding of the psychological development of individuals.

8. This interaction might be as biologically complex and difficult to understand as hormonal influences on the brain or as social as the differential response men and women make toward other men and women (an indication of different expectations concerning behavior).

9. To suggest that there are differences does not require one to label them "good" or "bad" or "inferior" or "deviant." Differences can exist between individuals and between genders that merely point out diversity. Historically, of course, we have used the male prototype, and when women differed they were considered "deviant" or "inferior." In this work we suggest that because mammals are prototypically female, it is the male that is deviant from the norm.

10. Referring to androgens as the male sex hormone and estrogens as the female sex hormone is somewhat misleading because both androgens and estrogens are produced in both male and female bodies and both are needed for the development of secondary sex characteristics at puberty.

11. There are, of course, abnormalities that affect females also—for example, Turner's syndrome, in which a female has only one X chromosome instead of two. It has been estimated that only 1 in 700 females is affected by a gender defect, whereas 1 in 500 male infants is born with some chromosome anomaly (Hoyenga & Hoyenga, 1979).

12. There are also sex-limited traits, but these usually find expression specifically in one or the other sex. For example, milk production in the female and beard growth in the male are examples of sex-limited traits.

13. Sex-linked traits, carried on either the autosomes or the sex chromosomes, are displayed in females when both X chromosomes, the one from the father and the one from the mother, contain a recessive gene for the disorder.

14. Chromosomes are categorized into sex chromosomes—those which determine the biological sex of the individual—and autosomes—the other twenty-two pairs of chromosomes which we inherit from our parents.

15. Carter (1972) has noted that the data making ichthyosis hystrix a sex-linked trait are equivocal. He suggests that only hairy ears is truly sex-linked.

16. A sex-inverted male is an XX chromosome individual who, evaluated by physical genitalia, is a male (Polani, 1972).

17. This difference in conception and mortality rate is apparently consistent in other animal species (Hoyenga & Hoyenga, 1979).

18. Androgen and progesterone production may explain part of the susceptibility of men to disease and their higher mortality rates; castration appears to increase longevity and health in humans and animals lower on the phylogenetic scale than humans (Hamilton, Hamilton, & Mestler, 1969; Hamilton & Mestler, 1969). New research with estrogen-replacement therapy suggests that the continued use of estrogen after menopause increases women's health, particularly protection against heart disease.

19. Research has not supported the prediction that as more women enter the workforce the frequency of serious disease would increase (Baum & Grunberg, 1991; Eaker, Packard, Wenger, Clarkson, & Tyroler, 1988; Markides, 1990).

20. Personal communication, Susan Bailey, Director of the Women's Research Study Center, Wellesey College, September 1989.

21. That male humans have been identified as more aggressive than female humans is consistent with observations about other animals also, including mice, hamsters, and nonhuman primates (Houser, 1979; McGuinnes, 1985; Mitchell, 1981). As with humans, however, there are differences in the degree of aggression in the population of males—that is, one male may not be as aggressive as another male (White, 1983). Recent evidence concerning male-female relationships among baboons suggests that less aggressive males are more successful in mating (Strum, 1987).

22. Goldberg & Lewis (1969) found that those mothers who touched their boy babies at six months had sons who touched them more than the average at thirteen months also. It appears that the closeness of male children to their mothers is partly related to the mother's early behavior.

23. Interestingly, the reverse seems to be true in the human primate population.

24. These data are supported by nonhuman primate research (Draper, 1985; Mitchell, 1981).

25. The case material indicates that Larry was similarly dependent in his relationship to men, notably with his probation officer and his housemates. In both cases the men provided assistance in Larry's being employed—efforts which had the positive effect of facilitating an adult, autonomous life. In all his relationships with women, on the other hand, Larry sought dependency gratification as an end in itself.

4

Sociocultural Influences and Stereotypes

Men do not become what by nature they are meant to be, but what society makes them. . . . Generous feelings . . . are, as it were, shrunk up, seared, violently wrenched, and amputated to fit us for our intercourse with the world, something in the manner that beggars maim and mutilate their children to make them fit for their future situation in life. (Colby, 1925, p. 82)

While psychobiological processes and constitutional differences,[1] with their sequential priorities and maturation rates grounded in programmed genetics, obviously influence the development of human personality, child development occurs in the context of a cultural and social structure, where agents (usually parents) are assigned to effect the learning and training of the young (Thomas & Chess, 1980). In this chapter we deal with the sociocultural forces that shape personality development: the cultural values and myths that provide ideal stereotypes and the social-interactive and social-structure[2] variables that impinge upon caretakers. In the next chapter we treat the direct, mediating effects of socialization and parenting, which provide the experiential application of these external factors.

CULTURAL PATTERNS

In 1952 Ralph Linton provided a list of values that are "universal"—found in all known societies. He includes the distinction between good and bad; prohibitions against rape, murder, and other forms of violence;

the expectation of the care and training of children; regulation of relation-ships between family members; and the prohibition of sex between mother and son. Although this list is less specific and much shorter than Murdock's (1975), it is clear that, despite variations in the how, why, or who, almost all important human activity is to some degree regulated and controlled by a culture's definition of what is right and wrong, with sanctions against behavior that is considered unnatural or sinful.

Although values preexist any particular individual of the culture and he or she is usually not able to change the values or even exert veto power, individuals who are "civilized" (or enculturated) are expected to internalize the value judgments. These value judgments then become incorporated as part of the "self"; individuals shape their personality around the stated values of the society. As Thomas and Chess (1980, p. 185) observe, in our society where "hierarchical value judgments are made on the basis of sex, color, religion, national origin, and socioeconomic class, these aspects of an individual's identity become important attributes of the self." While the radical cultural approach usually minimizes the amount of deviance permitted by a given society or the existence of "variant" value orientations (Kluckhohn & Strodtbeck, 1961), there is little question, based upon the existence of guilt feelings, value conflicts, battles over such moral issues as abortion, and of choices that are labeled psychiatric disorders, that values exert a strong personal influence on individuals, even individuals who live in a rapidly changing, "multicul-turally diverse" society.[3]

The role of values in establishing the objectives of child-rearing is of particular importance in the development of personality. Not only do the values dictate the behaviors that are to be inculcated in the new member of the society, but some times the values also play a factor in shaping the physical aspects of individuals. For example, Montagu (1974b) notes that steatopygy (an excessive amount of subcutaneous fat in the buttocks), a highly valued sign of beauty, is found in a high proportion of Bushman women in Botswana. Mothers encourage the condition by feeding their girl children a diet high in animal fat.

Male domination of females, a common characteristic in all recorded cultures, has its origin in males' greater physical strength; in fact, Ward (1916) suggests that sexual selection changed from female to male control when males noticed that they were bigger than women and the first rape occurred.[4] Because of culturally determined distinctions, males are en-couraged to be assertive, competitive, and dominant and females to be dependent, passive, and submissive. There is an expectation that the male should have superior status, be dominant in relation to females, and assert leadership functions in society. However, the "general law," which states that "whenever one sex is larger or stronger than the other, the larger or stronger sex will occupy a position of dominance with respect to the smaller or weaker sex" (Montagu, 1974b, p. 142),[5] is anachronistic and maladaptive in the case of modern Western societies. The unequal distribution of power persists in the value-system because of the myth of male physical superiority in spite of the plethora of evidence that suggests that in a majority of important biological aspects females are, in fact, superior to males.

Besides having differential expectations for the general behavior of men and women, all known societies provide for a division of labor (Murdock, 1975) and almost always there is some distinction of assigned tasks based upon gender (Benedict, 1938). The traditional explanation is that differences in reproductive function result in different work demands. Women carry and then nurse infants and, therefore, must be near the hearth. Men, on the other hand, free from child-care responsibilities (until recently men have been seen as unfit for child care, as well as inept), were required to hunt and protect the female and her offspring. While no one can deny that childbearing is exclusively a female function, there is considerable cultural variation in the caretaking and training of the young (Mead, 1935) and no biological reason for the low value placed upon childbearing as work for the common good of the society (Montagu, 1974b). In most societies childbearing is perceived as almost a disability: "If the female of the species were the more powerful animal, it is almost certain that childbearing would, in all societies, be esteemed yet another of the physical advantages of the dominant female as compared to submissive male" (Montagu, 1974b, p. 143).

Children are not born knowing their proper place within the culture; they must be taught. While it is intuitive that mothers and fathers treat their sons and daughters differently—after all, the gender roles for each are distinct—Eleanor Maccoby and Carol Jacklin (1974), in a review of experimental literature in psychology, came to the conclusion that there are only minimal differences between boys and girls in both the behaviors they exhibit and the care provided them by parents. Accounts by anthropologists and a wealth of data from clinical studies and sociological reports, on the other hand, suggest that gender is an important variable in parenting behavior (Benedict, 1938; Goodheart, 1992; Mead, 1935; Stoller & Herdt, 1982). Not only do different cultures have different expectations about appropriate gender-role behaviors that adults selectively reinforce, but within a culture there are differences among various socioeconomic classes (Whiting & Edwards, 1988).

In less technologically oriented cultures, where labor is clearly divided by gender, children are taught their appropriate gender role by performing the behaviors that will be necessary for them as adults; for example, boys hunt small animals and girls cook or help in hut making (Benedict, 1938; Whiting & Edwards, 1988). In our culture, where labor is not clearly divided by gender, parents spend a great deal of time delineating appropriate behaviors for their child and then selectively reinforcing and/or punishing congruent or incongruent actions.

MYTHS AND ARCHETYPES

The dark side of men is clear. Their mad exploitation of earth resources, devaluation and humiliation of women, and obsession with tribal warfare are undeniable. Genetic inheritance contributes to their obsessions, but also culture and environment. We have defective mythologies that ignore masculine depth of feeling, assign men a place in the sky instead of earth, teach obedience to the wrong powers, work to keep men boys, and entangle both men and women in systems of industrial domination that exclude both matriarchy and patriarchy. (Bly, 1990, preface, p. x)

The values that determine the form of any society can be found through an examination of the culture's myths and stories; they represent the ideology of a culture in story form. Myths may be structuralized and written down—for example, the Creation myth of the Old Testament and the Oedipus myth, or they may be reflected in whole value systems, such as, the Ten Commandments and the Declaration of Independence. Myths are mostly "unconscious" for individual members of a culture (Jung, 1968), but myths, particularly those which reinforce religious and moral values, are very powerful transmitters of culture. The most effective, emotion-evoking of these traditional tales focus on a protagonist. The protagonist is often a heroic personality (Rank, 1908), who presents a "mythic image" of singular importance to the psychology of the culture. Carl Jung (1958) has called these mythic images archetypes.

Archetypes

More than merely main characters in value-transmitting moral dramas, archetypes are thought forms that are universal, motivational personas, which provide the bridge between culture and individuals—the "collective" or "racial" unconscious (Jung, 1954). Despite psychology's calculated neglect of Carl Jung's theory generally, in part because of Jung's reliance upon Lamarckian conceptions of evolution (Hall & Lindzey, 1957), his notion of emotional-evoking myth personifications has had a profound and continuing influence on American literature.

The studies of cultural myths and archetypes published by English professors and poet-storytellers with a Jungian orientation have become very popular, especially the books of Joseph Campbell (1949, 1962, 1988). Interestingly, two of the best-received collections of myths emphasize the influence of myths on gender differentiations: Clarissa Pinkola Estes (1992) writing from the point of view of a feminist and Robert Bly (1990) contributing to the psychology of men.

[Archetypes] represent the projection into the daylight world—in forms of human flesh, ceremonial costume, and architectural stone—of dreamlike mythic images derived not from any actual daylight-life experience, but from depths of what we now are calling the unconscious. And, as such, they arouse and inspire in the beholder dreamlike, unreasonable responses. (Campbell, 1988, p. 56)

Archetypes provide "inner predispositions to perceive the world in a certain manner" (Hall & Lindzey, 1957, p. 82), or culturally determined expectations of how a person who occupies a particular role "ought to" behave. Among the archetypes identified by Jung are the hero, the child, the earth mother, the demon, and the old wise man (Jung, 1954). More recently, Jung's notion that archetypes are transmitted genetically, an idea incompatible with older, simpler conceptualizations of evolution, has been taken up by evolutionary theorists, such as Eugene d'Aguili and Charles Laughlin (1979), who suggest a biological basis for the need to establish perceptual predispositions and for the mechanisms that produce mythic images.

There is some disagreement about whether archetypes are "universal" or part of the mental apparatus of a specific culture (or "race," as Jung would have it). Whether they and other aspects of culture are transmitted from generation to generation through teaching of traditions—that is, are learned, or are so adaptive, so useful in the conduct of human affairs—that they have become ingrained in the chromosomes is probably not a meaningful question.[6] But the implications of the work of archetypes and of the contributions of cultural anthropology are obvious. An individual's value and belief systems, often influenced by irrational forces that transcend actual social experiences, reinforce social norms and role definitions and provide idealized models of behavior, which guide the individual to organize, order, and understand her or his "daylight-life experiences."

The theory of archetypes suggests that a child responds not only to its actual mother, but also to the archetypical mother image.[7] The reciprocal feelings of love between mother and child and the special, intensified quality that characterizes their bond do not, thus, depend entirely upon the personality of each or upon the actual experiences they share. Identifying your primary caretakers with the earth mother archetype, for example, will lead to an evocation of primitive, preprogrammed emotions toward her. Similarly, for mothers, identifying your child with the archetypal child will lead not only to a realistic appraisal that it is a person who requires care and protection, but also to an unlearned intense desire to nurture the child (Jung, 1968).

Jung often focused on the influence of culture upon gender-role distinction. Unlike Freud (1905), who taught that individuals are at birth "bisexual" in identification and must learn the socially accepted definition of their gender, Jung (1968) believed that psychological adjustment involves the integration of the masculine and feminine aspects of personality. While for the Jungians and cultural anthropologists the existence of cultural values, ideas, and perceptual sets that do not require learning in any formal sense provide an important influence upon personality development, American psychology generally has been far more interested in social structures, such as norms and role definitions, which are acquired through social interactions.

Myths of Mothers

> The mother is first, giving birth to the child; but without the child, without the son, the mother is not. Thus, in a sense, they give birth to each other, justify each other and then—are sufficient unto each other. (Lederer, 1968, p. 119)

Myths present the characteristics and determinants of a culture far better than its written history (Benedict, 1938; Bettelheim, 1962; Freud, 1913; Lederer, 1968). Myths illustrate the fears, frustrations, and fascinations of a society; they speak to the deepest desires and anxieties of humans; they address human passion; and they not only reveal the attitudes that members of a society have toward the social order but also justify the social order. "Myth is the primordial language natural to these psychic processes, and no intellectual formulation comes anywhere near the richness and expressiveness of mythical imagery" (Jung, 1968, p. 25).

Although one might expect that myths and folklore differ across cultures, there is considerable cross-cultural consistency, particularly in the area of myths about mothers. Detailed analysis of cultural myths reveal that, in general, they are more similar than they are different—even between distant cultures such as Polynesian versus African—thus suggesting a common human condition (Lederer, 1968; Neumann, 1963). For example, the story of the goddess who bears a son who becomes her consort and then her victim is common to several cultures. The idea of a virgin giving birth to a hero who saves humankind dates back to Summerian literature and is also found in many Western and Asian stories (Rank, 1908).

Worship of the Great Mother, as the first god, is common across cultures and dates as far back as the Neanderthals. The adult male "primitive's" perspective of women as frightening creatures—because, for example, they bleed without dying and produce progeny "at will"—paired with the child's experience of the all-powerful mother—who appears "godlike"—results in awe, if not fear, and has led to the reverence and mystification of women. All preindustrialized cultures—for example, the Greeks, Romans, and Egyptians—paid homage to women. Goddesses have reigned five times as long as any other deity (Bachofen, 1861; Brenner, 1950; Briffault, 1927; Gimbutas, 1989; Lesse, 1979; Neumann, 1963; Thompson, 1964; Warner, 1976).[8]

Goddesses are functionally associated with sex and pregnancy, life and death; their color is red; blood is the life source.[9] Goddesses control the continuation of the species and are responsible for good harvests. Goddesses have no husbands, although as we get closer to Christianity, goddesses frequently have young male consorts. Goddesses are usually protrayed as nurturant; the Babylonians called her "The Mother with the Faithful Breast" (Collum, 1939), and in Palestine, which was known as the land of milk and honey, honey flowed from her breasts (Neumann, 1963). As a reflection of the imperviousness of the image of mother as provider for all and of all, in contemporary society we have deep regard for our "alma mater," that institution which provides succorance to scholars by feeding them wisdom, and we talk of our "motherland" and "mother tongue."

Mother goddesses did not always have positive attributes; there are the good and the bad mother goddesses. The good mother provides for her children and the bad mother brings plagues, droughts, and other natural devastations. Myths of the violent or hostile mother include Hera rejecting Herakles for biting her breast and the South-German legend that describes baby stealers who offer either a breast filled with milk or pus to infants (Rank, 1908). One common thread among myths of the bad mother is the idea that she will devour children. American Indian folklore, as well as English, Australian, and Polynesian folklore, has stories in which witches kill and eat children (Farrand, 1902; Lea, 1887).[10] Colloquially, one can hear mothers say to children, "I'm going to eat you up."[11] To appease the bad mother, primitive cultures sacrificed either humans or animals or both; in India, until 1835, a male child was sacrificed to Kali every Friday (Campbell, 1962).

Universal to human ideas about women are these generalized attributes of the goddess, that they are powerful and dangerous. To protect oneself from the danger of women, men made them tabu and created elaborate restrictions for both women's behavior and women's dealings with men. The most common tabus restrict women when they are at their most magical—when menstruating or pregnant.

During menstruation, labeled an unclean state by men, the restrictions kept women separated from the main part of the tribe. Women have been relegated to the wilderness, forbidden to look upon men, hidden in dark huts, suspended in cages, fumigated and/or roasted in attempts to make sure that men did not fall ill or die because of exposure to them (Delaney, Lupton, & Toth, 1976; Lederer, 1968). We suggest that the attribution of "uncleanness" to women is an illustration of males' reaction formation. Because the "willful" ability to bleed without dying and the ability to produce other living creatures are such awe-inspiring abilities, indicative of a powerfully magical person, primitive men made her unclean; by designating her unclean, men protected themselves. The idea that women are unclean has not disappeared with civilization and technology; television commercials that suggest the vagina needs cleansing and/or perfuming are current manifestations of this idea.

Similar fears have been associated with pregnant women. In Costa Rica, for example, pregnant women were held responsible for deaths in the neighborhood (Graves, 1948). In Hindu culture, as well as in Orthodox Jewish and African cultures, women are unclean after birth and must avoid their family anywhere from sixty days to six months. The Bantu, in particular, went to great pains to hide the afterbirth so that a cosmic disaster would not occur (Frazer, 1922).

Couvade is probably the most illustrative example of what Karen Horney (1932) called "womb envy." Couvade, beginning some time after the third month of pregnancy, includes as symptoms the male's becoming nauseated and having abdominal distention. As birth draws near, men take to a bed, too sick to function.

After an era in American culture when, in polite company, one was not supposed to mention pregnancy, the current practice of making pregnancy a medical problem, primarily guarded by male gynecologists, might also be considered a manifestation of these earlier fears. Only now, instead of withdrawing from the birth process, men wish to control it.

The Mother-Son Dynamic

> He shall be found at once brother and father of the children with whom he consorts; son and husband of the woman who bore him; heir to his father's bed, shedder of his father's blood. (Sophocles, *Oedipus Rex*, cited in Mullahy, 1948, p. 358)

Freud used the Oedipus story to suggest that boys lust after their mother, but eventually give up this lust and identify with the father—the aggressor—because of castration anxiety.[12] However, another interpretation of this story might be that the point of Oedipus was to remind males that they need to remain chaste, in relation to their mother, because of being physically inadequate to give her sexual fulfillment.[13]

> The boy . . . feels or instinctively judges that his penis is much too small for his mother's genital and reacts with the dread of his own inadequacy, of being rejected and derided. . . . His original dread of women is not castration anxiety at all, but a reaction to the menace to his self-respect. (Horney, 1932, p. 142)

GENDER-ROLE STEREOTYPES

While roles are taught to a child generally as part of the entire socialization process, they have an existence external to the mother-child interaction and are part of the more global social structure. Roles refer to expected or prescribed patterns of behavior and attitudes that persons in a given situation are supposed to exhibit (Chavetz, 1978). Because all cultures supply ideal gender-role concepts (which may have the emotional impact of archetypes), they frequently encourage gender-role stereotyping: "rigidly held and oversimplified beliefs that males and females, by virtue of their sex, possess distinct psychological traits and characteristics" (Basow, 1980, pp. 4–5).

In general, because roles develop through the actual, social interactions of members of a society, their definitions can undergo change more rapidly than the more conservative value system (which is relatively impervious to political and social events). It is interesting, therefore, that despite the feminist revolution and the advocacy of the value of androgyny, there seems to have been only slight modification in gender-role stereotypes and in the socialization practices by which they are transmitted (Doyle, 1989; Meth & Pasick, 1990). The gender distinctions inherent in the ideal types, which provide goals for socialization, have not changed as much as social scientists had expected and desired: compared to females, males are still socialized to become more independent, unemotional, instrumental, and dominant and less in need of social support and security.[14]

Social-role definitions are tied to status considerations. In almost every study that included the "social desirability" of traits, most of the highly valued traits are "masculine" (Bem, 1974; Broverman et al., 1970). Because of the differing value attached to "masculine" traits, the gender stereotypes, in most cultures, perpetuate the lower social status of females.

Besides the status differential favoring male traits, male children have historically been more valued (Williams & Giles, 1978):[15] parents note a preference for male children, males are the usual inheritors of property, and males are often pampered and catered to. We suggest, however, that attitudes toward boys that result in behaviors identified as pampering, especially those that are tied to male gender-role socialization, are in reality a subtle form of ostracism that significantly affects the emotional well-being of males. For example, one consequence of pampering is that boys often believe that they and the other males in the family have power. Farrell (1986), however, suggests that if power is control over one own's life, men have very little real power because external rewards fail to satisfy psychological needs such as inner peace, emotional expression, or sexual fulfillment.

Once a set of specific gender behaviors and characteristics has been determined by a society, these behaviors become the "norm" and are taught, gender specifically, to all children. Concern that your child will "fit in" to society with the appropriate gender role is a powerful, albeit probably unconscious, motive for parents. Ideas about "maleness" and "femaleness" influence parents from the first day of awareness of pregnancy, when they plan their forthcoming relationship with the new child, and continue to influence their behavior toward the child. Seeing the child as possessing appropriate gender characteristics often overwhelms an accurate evaluation of the child's idiosyncratic characteristics.

Along with various reasons, both conscious and unconscious, which are tied to the decision to become pregnant, for example, a woman may decide to become pregnant so that she can be recognized as an adult in the society, give a "gift" to her husband, or, as several teenage mothers currently report, have someone to love, mothers and fathers also have expectations about what parenting will be like and what their new child will be like (Kitzinger, 1978). Several researchers have reported that these expectations about the new child usually relate to traditional gender-role stereotypes and are in place prior to the birth of the child. For example, in a study where first-time parents of newborns were asked to describe their hours-old child, they reported that their daughters were beautiful, delicate, and weak, while their sons were firm, alert, strong, and coordinated (Rubin, Provenzano, & Luria, 1974); male infants in general are perceived as more active and aggressive (Lansky, 1967; Rubin et al., 1974). Another study revealed that adults also play with children differently when they believe that the child is a boy or a girl. Frisch (1977) reported that adults who played with a fourteen-month-old child engaged in more active play when the adults thought that the child was a boy than when they thought the child was a girl. When the child was thought to be a girl, not only did they play more quietly but they were also more likely to choose a doll rather than a ball for "her" to play with.

To ensure that their child matches their expectations, and is therefore considered acceptable to them and to other members of society, parents spend a considerable amount of time and energy eradicating unacceptable behavior and encouraging acceptable behavior. General gender-role socialization for boys includes their being taught to be stoic, not to cry, not to be nurturant, and not to be a "sissy"—that is, to deny any component of their behavior that might be construed as feminine. One of the prime aspects of a boy's gender-role development is to teach him to be not-feminine (Chodorow, 1971; Meth, 1990; Pleck, 1981).

We find that they [boys] believe grown-ups expect them to be noisy; to get dirty; to mess up the house; to be naughty; to be "outside" more than girls are; not to be cry-babies; not to be "softies;" not to be "behind" like girls are; and to get into trouble more than girls do. Moroever, boys are not allowed to do the kind of things that girls usually do, but girls may do the kind of things that boys do. (Hartley, 1959, p. 461)

To ensure that little boys and girls grow up to meet these objectives, parents encourage differential behaviors for boys and girls; girls are reinforced for intellectual pursuits—specifically reading—and for cooking and various household chores, and are taught to be passive, nurturant, and dependent (Parson & Bales, 1955). Little boys are socialized to become proficient at out-of-door activities, insensitive to the emotional needs of others and themselves, obstreperous, and convinced of their own invincibility.

SUMMARY

At every stage in the maturation process, biological aspects of an individual interact with social forces, which anthropologists refer to as the sociocultural matrix. Cultural values, which are in part transmitted by myths and archetypes, provide the goals for personality development and establish standards for the conduct of individuals who share the culture. In addition they may introduce perceptual predispositions that influence the emotional attachment to the mother and the nature of the mother-child bond. The social structure commonly divides its province into "masculine" and "feminine." One can discern the influence of culture, which provides traditional ideal types for each gender, and of the social structure, which establishes gender-role stereotypes to direct gender-specific socialization practices, upon the actual gender distinctions that children learn and internalize. What are perceived as masculine traits—individualism, independence, competitiveness, competence, and the like—are highly valued in a society that has long been dominated by males. The women's movement, which has tried, relatively unsuccessfully, to change gender-role stereotypes for several decades, has rightly categorized the gender distinctions of this society as unfair. Some feminists and advocates of the new men's movement, have further argued that, while possessing "masculine" traits has certain economic and political (power) advantages, the socialization practices of this society create men who are emotionally crippled.

It is our contention that the stereotypes and child-rearing practices are worse than unfair; because they are inconsistent with the sex differences in biology and physical maturation, the social forces affecting gender distinctions create males who are uniquely unprepared to deal with separation and cannot accept their dependency needs.

NOTES

1. The recent entrant to nature-nurture scholarship, evolutionary psychology, suggests that many human behavior universals, for several decades attributed to "culture" by American social scientists, may also be a function of biology (Tooby & Cosmides, 1992).

2. This distinction between culture, with values as its primary control mechanisms, and society, with norms as its mechanisms, is very common in the works of sociologists and anthropologists from roughly 1950 to 1980. One of the briefest, most concise, definition of terms appropriate to the distinction between culture and society appears in Linton (1959). Maintaining Linton's definition, Kluckhohn and Murray (1962) present the concepts in an interactionist personality theory.

3. That dominant values are continuously challenged in this society suggests some erosion in the potency of the values as instruments of social control. Many of us have

questioned the adaptation value or fairness of this culture's judgments and in the main they have proved to be far less resilient than anthropology would have predicted.

4. Apparently in almost all species of animals, females select large and strong males with whom to mate (Dawkins, 1986).

5. An apparent contradiction to this "law" was presented by the observations of the Tchambuli made by Margaret Mead (1935). The more recent study of this society by Deborah Gewertz (1981) suggests that Mead's conclusions were inaccurate, and that there was no history of female dominance over males except for a very brief period after the Tchambuli returned to their territory following their exile (it was then that Mead studied the society).

6. A "meaningful question," as in the Positivist tradition.

7. Colin M. Turnbull (1972) has presented a most poignant description of what appears to be an innate belief or desire to be loved and cared for by one's parents.

8. The tradition of paying homage to female deities continues with Maryology in the Catholic Church. An increase in citings of Mary in various cities across the United States was reported in a recent article in *The Day* (12 December 1992), a New London, Connecticut newspaper.

9. Frequently, primitive tribes used red ocher in their rites and Neanderthals used red ocher in their burial rites.

10. This theme is quite common in fairy tales that are still told to children today in America—for example, Hansel and Gretel and Little Red Riding Hood.

11. There are various myths and stories that deal with *vagina dentata*, which also may have influenced the fear of oral incorporation (Lederer, 1968).

12. Rheingold (1964), among others, suggests that while the *classical* story of castration suggests fear of a castrating father, in clinical practice it is significantly more likely that the boy fears castration *by the mother.* "The mother cares for and disciplines the child and it is her attitudes toward excretory function and the genital organs and autoerotic activity that basically determine the child's fears" (p. 86).

13. In a recent reinterpretation of Malinowski's (1927) theory that the Oedipus complex is absent in matrilineal societies, Spiro (1982) presents evidence that manifestations of the Oedipus complex in the Trobriands is very subtle but, nevertheless, present. Earlier, Kathleen Gough (1953), in a study of the matrilineal Nayar, reported a normal Oedipus complex. For a discussion of universal human characteristics found across cultures, see Brown (1991).

14. Research generally confirms that there is a clear consensus about gender-role stereotypes in the United States. In the classic study by Broverman et al. (1970), approximately 75 percent of their college student subjects agreed which traits are "masculine" and which are "feminine." Masculine traits included being very aggressive, independent, active, competitive, and direct, while feminine traits included being not aggressive, independent, or competitive but being very passive, submissive, and dependent. Some newer research (Stevens, Gardner, & Barton, 1984) suggests that there have been only slight modifications of the characteristics that college students believe to be typical of women and men.

15. The ambivalence parents have toward children was considerably more obvious in earlier eras. Infanticide, as a means of population control or to rid oneself of unwanted children—or unwanted girl children, in particular—reaches as far back as the Paleolithic era (Birdsell, 1975). It has been only in fairly recent times where we know, because of written restrictions, that infanticide has been discouraged. There are rumors, of course,

that infanticide of girl children still occurs in China and India (T. H. Maugh, "Infanticide in India," *L.A. Times*, February 9, 1992; *Washington Post*, October 24, 1991). There are also reports of infanticide in various nonhuman primate groups, often when a new high-ranking male enters the group.

5

Socialization and Parenting

Your child is at your mercy. It is up to you to make him/her a happy, cheerful person or to thwart his/her possibilities of development. Your behavior during the first years of your child's life lays the foundation for its character. (Haussler, 1976, p. 35)

The most influential, direct mediating process by which social forces shape personality development is socialization, which has been defined as "the whole process by which an individual, born with behavioral potentialities of an enormously wide range, is led to develop actual behavior which is confined within a much narrower range—the range of what is customary and acceptable for him according to the standards of his group" (Child, 1954, p. 655).

Ralph Linton (1952) and Abram Kardiner (1945), two cultural anthropologists, have presented concepts of how cultural forces influence the development of "basic personality." Their postulates, which provide a rationale for the environmentalist position, have been paraphrased by Florence Kluckhohn (1962, pp. 343–344):

1. That the individual's early experiences exert a lasting effect upon his personality, especially upon the development of his projective system.
2. That similar experiences will tend to produce similar personality configurations in the individuals who are subjected to them.

3. That the techniques which the members of any society employ in the care and rearing of children are culturally patterned and will tend to be similar, although never identical, for various families within the society.
4. That the culturally patterned techniques for the care and rearing of children differ from one society to another.

In this society, as in all known cultures, there are formal procedures for socialization of the young (Murdock, 1945, 1975). Despite the acknowledged influence of the school, church, mass media, and occupational and social status, the family remains the major agent of socialization (Anshen, 1959; Clausen, 1966),

[the] primary group whose close, intense, and enduring attachments are . . . crucial not only as the prototypes of subsequent ties, but also for adequate socialization and emotional development of the child. The family is the first unit with which the child has continuous contact and the first context in which socialization patterns develop; it is a world with which he has nothing to compare. (Elkin, 1960, p. 47)

When sociologists speak of the "family" in this regard, however, they may as well refer to the mother, since in contemporary society in the United States she is, for practical purposes, the sole responsible socialization agent.[1] Her ability to teach the values, attitudes, and socially acceptable behaviors and to train the child in accordance with sociocultural guidelines is the most significant determinant of "normality" in individual children.

As we noted earlier, because there is likely no genetic imperative in the form of a specific maternal instinct to guarantee that a child will receive adequate care, there is considerable variation in parenting. Although there are sanctions against severe neglect of children in our enlightened age, extremely poor parenting is not uncommon, as the incidence of children who "fail to thrive" attests. The most drastic form of socially sanctioned antiparent practice is, of course, infanticide. Even when justified as population control, the practice of ridding the family of an unwanted child (which historically has almost always meant an unwanted girl child), a practice for which there is evidence as far back as the Paleolithic era (Birdsell, 1975), would be classified as "unnatural" and maladaptive in terms of species survival. Infanticide is, nevertheless, observed in a variety of primate groups, when a new high-ranking male enters the group, in rituals of bizarre cults, and in rural areas of China (Bakan, 1979). According to the values of western civilization, however, infanticide and less drastic examples of refusal to fulfill the obligations of parenthood are considered pathological and criminal.

TRAINING YOUNG CHILDREN

The training routine of young children is, in its broadest aspects, similar to all societies. All children must learn, for example, to feed themselves, to control elimination functions, to become independent and competent, and to learn the rules of status and role, particularly gender roles, of the society. Social scientists have long recorded that, despite the regularities of biological maturity of children, the specifics of early socialization practices exhibit considerable variation. It has been common to consider, as sources of this variation, social-class membership (Hess, 1970; Keller-hals & Montandon, 1992; Zussman, 1978) and the vagaries of individualistic parenting patterns. It is far less common to focus on what is probably the most important determinant of differences in child-rearing practices: the gender of the child. At every developmental stage, beginning with early ego-identity differentiation, parents behave differently—and are expected to behave differently—to boys and girls.

Give me a dozen healthy infants, well-formed, and my own specified world to bring them up in and I'll guarantee to take any one at random and train him to become any type of specialist I might select—doctor, lawyer, artist, merchant-chief, and yes, even beggar-man and thief, regardless of his talents, penchants, tendencies, abilities, vocations, and race of his ancestors. (Watson, 1925, p. 82)

This oft-quoted credo of Watsonian behaviorism, presenting a clear statement of radical, naive environmentalism, overstates the ability of "training" to mold children. Genetic and other individual differences set real limitations on the intentions of mothers and other socialization agents, including child psychologists. A second agency (secondary in terms of chronology if not influence), the formal educational system, which has been uniformly behaviorist in orientation for the past several decades, has been singularly unsuccessful in meeting its stated goals in the United States, in part because it ignored the talents, penchants, tendencies, abilities, and social realities of schoolchildren, confusing, for example, equality of opportunity, which is dictated by democratic ideals, with equality in intelligence and motivation.

Another complicating factor is that there is far from unanimity about the goals of training and there have been "fads" in child-rearing philosophy (Montagu, 1974b) that reflect historical and political changes. As we noted in Chapter 2, surveys of child-rearing advice in this country demonstrate how the specific suggested practices will vary from time to time (Clausen & Williams, 1963; Escalona, 1949; Stendler, 1950; Vincent, 1951).

Clausen and Williams (1963, p. 78) have noted that, at least from the mid-nineteenth century to 1963, some beliefs concerning child-rearing practices have persisted: "the emphasis upon and concern with early cleanliness and training; the advocacy of early weaning; concern with the evils and dire consequences of masturbation; the desirability of activity and opportunities for the child to explore."

It is interesting that in none of the surveys of changes in child-rearing philosophy is there mention of gender differences. Feminists have long maintained that when developmental psychologists refer to "the child," they usually mean "the boy child," but there is no specific mention of one practice being advocated for boys, another for girls, in any of the surveys. Even the psychoanalysts, who have long been accused of gender bias in their developmental theories, do not suggest much gender differentiation in children under three years of age. There is some good evidence, however, that ignoring gender differences in infant care may be a mistake.

ATTACHMENT DURING THE ORAL STAGE

When the Freudians presented their five-stage theory of personality development,[2] few variables were presented, except for the mother's psychopathology, which would account for variations and deviations in development during the first stage. Children needed to be fed, and while other biological and psychological needs that occur during the first year of life were recognized (e.g., need to gratify the sucking impulse, need for tactile stimulation, and need for security), the orthodox Freudians and child-development specialists at first focused upon feeding.[3] Since providing nutrition is so bound to the survival and health of infants, who are almost completely unable to obtain nutrients on their own, advice on child-rearing through history tended to deal with nuances such as bottle vs. breast, self- vs. demand-feeding, and early vs. later weaning.

Later, other psychoanalysts would emphasize psychological phenomena related to socialization during the oral stage for which the practices around feeding have little direct relevance. The socially prescribed parental behaviors involved in bonding and attachment of infants, for example, have been well researched in the past twenty years. What may be the most significant finding in this research is that there are "perceptable differences between typical patterns of mother-daughter and mother-son interactions" (Cahill, 1986, p. 168). Basing his conclusion on the individuation research of Michael Lewis and his associates (1985), Cahill takes the position that the differential treatment of very young children is a result of prescribed socialization practices, rather than gender-linked differences in maturation, in helplessness, and in aggression of infants.[4]

Taken together, the findings of such observational studies indicate that up until their infants are six-months-old mothers look at and talk to daughters more than sons but touch and hold sons more than daughters. After their infants are approximately six-months-old, however, mothers tend to give daughters both more nontouching and more physical contact than they give sons. By responding to male and female infants differently, of course, mothers invest them with different natures. For example, mothers apparently invest six-months-old females with sociability and six-months-old males with autonomy. (Cahill, 1986, p. 168)

Gender differences in socialization during this very early separation/individuation stage (Olesker, 1990) have another consequence: the abrupt change toward boys, who are now encouraged or even forced to separate from mother, at least briefly, constitutes a discontinuity in the attachment process. It is interesting that males, even in very different cultures, are more subject to discontinuities in training than female children (Benedict, 1938). It is our contention that boys, for whom forced separation is experienced as traumatic, are likely to develop a dread of abandonment.

TOILET TRAINING AND ENFORCED CONFORMITY

The boy's self-image from birth has been influenced by parental expectations that he will be wilder, rougher, and more difficult to control than a girl child. Indeed, he has been more aggressive on the average, perhaps in part because of innate biological differences between the sexes, although this remains to be proven, and in part because of a less precocious, less rapid advance in the development of ego controls as compared with girls (again, it is difficult to know to what extent this difference is innate and to what extent it results from a difference in environmental expectation). When demands for self-control are applied during the sadistic-anal period[5] of toddlers and younger children, greater compliance is expected for girls than from boys. Girls tend to become toilet trained significantly earlier than boys, probably not only because of intrinsic factors but also because of mothers' tendency to be more stringent in their expectation that their daughters be neater and cleaner than their sons. (Silverman, 1986, pp. 438–439)

In considering the various aspects of socialization, it becomes apparent that there are degrees of conflict within the general area of socialization: some training results in more conflict between parents and children, and others less. Training the child in proper dining behavior, for example, comes early in the socialization process and is usually *not* a traumatic event for the child or the parent. While eating demands the adoption of utensils as a substitute for fingers and neatness as a substitute for the sensual pleasure of messiness, correct eating behavior does not often evolve into a conflict over control. Toilet training, on the other hand, which occurs during the stage of autonomy-striving and requires that the child gain control over her or his concealed physiology and relinquish a part of his or her self to another, is fraught with frustration for both parents and child. Toilet training is often complicated by the child's fears and feelings of aggression and hostility.

The guidance that has been provided for parents on toilet training has an interesting history. In the early part of this century, it was suggested that bowel training should begin "by the third month or even earlier" (U.S. Children's Bureau, 1914). By 1921, mothers were encouraged to begin training "as early as the end of the first month . . . as soon as the mother takes charge of the baby after her confinement she should begin upon this task" (U.S. Children's Bureau, 1921). From 1929 to the current time the trend in toilet training has been reversed; parents are now told that they should wait until the child is maturationally ready before they begin this arduous task. *Infant Care* of 1951 suggests that "babies are not ready to start learning bowel control by the end of the first year. One-and-a-half or two years is a much more common time for them to learn willingly" (U.S. Children's Bureau, 1951). It should be noted that expert advice concerning the optimal period for the onset of toilet training, which frequently ignored the limitation caused by the relatively late myelinization of sphincter muscles, was more concerned with cleanliness than fostering good mental health for infants.

Not only has the severity of toilet-training advice varied for different eras, but research suggests that the severity of toilet-training practices differs according to the socioeconomic status of the parents: middle-class mothers begin toilet training later than do lower socioeconomic status mothers, and middle-class mothers in general are less punitive and "somewhat warmer and more demonstrative" (Davis, 1943; Sears, Maccoby, & Levin, 1957).[6] Regardless of the motives of the experts in recommending training before muscle control was possible for most infants, or the differences in attitude toward toilet training by parents of different socioeconomic strata, a too early demand for conformity has deleterious consequences for the individuation process.

Toilet training is even more problematic for boys. Since we know that boys are maturationally retarded in comparison to girls, that their toilet training takes longer to complete, and that parents are more punitive generally toward boys than girls (Feinman, 1974; Sears et al., 1957), we can assume that the mother-son relationship becomes particularly conflict-filled and stressful during the toilet-training period—in our society usually the second year of life. Mothers are likely to become resentful toward boys and to become overly punitive because of their failure to comply with the demands of this phase of socialization (Bardwick, 1971; Sears et al., 1957).

Problems in toilet training have specific consequences for the individuation process and can be the occasion for a repetition of earlier separation anxiety. Rather than being loved for merely being himself, the small boy learns that in order to maintain mother's approval, he must perform as she wishes. Awareness of this mandate can lead the boy to become unsure of himself.

If the child is punished too frequently, he will feel that it is safe to make responses only when he is certain that they are correct (i.e., in conformity with his parents' expectation of him). He may become inhibited, timid, afraid to attempt responses that are not specifically approved by his parents. (Mussen, Conger, & Kagan, 1969, p. 264)

Maladaptive behaviors, such as temper tantrums, hostility toward parents, and lack of control, are not unusual reactions to inadequate toilet training. The long-term effect of a perceived negative toilet-training experience on the child is not only the child's timidity, but resentment from the child toward the person responsible: the primary caregiver—most often the mother (Kessler, 1966). One possible consequence, for a boy, is that general hostility and resentment toward women will be reinforced: anger toward the punishing-controlling mother and toward the favored sister, whose biology makes toilet training earlier, easier, and more successful.

That boys more than girls feel the negative consequences of toilet-training conflict specifically is suggested by their much higher incidence of enuresis and encopresis. They also become the recipients of more severe discipline, are more often subject to parental efforts at behavior control, and, we submit, are more vulnerable to psychological problems involving autonomy, security, and the fear of abandonment.

GENDER ROLE

Beyond training a child to eat correctly and to dispose of bodily wastes appropriately, the most important element in the socialization process is that the new "human" be taught to conform to the appropriate gender role for his or her culture. Gender functions as a social category (Grady, 1977). It is, in fact, one of the first categories about the world that a child learns—a child of eighteen months is able to differentiate between girls and boys (Money, 1961). The first characteristic about a person that another perceives, gender is the usual determinator of one's place within the social structure, defining sanctioned and unsanctioned behaviors. Interestingly, while changes in basic socialization practices—for example, how to teach eating behavior or toilet training—have been suggested over time, there seem to have been few modifications in gender-role socialization over the last decades in spite of the increased discussion of concepts such as the value of androgyny (Doyle, 1989; Meth & Pasick, 1990). With only slight modifications among a few individuals, gender-role socialization has remained constant. In fact,

almost half of the adults who favor changes in women's roles are not socializing children to acquire sex roles in accordance with their own ideology about the women's movement. (Lackey, 1989, p. 280)

Gender-role socialization begins at birth, continues through adulthood, and is rigid and unyielding in extracting conformance from children. Prior to behaviorism, which had a significant hold on American psychology until fairly recently, theories of gender-role socialization were either biological or psychoanalytic in nature. Biological theories suggested that fulfilling adult gender roles was merely a function of biology, and biologically oriented theorists tended to ignore the influence of social situations. Psychoanalytic theory, exemplified by Freud's (1905) offering, *Three Essays on the Theory of Sexuality*, on the other hand, recognized that for a positive resolution of the Oedipus complex, and, therefore, gender-role solidification, some discussion of the interaction within the family was necessary. Other theories of gender-role socialization include Mischel's (1966) social-learning theory, an elaboration of basic behaviorist notions of the effects of reinforcement and punishment on gender behavior acquisition; Kohlberg's (1966) cognitive-developmental theory, which lies on a foundation of Piagetian ideas about mental development; Cahill's (1986) sociologically oriented theory, which suggests that gender identity develops in five stages, spurred on by the motivation of the child to be perceived as a socially competent person; and Lynn's (1969) interactive theory, which explains why boys have a more difficult time with gender-role socialization than girls.

It is a universal and psychobiological necessity for all infants to establish their first affectional tie to mother, and mother has been and continues to be, for most families, the primary caregiver and, as such, the principal socializer. The task of socialization is fairly easy with girl children because they are like mother both biologically and in terms of their prospective gender role. However, male children are a problem for mothers because of their difference and her belief that she needs to "turn this little boy into a little man." The essential problem of individuation—to break the tie with mother—becomes a serious problem for males, who must come to identify with the father, often in the absence of a father. "The boy's affectional tie to his mother is deep, and it takes time before the boy's self-conceptual or sex role identity considerations can lead him to subordinate it to the development of a tie to the father" (Kohlberg, 1966, p. 135). Making a child "the other," especially in a culture and time when the range of acceptable gender-role behavior is wider than in the past, is difficult. Unfortunately, it is the boy who is most likely to be damaged or hurt by this difficult task.

In technologically less sophisticated societies, where men and women occupy separate spheres and have tabus and restrictions concerning their interaction with each other, men are active participants in the everyday lives of children, and what an adult male is is as obvious to a small child as what an adult female is. These societies also have *rites de passage* where the young man, after suffering through rigorous trials, passes from the world of the child into the world of the adult; male children are sometimes "stolen" from the women's hut and are then "reborn" from men (Stoller & Herdt, 1982). These rituals emotionally attach the adolescent to the culture of the adult male and provide a replacement tie for the one that has been broken with the mother.

A current problem in male gender-role socialization in our culture centers on the lack of male role models for little boys (Dinnerstein, 1977; Friedman & Lerner, 1986; Hartley, 1959; Lynn, 1969). David Lynn (1969, pp. 33, 36) has succinctly stated the problem: (1) "both male and female infants usually establish their initial and principal identification with the mother"; (2) "males tend to identify with a culturally defined masculine role, whereas females tend to identify with their mothers [a real person]"; but (3) "the boy . . . must restructure [his experiences] . . . in order to abstract the principles defining the masculine role." What Lynn suggests is that in our society, particularly since the industrial revolution, men have been more and more removed from the everyday lives of our children and thus male children are socialized to conform to a stereotype of appropriate male behavior rather than to a real adult male. Moreover, children see only tired males, overworked males, or "fun-loving" Saturday males, a fragmented picture of what the male role truly is.

Male children are removed from viewing the emotional component of the adult male role and are thus hampered in their ability to form a self-concept that includes recognition of their need to attach to others.

The boy has a distinct problem in shifting from mother identification to an identification with the father because of the relative lack of salience of the father as a model. Typically in this culture the girl has her same-sex parental model for identification (the mother) with her more hours per day than the boy has his same-sex model (the father) with him. Moreover, even when home, the father does not usually participate in as many intimate activities with the child as does the mother, e.g., preparation for bed and toileting. The time spent with the child and the intimacy and intensity of the contact are thought to be pertinent to the process of learning parental identification. The boy is seldom if ever with the father as he engages in his daily vocational activities, although both boy and girl are often with the mother as she goes through her household activities. Consequently, the father, as a model for the boy, is analogous to a map showing the major outline but lacking most details, whereas the mother, as a model for the girl, might be thought of as a detailed map. (Lynn, 1969, p. 24)

While there are not a lot of "real" men for children to observe in their lives, children do see a great number of males on television and in comic books. The behaviors, attitudes, and values of these males, however, are most often overblown versions of our cultural stereotype of what a male is thought to be like. What children do see is a compilation of stereotyped male characters, including animated superheros, who are strong, independent, brave, and "able to leap tall buildings in a single bound."

This stereotyped picture includes the ubiquitous belief that men and women *should* be different (not merely in reproductive functioning) and *are* different. The stereotype includes the belief that women are the inferior gender, weaker, less intelligent, and more prone to moral degeneracy.[7] Males, on the other hand, are perceived as being very aggressive, independent, objective, dominant, active, competitive, logical, worldly, direct, and self-confident—traits that would suggest a person who has an independent attitude and who participates in external, goal-directed activities.

Although the criticism that only stereotyped characteristics are shown on television, in comic books, and in the movies holds also for the women portrayed, because of the presence of "real" women in the lives of children, children can more readily notice the discrepancy between the women they know and the roles actors play. Children are aware of what a real woman is like and little girls feel attached to the core group of women in the culture.

Although Lynn's theory is sociopsychological and focuses more on the environment in which the child finds himself than on the intrapsychic phenomonology of the child, his notions about contemporary gender-role socialization agree with psychoanalytic theory. Rank (1924) had earlier suggested that the mother is the center of the child's world and is the person with whom the child initially identifies. Separation from the mother and the creation of the boy's gendered-appropriate self is the primary developmental goal of the child, but Rank emphasizes the difference between being separated and separating. Separating, when the boy parts from the mother at his own rate, is not as potentially traumatic as *being* separated. Being separated, when the mother forces the child away, may lead to feelings of abandonment. In our society, the male child is perceived as the "other" by the mother, his identification with her is considered negative, and subsequently the mother works hard to turn the little boy into a "man." In this process, the mother may both psychologically and physically push the young boy away.[8] As the father is often unavailable, the young boy, in our culture, is frequently left all alone.[9] "Sex-role typing . . . is debilitating and constrictive to growth. . . . Male victims of sex-role typing are unable to be fully feeling individuals. They are crippled in their expression of needs for nurturance, love and dependency" (Wainrib, 1974, p. 36).

Heaped upon these contra-intuitive instructions, boys are also taught that their main function in life occurs outside of the home, in the "real world." As a part of the external life, the man may feel connected to the greater masses of humanity and part of "masculine history" (Tolson, 1977, p. 47), but he does so at the expense of sensitivity and connectedness to the real work of life that occurs within the family.

Of course, some cross-gender behavior is allowed (Fling & Manosevitz, 1972; Hartup, Moore, & Sager, 1963), while others are punished more severely. For example, if a girl is a tomboy she might receive some admonition, but she may also receive some praise for her abilities and her behavior will be perceived as "cute." However, if a boy participates in cross-gender behavior—for example, playing with dolls—he is frequently called a sissy and is severely ridiculed or punished (Green, 1980; Lynn, 1969; Stoller & Herdt, 1982).[10]

MOTHERHOOD AND MASCULINITY

The earliest experiences of a male and his mother play a crucial role in the dynamics underlying the overreaction that men have toward being abandoned by their wife or significant other later in life.

It is the specific unconscious need of the mother that activates, out of the infant's infinite potentialities, those in particular that create for each mother "the child" who reflects her own unique and individual needs. This process takes place, of course, within the range of the child's innate endowments. (Mahler, 1967, p. 750)

Contributing to the problem that the boy may have in relating to his mother, of course, is the "ideal" conceptualizations that we all have about our relationship with our mother (an archetype in Jungian terms). If our ideal image of what our mother should be like is not matched with the reality of our experiences, our anger may be internalized, as in depression, or externalized, as in violent behavior.

The first person with whom the child identifies is the mother, and most boys want to maintain their close relationship with mother and wish to be like her. Not only is the desire to be a woman in evidence in the behavior and verbalizations of small boys, there have been cases of fantasy or enacted pregnancies in adult males (Freud, 1909). In her radical reconceptualization of psychoanalytic theory, Karen Horney (1932, 1934) suggests that young boys develop what she calls "womb envy," the most direct manifestation of its influence on adult males being a wish to control the reproductive function of their wife (Thompson, 1964). This envy of the mother contributes to the boy's ambivalent feelings toward his mother.

It is clear that such envy not only assigns to women a superior position which, since she may abuse it to dominate, is in itself anxiety-provoking; but that the resentment of such superiority must give rise—by way of projection—to the supposition that, where one hates, one is also hated, and where one is hated, one needs to be afraid. (Lederer, 1968, p. 5)

The degree to which a woman can become a "good" mother is limited by her own needs and her parents' abilities to be good parents. In the genre of pop psychology, probably the most famous indictment of contemporary motherhood was included in Philip Wylie's *Generation of Vipers* (1961), where he blames the deterioration of American culture on the stereotype middle-class urban wife who he suggests is indulgent, mercenary, materialistic, and controlling of both husband and children.[11]

In a more psychoanalytic approach, Karen Horney has described a particular woman, the "feminine type," who because of her own neurotic tendencies contributes to bad mothering. The "feminine" woman derives her complete sense of self from ministering to others and vicariously through the works of the man to whom she is married or of the male to whom she has given birth. The personality of this woman fits, more or less, the stereotypical notions about women. In "Overvaluation of Love," Horney suggests that this artificial personality produces a woman who is unfulfilled and angry and copes with her anger by hostilely attempting to control others, usually her husband and children.

The neurotic will desire to have control over others as well as over himself. He wants nothing to happen that he has not initiated or approved of. This quest for control may take the attenuated form of consciously permitting the other to have full freedom, but insisting on knowing about everything he does, and feeling irritated if anything is kept a secret. (Horney, 1934, p. 167)

The problem is cyclic. Women who fall into the category of the "feminine type" produce sons who are unable to live full emotional lives and who continue to search for a woman who will provide for them the type of relationship that they could not have with their own mothers. The severity of the consequences of the "bad mother" is, of course, a function of both the child's ability to biologically withstand stress and the gender of the child. Boys, because they are biologically inferior and "the other," and therefore "rejected" by mother, will always be more susceptible to early childhood experiences that lack enough support and nurturance.

GENDER-ROLE SOCIALIZATION AND ABANDONMENT

The range of acceptable behaviors included in the traditional gender-role definitions is quite narrow. To deny to men their needs for dependency, security, sensitivity, relatedness, and warmth severely constricts temperament development. "Feminine" behaviors in little boys are punished and little boys are "pushed" away from the nurturant and supportive care of their mothers. As a consequence, while males will go to any extreme to deny their femininity, they forever seek a mother replacement. Because denial of one's "feminine" characteristics is unnatural, turning boys into "men" is a difficult and arduous task. Research confirms that boys are more harshly punished for deviations from stereotypical behaviors than are girls, males from fatherless homes have a more exaggerated notion of what masculinity is than boys who have fathers, and boys in male peer groups advocate a more exaggerated, narrow role of acceptable behaviors for males (Feinberg, Smith, & Schmidt, 1958; Pope, 1953; Tuddenham, 1952).

In addition to the conflicting messages that little boys receive—that they are valued but rejected and that they are loved but must produce something or act in a particular manner to gain approval—little boys are instructed that their main function in life occurs outside of the home, in the "real world." Little girls, on the other hand, learn that they are valued for "being" and that relationships are important—skills which regardless of whether they are homemakers or professional women provide them with greater flexibility in their adult life. Interestingly, these skills that women learn—for example, caring for others and listening to what others say—are currently being identified as useful skills in the business world. Boys, on the other hand, are being trained as if we still lived in a hunter-gatherer or agrarian society; the aggression and muscle mass of males might have been useful at one time, but in contemporary society they are dysfunctional.

In an attempt to compensate for the anxiety produced by individuation problems, men created a world that, on the surface, provides them with security and importance. Psychologically, however, men with individuation problems not only suffer from separation anxiety but also harbor repressed feelings of hostility toward their mother who "rejected" them when they needed comforting the most.

Specific problems that may arise for males who are too well trained in the stereotypical male gender role include excessive strivings for dominance and competitiveness, an overemphasis on work, violent and emotional conflicts, the machismo syndrome, and sexual discrimination. Typically men have general problems dealing with women and interpersonal friendships (Franklin, 1984). If a man questions the goodness of fit between himself and the stereotype, it is likely that feelings of inferiority, anxiety, and lower self-esteem and self-confidence ensue (Meth & Pasick, 1990).

DRILL SERGEANT

Rick Baker was born to well-off, socially prominent parents in southern California. Politically conservative and involved in numerous civic and social organizations, the senior Bakers were constant party-goers. Delighted with her pregnancy and relieved that, after two daughters, she had produced a son, Mrs. Baker soon realized that she no longer had the time or enthusiasm to care for a young child. She recalls that she would hand

Rick to a nurse because she did not like the smell of milk and did not want to risk a leaky diaper.

Although Rick was a healthy and husky baby, he is described as having been cranky and demanding, energetic and aggressive. His father, who owned a very successful automobile dealership, describes Rick as a "real boy," by which he means rugged and fearless. His parents were proud of his success at football, although they were too genteel and class-conscious to attend any of the games.

Rick was popular at school but indifferent to his studies. His best friends were athletes, whose families were not known to the Bakers. Except for fighting, Rick was seldom in trouble in the community until he was involved in some kind of "rumble." His parents, unconvinced that the infraction was serious and warranted probation, put him into a Jesuit high school. Rick joined the Marines as soon as he graduated.

He loved the Marines and attained the rank of Sergeant. On leave, his mother, with whom he developed a close relationship, would show him off. He and his parents were disappointed that his work—training recruits—prevented him from serving in Vietnam.

Civilian life, after discharge, bored Rick. He could not find a job that satisfied him and he lived at home. He dated frequently and was married, when twenty-seven, to a young woman he had impregnated. Despite the responsibilities of a family, Rick did not settle down. After each brief attempt to earn a living, almost always ended by Rick's temper outbursts at work, he seemed to be spending increasing amounts of time at a neighborhood bar with his male friends.

His wife Anne was ambitious, and after her second child was born, she began to take college courses. Her mother-in-law seemed happy to look after the children, although she would secretly confide to Rick that she did not believe that Anne was a conscientious mother. Mrs. Baker, who had some earlier problems with her own husband's infidelities, would stir up Rick's jealousy by hinting that Anne was probably having an affair with one of her professors.

Anne's dissatisfaction with her marriage had to do with Rick's inability to maintain stable employment and with his drinking and partying. She also resented the continual "handouts" from Rick's parents. In her last semester, as she left for class, Anne informed him that she was going to get a divorce if Rick did not agree to marriage counseling. That afternoon the security people at the college apprehended Rick, who was apparently rushing around the psychology building, accosting every male he en-countered and threatening to "off" the professor who was having an affair with his wife.

Rick, who had controlled his belligerence when drinking, became increasingly abusive at home toward Anne, verbally and physically, in an attempt to discover who was cuckolding him. Thoroughly distraught and fearing for her safety and that of the children, Anne moved back into her parents' home. Rick returned to his family home.

Although his parents sympathized with him during his first few days with them, they became apprehensive about Rick's obsessive interest in firearms. He had always had a small collection of guns, but now he spent an inordinate amount of time cleaning and oiling them and speaking, almost incoherently, about following Anne in the evening to catch her with her lover.

Rick's rage did not erupt until the day he was to appear in court for the divorce hearing. Pulling into the parking lot, he saw Anne talking to a man. Convinced that this was her paramour, Rick took a pistol from his glove compartment, rushed over to the couple, and shot at his wife and her attorney. Miraculously, all four shots missed—although he was at fairly close range. Rick sped away, eventually making his way to Mexico.

Although "old money" does not have to be very old in southern California, the senior Bakers were accepted members of the genteel upper-middle class there and, much like the British landed gentry, held somewhat exaggerated values and standards of behavior. East of Beverly Hills and Hollywood, the social group to which they belong is quite small in numbers and it is possible to be acquainted with almost all the "right people." Emotional distancing from infants, even the favorite child, is not shameful or criminal to this group; it is commonplace. This is true particularly, as in the case of the Bakers, when the parents are somewhat older and fully involved in social affairs. Turning Rick over to the care of nannies was normal, and he appeared to be the type of boy who did not crave affection or attention.

Actually, the behavior ascribed to the young Rick, by parents and caretakers, resembles the symptoms of attention deficit disorder (ADD). He was very active, for example, and always "into things," but the condition was not diagnosed and his school problems were assumed to be due to poor motivation. When he was a toddler, Rick's adventurousness and aggression were seen as positive attributes and were subtly encouraged by his parents.

In dealing with the ambivalence of separation, he had almost no attachment ties to interfere with autonomy striving. Life outside of the home was appealing to him and he was successful in engaging in activities consistent with the male gender role. There is evidence that a firm connection to his parents was missing from his developmental years, since

Rick seemed to be seeking a replacement family in his peer group, team, and the Marines. Also, after he left the service and when he was abandoned by Anne, he returned to live with his parents. His "close" relationship to his mother began when Rick was an adult. Something was, nevertheless, incomplete in the personality structure of this highly competitive, aggressive man who somewhat exaggeratedly played the gender-role stereotype.

Although one would have expected that his earliest experiences and his temperament would make him vulnerable to problems with intimacy, team spirit and loyalty, and other manifestations of homonomy needs, the strength of his autonomy motives, competitiveness, leadership qualities, and athletic prowess obscured his unmet needs. When his pathology emerged, it took the form of overwhelming sexual jealousy. While the vulnerability had its source in "orality," the pathology seems to have its basis in "genital stage" fixation. His mother's response to Rick's marriage suggests an Oedipal conspiracy: she incited jealousy feelings in an obvious attempt to have Rick leave his wife.

Like any pasha, Rick believed that it was his right to control his wife, particularly her reproductive functions, and Anne's assertive decision to go to college challenged his right to dominate her. Rick's socialization did not provide for a wife's willful disobedience, and he believed that real men do not sit passive when cuckolded. To the senior Bakers, misbehavior, even sin, was tolerated if done discreetly; one does not, after all, wish to have scandal associated with the family. Having a son stalk his estranged wife while he carried a loaded gun might lead to such a scandal.

For much of his life, Rick was able to channel his aggressiveness and resentment in socially acceptable ways. He succeeded in playing the one-sided gender role prescribed by his society primarily because he was similarly one-sided. He was unsuccessful in his marriage, not only because he was unable to accept the responsibility of supporting his family financially, but also because his wife eventually refused to play her role; role behavior is achieved when the "other" plays the reciprocal role as socially determined. The traditional husband role provides for dominance in the relationship; he makes the important decisions and is in control; he enjoys the benefits of nurturance and care. Anne's rebellion, her decision to change the course of her life, subverted the marital roles and Rick was too much of a man to allow that.

NOTES

1. No matter the rhetoric about the way the world "should be," the overwhelming evidence is that mothers, even in two-parent families, are disproportionately responsible

for child care (Björnberg, 1992; Kutner, 1992). The number of mothers raising children is even greater when we remember that approximately 29 percent of all families with children, in 1991, were single-parent families and women head 90 percent of all single-parent families.

2. The oral, anal, phallic, latency, and genital stages. A number of substages have been suggested by various theorists.

3. One of the earliest attempts to expand the oral stage and describe psychological interactions between mother and infant beyond those involved in feeding was Frenczi's (1950) paper on the "stages in development of a sense of reality." A better known expansion occurs in Erikson's (1950) "eight ages of man" reconceptualization of Freud's psychosexual theory. Erikson presented the conflict of basic trust vs. basic mistrust as the result of experiences during this stage, consequences only partly determined by self- vs. demand-feeding.

4. This last suggestion is the conclusion of Moss (1974).

5. In modifications of psychoanalytic theories of development the anal stage is usually divided into an earlier, sadistic stage and a later retentive stage (Erikson, 1950). Although an approximation, the anal-sadistic stage is said to occur normally in the first few months of the second year. Consequently, Silverman's boy child who exhibits characteristics of anal sadism after toddlerhood would be likely showing symptoms of fixation (or regression).

6. Punishment as a function of both gender and socioeconomic status, in a variety of situations, has been repeatedly reported (Hess, 1970; Zussman, 1978). Kellerhals & Montandon (1992) report that similar differences in child-rearing attitudes, techniques, and goals are still a function of social class, at least in Europe.

7. Assessment of male and female characteristics has had a long history in psychology (Broverman et al., 1972; Rosenkrantz et al., 1968). A recent reanalysis of the factor structure of the Rosenkrantz et al. scale, however, does suggest that there may be a slight modification of what college students consider to be male and female traits (Stevens, Gardner, & Barton, 1984). While noting some movement toward egalitarian beliefs, research still reports that more individuals hold traditional attitudes (Antill, 1988; Zammuner, 1988).

8. There is evidence from the study of primates that primate mothers push away their male offspring earlier than they do their female offspring, even though male primates mature later than do females (Strum, 1987; van Lawick-Goodall, 1971).

9. An extreme example of mothers pushing away boy children occurs in Herero, a pastoral preliterate culture in the northern Kalahari, where the death rate for boys is between two and three times greater than for girls. That the Herero mothers "take their daughter to their hearts but refuse their sons" is offered as an explanation (Cronk, 1991, p. 405).

10. Since male behavior has higher value, girls who are tomboys are considered to be aspiring toward higher status themselves. Boys, on the other hand, who participate in low status sissy behavior would be considered aberrant.

11. See Dubbert (1979) and Kitzinger (1978) for a discussion of the history of motherhood.

6

Self-Identity, Attachment, and Separation Anxiety

Before the child is able to recognize the perceptible and visible body parts as belonging to the self, many experiences must be passed through. These experiences are often associated with painful feelings. Pain will lead the child to self recognition. Pain is the most powerful teacher of differentiation between the subjective and the objective.... Only when words are used will the more complex concepts such as the "I" (i.e., Ich) become defined. However, the common assumption that the "I-feeling" (i.e., Ichgefühl) only emerges from the moment that the word "I" is used is completely erroneous. Observations clearly demonstrate that the "I-feeling" is not evoked by the learning of words, but is present much earlier than this particular vocabulary. ... By means of language the comprehensible distinctions of the "I" are specified, and the cultivation—not the emergence—of the "I-feeling" is promoted. (Preyer, 1892, pp. 348–356)[1]

Self-identity is a product of the convergence of two broad developmental forces, homonomy and autonomy, which are both constrained and encouraged by biological maturation and social learning. Contemporary personality theories, stimulated by the interests of cognitive psychology, have revived a concern with the development of the sense of self as a unifying concept that *reduces the complexity* inherent in human maturation and *provides a reference point* for processes of psychological growth (Ross, 1992). The influence of social interactions and experiences, particularly pathognomonic ones, on the *emerging* self-identity of very young children has been well researched, while, with a few notable exceptions, there has been little work on the life-long sequelea of early experiences

(Bowlby, 1969). Separation fears and the dread of abandonment, which have their source in the earliest experiences of childhood, are nevertheless elicited repeatedly in the life of select individuals (Bowlby, 1969, 1973; Horner, 1975) with serious consequences for self-perception and feelings about oneself.

Interestingly, unlike the history in other areas of psychology (Shields, 1975; Stevens & Gardner, 1982), the history of research and theory development within the area of child development is notable for its lack of attention to gender differences. Similarly, for the most part, evaluation of what the differences owing to gender may be in the development of individuation, self-identity, or separation anxiety has been ignored, even when the researchers or theoreticians maintain an "anatomy is destiny" orientation (Erikson, 1968). However, because autonomy-homonomy issues are related to maturation and females mature, physically and emotionally, earlier than males, it is very likely that the individuation process is different for girls and boys.

THE DEVELOPMENT OF SELF-IDENTITY:
THE INTERACTIONIST POSITION

> The emerging ego identity . . . bridges the early childhood stages, when the body ego and the parent images were given their specific meaning, and the later stages, when a variety of social roles become available and increasingly coercive. A lasting ego identity . . . cannot begin to exist without the trust of the first oral stage; it cannot be completed without a promise of fulfillment which from the dominant image of adulthood reaches down into the baby's beginnings and which, by the tangible evidence of social health, creates at every step an accruing sense of ego strength. (Erikson, 1950, p. 218)

From its origins in the work of William James (1890) and George Herbert Mead (1934)[2] theoretical formulations concerning the development of self-identity have been primarily interactional, specifically noting that self-image is a product of a synthesis of polar forces. In psychoanalysis, for example, there has been a recognition in the theories of Erik Erikson, Margaret Mahler, and Heinz Hartmann that self-identity is affected by both nature and nurture, as well as by autonomy and homonomy in the theories of John Bowlby and Mahler. This is not to say that self-development theories enjoy unanimity; the controversies are, however, usually based upon a particular emphasis on determining factors. Among the major "schools" that have been traditionally involved in self-development research, for example, the psychoanalysts generally have emphasized constitutional (genetic) factors, while the social psychologists, who increasingly provide the laboratory research studies on self-formation, tend to emphasize environmental factors (including social interaction and cultural determinants).[3]

Almost every self theory concedes that there is some sort of "core" identity, an awareness of self that emerges from the earliest self-differentiation that occurs in the first few weeks or months of life (Lewis, Brooks-Gunn, & Jaskir, 1985), but beyond this almost nothing about the concept of self is simple. In addition to the fact that one's self-concept changes throughout one's life and is affected by such experiences as peer pressure (Scheier & Carver, 1983) and successful goal attainment (Bandura, 1986), research confirms that self-image is, at the same time, both malleable and relatively stable (Hull et al. 1988; Markus & Kunda, 1986; Ross, 1992).

Usually presented as a multifaceted "thing," a usage admittedly unscientific (Allport, 1937; Ross, 1992) but one which reflects a common, native feeling about the "core" (James, 1890), the concept of self is complex. It can include the perception of oneself as actor (Freud's *Ich*) or as an object (Freud's *Selbst*); the latter suggests that one's self is capable of being evaluated, compared, and loved or hated (Freud, 1930).[4] Social psychologists and sociologists, who emphasize environmental determinants, have focused on the objectified self-image, while Freudians, particularly the "ego" psychologists and object-relations theorists among them, tend to focus on an inner awareness of self. Heinz Kohut (1977, p. 177) suggests that "our sense of being an independent center of initiative and perception [are] integrated with our most central ambitions and ideals and with our experience that our body and mind form a unit in space and a continuum in time."

It is interesting that Kohut and his followers maintain that the core self guides and directs perception, while most others, including Mahler, Pine, and Bergman (1975), Bowlby (1969), Settlage (1971), Lewis, Brooks-Gunn, and Jaskir (1985), and Hartmann (1964a), emphasize that the development of self-identity is *dependent* upon the maturation of perceptual abilities. Because the core of feeling-oneself-an-actor concept stresses stability, there has been considerable reliance on Piaget's cognitive development scheme regarding the achievement of object constancy for an explanation of increasing stability in the sense of identity in infants (Hartmann, 1964b; Mahler, 1967). Cognitive maturation provides both a plausible psychobiological foundation[5] for the evolution of the sense of identity and a basis for a distinction between the dread of abandonment and separation anxiety (Settlage, 1971).

M. Brewster Smith (1978, pp. 1053–1054), presenting a concept of self in the context of "universal features of being a person," has written the following nonjargonistic definition of the multifaceted sense of identity:

Selfhood involves being *self-aware* or *reflective*; *being* or *having* a body (a large debate here); somehow taking into account the *boundaries of selfhood* at birth and death and feeling a *continuity of identity* in between; placing oneself in a *generational sequence and network of other connected selves* as forebears and descendants and relatives; being in partial *communication and communion with other contemporary selves* while experiencing an *irreducible separateness of experience and identity*; . . . *guiding* what one does and *appraising* what one has done at least partly through *reflection* on one's performance [italics in the original].

PSYCHOBIOLOGICAL FOUNDATIONS OF SELF-IDENTITY

The basic responses of the hunter-gatherers have metamorphosed from relatively modest environmental adaptations into unexpectedly elaborate, even monstrous forms in more advanced societies. Yet the direction this change can take and its final products are constrained by the genetically influenced behavioral predispositions that constituted the earlier, simple adaptations of preliterate human beings. (Wilson, 1982, pp. 93–94)[6]

While the stated purpose of sociobiology is to effect an integration of genetic predispositions and cultural forms characteristic of "advanced societies" (Wilson, 1975), the general approach has been to explain social behavior in terms of biological determinants. Although an over-emphasis on biology may lead to highly imaginative, artificial conceptions of what "earlier, simple adaptations" might be *sans* social factors,[7] postulating various biologically dominated growth processes—that is, making biological maturation primary—has been useful in developmental theories.

The component processes of self-identity are almost always presented as inevitable, universal, and psychobiologically determined; this has been the position taken in the case of differentiation (James, 1890), individuation (Mahler et al., 1975), and the trend toward autonomy (Angyal, 1941, 1965). For example, the genetic basis for separation fears has been made by Bowlby (1973) and by Piaget (1970) for the development of cognitive abilities, especially those that influence self-perception.[8] Temperament traits, which likely affect mother-child interactions during individuation and vary widely among individuals, also appear to be innate (Thomas & Chess, 1977).

Postulating a biological baseline for human development has certain advantages; for example, age norms, for a variety of perceptual and motor abilities, provide a basis for determining to what degree and in what manner biological development is encouraged or impeded by learning, parental attitudes, and culture (Dennis & Najarian, 1957; Landreth, 1967). Based on repeated observations of sixty infants, Schaffer and Emerson (1964) have provided normative data on the intensity of reaction to brief separations from caregivers, which can guide our assessment of deviant "protest" behavior in children and point out parental behavior that results in abnormal behavior in a child. A similar use of an "underlying, universal pattern" of development is observable in Levinson et al. (1979), where his study of the life cycle of adult males considers the unique shaping experiences of men in terms of "common developmental principles."

Many influences along the way shape the nature of the journey [the life process]. They may produce alternate routes or detours along the way; they may speed up or slow down the timetable within certain limits; in extreme cases they may stop the developmental process altogether. But as long as the journey continues, it follows the basic sequence. (p. 6)

Operating like "open" instincts (Tinbergen, 1951), the underlying mechanisms of identity development are innate and universal, although highly influenced by social forces. It is indisputable that humans are by nature "social" animals and that by virtue of their large, highly developed brains and superior communication ability are capable of an amazing variety of responses to stimuli. But humans are not merely products of social factors and learning; there are regularities in the form of species-specific universals that cannot be explained by the patterns of society and culture (Kluckhohn, 1953; Kluckhohn & Murray, 1962; Kluckhohn & Strodtbeck, 1961).

Currently, the primacy of what we have called psychobiological mechanisms has been affirmed in the promising, well-documented work of the evolutionary psychologists (Barkow, Cosmides, & Tooby, 1992; Brown, 1991). Evolutionary psychology, an interactionist position approach to understanding development, dispels many of the myths of radical cultural anthropology,[9] but is somewhat less "genetic" than sociobiology. Earlier interactionist anthropologists, such as Clyde Kluckhohn, had sometimes expressed similar views of universals—for example,

The members of all human groups have about the same biological equipment. All men undergo the same poignant life experiences such as birth, helplessness, illness, old age, and death. The biological potentialities of the species are the blocks with which cultures are built. Some patterns of every culture crystallize around focuses provided by the inevitabilities of biology: the difference between the sexes, the presence of persons of different ages, the varying physical strength and skill of individuals. The facts of nature also limit culture forms. No culture provides patterns for jumping over trees or for eating iron ore. (Kluckhohn, 1965, pp. 26–27)

One may assume that a universal is biologically dominated when:

1. the mechanism appears in all humans and may be said to be characteristic of humans;[10]
2. it occurs in all known societies, where it may be modified by "variations in the rules by which societies attempt to govern the behavior of their members" (Ford & Beach, 1951, p. 3);[11]
3. there is good reason to suppose that there is a specific physiological or neural basis for it;[12]
4. similar manifestations can be cited, beyond analogies, in other species that are relatively alike morphologically;[13]
5. although "learning" may shape the behavior under the control of the mechanism and influence the "triggering" of behavior dependent upon it, the adaptive function and the inevitability of the behavior appear relatively unmodified by learning.

The foundation of personality development is to be found, therefore, in psychobiological processes, differing for each gender, which provide the "direction" and "constraints" of the growth process. Impelled by the need to adapt to one's environment, we find the universals of human nature provide adaptive, necessary functions that smooth the operation of responding to experiential situations.

Social imperatives, from cultural values and social norms, particularly those manifested in child-rearing practices, determine what is considered to be *normal* or *abnormal* in any culture. When the smooth development of human beings along lines dictated by psychobiological mechanisms is interefered with, by either social interaction or environmental pressure, the resulting development or behaviors can be seen as *unnatural*.[14] For example, if toilet training, usually initiated by middle-class parents when a child is about two years old (earlier in working-class families), is postponed until the child is five years old, the parents' behavior (and possibly their child as well) will be seen as abnormal. Similarly, at the other extreme, if parents begin toilet training before sphincter muscles have myelinated—say, when the child is around one year old—*their* behavior may be also deemed "unnatural."

Common deviations from psychobiological timetables that affect the development of self-identity include unreliable mothers, when the child is in early infancy (Erikson, 1950; Mahler, 1963); separations from mother, particularly before object constancy is attained (Mahler, 1968; Settlage, 1971); encouragement or lack of support for cognitive development (Piaget, 1970); conflict between parent and child, primarily because of a temperament mismatch (Thomas & Chess, 1977); failure to provide comfort when a child experiences separation anxiety (Bowlby, 1973; Mahler, 1968); and maternal overprotection of passive boys (Kagan & Moss, 1962).

ATTACHMENT

When separateness is radically persued, it is achieved at the expense of the normal human needs [sic] for interrelatedness . . . The overvaluation of separateness is reflected in a theory [psychoanalysis] that contrasts autonomy as a hallmark of mental health with dependence as a sign of developmental arrest. (Spieler, 1986, p. 53)

Despite the evidence that at every stage of development there is an interrelatedness of homonomy and autonomy, the usual emphasis for theories of self-identity development is upon separateness, individuation, and independence; this orientation, however, has serious consequences for males in this society.[15] As early as 1962, in the longitudinal study conducted by the Fels Research Institute (Kagan & Moss, 1962, p. 58), it was noted that males suffer life-long conflicts over their felt dependency needs and passivity behaviors because "a passive orientation to problems is inappropriate for the male role." Males are *supposed* to be assertive and self-sufficient and they are very aware of it (Ullian, 1981; Levinson et al., 1979; Kluckhohn & Murray, 1962).

In his classic, holistic approach to the etiology of neurosis, Andreas Angyal (1965) anticipated contemporary concerns about the effect of the psychological denial of dependency needs on the self-image of adult males.[16] Consistent with Bowlby (1969) and Mahler (1963) that the need to form attachments is innate and necessary for psychological survival, Angyal adds that the recognition of being in a "state of isolation" is anxiety producing and contributes to the development of neurosis. Angyal's theory of the developmental process involving homonomy resembles that offered by psychoanalytically oriented theorists to explain the persisting influence of separation anxiety.

Although an "excessive" need to establish dependency relationships and receive love remains high on the list of indicators of immaturity,[17] the importance of attachment in the development of infants and conversely the detrimental effects of maternal separation have gained more than general acceptance; they have become popular ideas. In a book written for the lay public on psychopathic personality development, for example, the authors attribute the "growing" incidence of children "without a conscience" to the failure of infants to make appropriate attachment relationships (Magid & McKelvey, 1987): "It is now clear that one of the primary causes of rapidly increasing crime, particularly by children, is unattachment. Indeed, it may be at the very heart of the crime wave the nation is now experiencing" (p. 63).

There is abundant research to confirm the relationship between early self-development (that is, differentiation and self-recognition) and the quality of attachment (Trad, 1987). Data suggest that children between six and eighteen months of age who are even temporarily separated from their primary caregiver develop symptoms of depression (Harmon, Wagonfield, & Emde, 1982; Robertson & Bowlby, 1952; Spitz, 1945; Spitz & Wolf, 1946).

Mary Ainsworth and her colleagues, after several years of research using her Strange Situation Procedure, have been able to confirm many of the theoretical ideas of Bowlby (1969), Mahler (1963), and Angyal (1965). Additionally, her research supports the notion that one aspect of maternal protection and security (homonomeity) is to encourage exploratory behavior (autonomeity) and to comfort fears of strange situations (Ainsworth & Wittig, 1969). Ainsworth has described three types of attachment: *A* (Avoidant attachment), where the child treats the mother and strangers alike, at twelve months of age shows no distress when separated from the mother, and shows no tendency to interact with the mother;[18] *B* (Secure attachment), where children show a desire to interact with and maintain physical contact with the mother and a moderate amount of distress when separated from the mother;[19] and *C* (Anxious attachment), where the child may show ambivalence toward the mother (clinging and hitting), distress during separation, and passivity or lack of exploratory behavior.[20]

Attachment, whether the product of an innate predisposition or a learned drive associated with nurturance and protection provided by the primary caregiver, is an indispensable and inevitable factor in the development of a sense of autonomy and of self-identity. Although disparaged as an enduring trait, particularly for males, dependence upon a caregiver at critical periods of self-development not only encourages autonomy but allows autonomy and self-regulation to develop (Trad, 1987). Most of the research on attachment focuses on the variables that influence the quality and strength of attachment, such as the age and cognitive ability of the child, the temperament traits of the child and/or of the parents, and the quality of the mothering. There has been somewhat less interest in the effects that attachment may have on infantile experiences and personality growth.

THREATS TO SELF-IDENTITY: PARENTAL ABSENCE AND ABUSE

A tendency to react with fear to each of these common situations—presence of stranger or animals, rapid approach, darkness, loud noises, and being alone—is regarded as developing as a result of genetically determined biases that indeed result in a "preparedness to meet real dangers." . . . Such tendencies occur not only in animals but in man himself and are present not only during childhood but throughout the whole span of life. Approached in this way, fear of being separated unwillingly from an attachment figure at any phase of the life-cycle ceases to be a puzzle and, instead, becomes classifiable as an instinctive response to one of the naturally occurring clues to an increased risk of danger. (Bowlby, 1973, p. 86)

Separation from primary attachment figures is inevitable and necessary for personality maturity. The interactionist position of evolutionary psychology suggests that, while the universal mechanisms impelling autonomy-striving are determined primarily by psychobiological factors, environmental or situational variables influence the individuation process at every phase. The most general categories of such variables involve qualities of mothering related to the "opposing" or polar homonomy tendencies, which may also be innate *en toto* (Mahler, 1952) or be motivated by a "genetically determined" fear of separation (Bowlby, 1969, 1973). The core of many interactionists' position is an available, protective mother, who provides "safe anchorage" (Mahler, 1967). This safe anchorage facilitates the child's outward movement, exploration (Ainsworth & Wittig, 1969), and risk taking behaviors (Bowlby, 1973).

Counter to the ideal of mother-as-safe-anchor are the very real situations where caregivers are less than ideal. Common types of nonideal parents or caregivers include those who are absent, either physically or emotionally; those who are abusive; and those whose temperament is a mismatch with the temperament of the child.

The most noted parent variable in relation to unavailability has been, of course, the simple physical absence of the parent. The findings of the classical study of the effects of separation after "bonding"[21] (Spitz & Wolf, 1946) have been replicated in a few studies (Harmon et al., 1982; Robertson & Bowlby, 1952). An interesting and important finding in this regard is that children who are separated from their mothers shortly after birth (with impediments to bonding and attachment as a consequence) are more likely to suffer non-organic failure to thrive (NOFT) and child abuse than children who had been nurtured from birth by mother (Klaus & Kennell, 1976).[22]

However, there is also some negative evidence for the postulated three-phase behavioral reaction pattern to separation experience (protest, despair, and attachment), which suggests that physical absence may provide a more complicated influence on a child's history of attachment. The most frequently cited complication involves timing (the age of the child and the length of parental absence) and context (the three phases appear most notably in institutional settings where love and attention are not provided by substitutes) (Trad, 1987). Separation before bonding does not appear to lead to depressive symptoms, and several studies report that separation in infants earlier than six months of age does not result in immediate symptoms of grief (Field, 1977; Rode, Chang, Fisch, & Sroufe, 1981; Sroufe & Rutter, 1984). Similarly, when children, all of whom were old enough to have bonded with a primary caregiver, were separated briefly—ten to twenty-seven days—and were provided good mothering in foster homes, none developed acute distress syndrome (Robertson & Robertson, 1971).

Although the persisting effects of isolated (and usually brief) separation experiences upon attachment and secondarily upon self-development are controversial, there is no doubt that certain enduring parental attitudes and behaviors have a profound influence on attachment. Among phenomena studied have been abuse and rejection, neglect, and inadequate care because of cognitive deficiencies.

Parental abuse of children has uniformly been found to have a severely deleterious effect on later self-image and social behavior. While a cold and rejecting attitude on the part of a mother may impede individuation, in children six months old or older (Ainsworth, 1973; Mahler, 1972; Main, Kaplan, & Cassidy, 1985), it also appears to facilitate differentiation, an essential component in the ability to bond, in younger children (Lewis, Brooks-Gunn, & Jaskir, 1985). A similar age relationship is found in the case of the child who is physically abused and maltreated: there is clear evidence, in such children, of insecure attachment (Ainsworth & Wittig, 1969; DeLozier, 1982; Egeland & Sroufe, 1981; George & Main, 1979), poor social responsiveness and relatedness (Gaensbauer & Sands, 1979), and delayed speech development and motor skills (Egeland & Sroufe, 1981; Kempe & Kempe, 1978; Martin & Beezley, 1977), particularly when abuse occurs after the child is six months old. Rejection, either by physical or emotional abuse, by a parent who is physically present may be more devastating than physical separation.

Although one might expect that parents who are below average in intellectual endowment are more likely to provide inadequate caregiving and perhaps to abuse children, the overall evidence is that low intelligence serves primarily as a "mediating factor" (Trad, 1987),[23] contributing only to poor or inappropriate care. More significant than low general intelligence, however, are specific cognitive deficiencies, particularly perceptual distortions and lack of awareness and comprehension in regard to aspects of the maternal function (Fredrick, Tyler, & Clark, 1985; Main & Goldwyn, 1984). Rejecting mothers, for example, are likely to have memory gaps for their own childhood, to maintain idealized representations of parents, who had nevertheless rejected them, and to be unable to describe their child's attachment needs in a "coherent" and accurate manner (Main & Goldwyn, 1984).[24] These researchers suggest that rejecting mothers perpetuate an "identification with the aggressor" while being relatively unconscious of the nature of the identification. Abusive and rejecting mothers have also been found to be more likely, than controls, to perceive anger in an audiotape of an infant's cry (Fredrick et al., 1985). There is a plethora of data that suggest that abusive mothers do not recognize what the impact of mistreatment will be on children (Gilligan, 1977; Smith, Hanson, & Nobel, 1973).

Less incidious, but perhaps more pervasive, is the detrimental result of a personality mismatch between parent and child. The suggestion of Thomas, Chess, and Birch (1968) that this mismatch, which may disrupt the smooth parent-child relationship,[25] has inspired considerable research. The value of "goodness of fit" between a child's temperament pattern, almost always measured indirectly through the mother's (or sometimes father's) *perception* of the child's temperament trait pattern, and his or her social environment has been demonstrated to influence attachment (Frodi, Bridges, & Shonk, 1989; Kemp, 1987), the development of self-regulation as opposed to learned helplessness (Donovan, Leavitt, & Walsh, 1990), and the production of mild, short-lived behavior disorders (Thomas & Chess, 1980).

Particularly noteworthy is the series of studies conducted by Wilberta Donovan and Lewis Leavitt and their associates at the University of Wisconsin. Using simulated child-care tasks and an audiotaped infant's cry as a stressor, the results indicate that a mother's perception of control influences and success or failure experiences in child care will influence her self-perceived competence and affect her coping behavior (Donovan & Leavitt, 1992). The Wisconsin research provides the intervening steps between attitudes, temperament traits, and expectations of parents and attachment and self-identity development of children with, their own, various temperament trait configurations (Donovan & Leavitt, 1985, 1992).

Gender as a Intervening Variable

There are real[26] or regularly perceived temperament differences between males and females at birth, parents' expectations and socialization practices tend to be gender-specific, and almost every phase of the separation individuation process shows the influence of gender differences. Yet few theorists and researchers have emphasized gender differences in the areas of attachment, separation anxiety, or the development of self-identity. There is ample evidence, however, that the delayed maturation of males and differential maternal handling—with a demonstrable discontinuity in the caregiving process—affect attachment and dependency needs.

Wendy Olesker (1990) collected data on twenty-two infants, nine to twelve months of age, and found that the superior cognitive ability (with the contribution of differential treatment by mothers) of females extended into self-other differentiation. Girls not only differentiated earlier than boys, when they became toddlers, girls perceived separation from mother earlier, and became anxious about it (Olesker, 1984). The significance of this latter finding is suggested by Olesker's description of those boys who were able to understand "separateness" at Mahler's stage of rapprochement:

Possibly, boys who show earlier awareness of separateness have a stronger tendency to identify with mother as a way to hold on to her at a time when other resources and coping mechanisms are not solidly developed. If so, such strong identification could interfere with establishing a masculine identity when awareness of anatomical differences subsequently take place. (Olesker, 1990, p. 343)[27]

Mahler failed to note that "girls seem to enter rapprochement earlier than boys"[28] (Olesker, 1990, p. 238), possibly because she was over impressed with the "locomotor" development of male toddlers and chose not to consider the superior maturation and more rapid rate of development in the physical, cognitive, affective, and psychic domains.[29] What was missed in the earlier work, because gender differences were ignored, is this: boys, who are pampered and protected in the first few weeks of life (and need it),[30] are encouraged to "push away" from mothers, explore, and become autonomous, while girls, who are superior developmentally but are also able to be aware of separation anxiety, are encouraged to stay close to their mother (Bergman, 1982; Bowlby, 1969; Chodorow, 1978; Fast, 1984; Garai & Scheinfeld, 1968; Kagan & Moss, 1962; Newson & Newson, 1986; Olesker, 1984, 1990; Rosenthal, 1967; Ullian, 1981).[31]

Earlier we noted that discrimination of self seems to be facilitated by rejecting, cold mothering (Lewis et al., 1985). The pushing away by mother of little boys, therefore, may at first glance suggest that boys would be precocious in attachment development. However, Lewis et al. (1985) suggest just the opposite. Children who have early self-awareness often behave with an "I don't care if you're around" attitude, which suggests that the security base, which attachment provides, is missing. Children who are missing this security perceive the environment as more threatening and more dangerous. By age six, children who had early self-awareness have a less positive image than those whose self-awareness was delayed, usually as a function of secure attachment (Lewis, 1986).

Rapprochement, according to Mahler, occurs generally after most children are more than eighteen months old, which is about when they are said to be developing "libidinal" object constancy (Mahler et al., 1975). These approximate ages must refer to boys; both rapprochement and object constancy occur much earlier in girls (Olesker, 1990). According to the theory of the Umbilicus Complex (cf. Chapter 7), parental handling in relation to cognitive development increases the likelihood that boys will develop a dread of abandonment, while girls suffer the more mature separation anxiety when mother (or mother substitute) is absent (Settlage, 1971). The discontinuous parental behavior—preferential pampering and protection followed by an abrupt pushing away—is almost sure to produce conflicts over passivity and dependency in males (Kagan & Moss, 1962).

SUMMARY

Like orthodox psychoanalytic theory, this society holds that males must become self-sufficient, competent, and self-regulating and must separate from the influence of mothers and other nurturing and protective persons if they are to become "mature." Because they come into the world especially helpless and underdeveloped, males are coddled, held, protected, and cuddled. Paradoxically, however, their cognitive development, including their ability to be aware of separateness and to attain object constancy, is not encouraged. When a male reaches nine months to a year of age, only dimly aware that separations may be temporary and mothers regularly return, he is strongly encouraged to move away from mother's protection. Whereas the dynamics for females are continuous and serve to produce anxiety if they are not in proximity to mother, the dynamics for males produce life-long conflict over dependence needs and a dread of abandonment.

The psychic development of males is a product of psychobiological factors interacting with experiential forces. While the most fruitful theories of the development of self have come from theoreticians who take a deliberate interactionist position, research findings from mainstream psychology are less in agreement with the broad theories than is usually recognized. Generally, the studies of attachment and separation "flesh out" the gross "stages" of psychoanalytic theories. The most current research indicates that individuation is a much more complex and significant developmental process—one that occurs much earlier than traditional theories suggest.

One of the principal reasons for the impressive lack of congruence between theory and research findings is that gender differences in child development have regularly been ignored. Individuation for males and individuation for females follow different timetables. These different timetables are a function of the differential maturation rates and the socially prescribed caregiving practices, which are gender-specific.

We agree with Susan Spieler that psychoanalysis, as well as western philosophy, is androcentric and fails to appreciate and value attachment and nurturing as positive personality components of adults. The problem is compounded when researchers do not recognize that divergence in development for the genders occurs, not at *three or four or five years of age*, but closer to *three or four or five weeks of age*.

NOTES

1. Stern (1985) has incorporated a similar idea in his theory of self-identity development where he postulates four "senses" of self: the *emergent self*, from birth to age two months; the *core self*, from two to six months; the *subjective self*, from seven to fifteen months; and the *verbal self*, which forms after that. Stern stresses that these are not "stages" in the typical idea of stage theory, but rather concurrent senses that remain with the individual, providing different aspects of the self, essentially making the "self" more and more complex.

2. The work of Preyer (1841–1897) predates that of the other, better known theoreticians in the area of self-identity. Mead's ideas on the development of the self-image have been a strong influence in sociology. His germinal essay, one of several lectures collated in 1927, was published in a highly edited book by C. W. Morris and appeared three years after Mead's death.

3. Psychoanalysts have, ironically, criticized both Erikson and Mahler for being too environmentalist in their conceptualizations. May (1986), for example, takes issue with Erikson's emphasis on social and cultural factors and his optimism. May calls these typical "American" values and comes close to accusing Erikson of pandering to an American audience. The argument posed by Kohut (1980) about Mahler's work was more subtle and technical. Because of her methodology, direct observations of interactions between mothers and young children, he asserted, Mahler was unable to research "mental representations" and, consequently, she underemphasized the inner, subjective aspects of self-perception. It is interesting, in this regard, that Bowlby (1973) questions Freud's biological orientation; he notes that Freudians make inherited characteristics related to the attachment to mothers (with direct relevance to self-development) "secondary," whereas, he believes, the fear of being alone is primary and innate. Bowlby, thus, categorizes Freud with social-learning theorists and suggests that he is not biological enough!

4. For Mead, the "I" represents the "unorganized aspect of human experience," while the "Me," the product of social interaction and the aspect of self that allows objectivity, "represents the incorporated other within the individual." Mead's concepts of I and Me are more collaborative than are Freud's concepts of Id, Ego, and Superego (Meltzer, 1972, p. 10).

5. Earlier the authors have observed that psychologists of interbellum Vienna, who were generally very environmentalist in approach, used the observations of biological maturation of infants to establish a baseline for psychological growth (Gardner & Stevens, 1992). Among the psychoanalytic self theorists who trained in interbellum Vienna are Mahler, Erikson, Hartmann, Anna Freud, Ernst Kris, and Kohut. Also in Vienna were a number of developmental and social psychologists, not identified with the Freudian movement, who were to make lasting contributions to self-theory and research; including Alfred Adler, Karl and Charlotte Buhler, Paul Lazarsfeld, Marie Jahoda, and Else Frenkel.

6. Wilson's earlier book *Sociobiology* (1975), recipient of the Pulitzer Prize, established him as a major influence on modern thought. Although his work is generally interactionist, Wilson has helped legitimize the geneticist position and has brought conclusions that have been unpopular among most social scientists to public attention. For the antisociobiology position the reader is referred to Hubbard & Lowe (1979), Tobach & Rosoff (1978), and Lewontin, Rose, & Kamin (1984). For the newer evolutionary psychology perspective, the reader is referred to Tooby & Cosmides (1992).

7. Earlier, the strict environmentalist position, denying that genetic predispositions were important determinants of complex social behavior, was presented by Linton (1959). He wrote that "instincts practically disappear by the time one reaches primates in the evolutionary scale" (p. 6) and suggested that human instincts are limited to "automatic unlearned responses" controlled by the autonomic nervous system, such as those involved in digestion.

8. Piaget's position, although interactionist, strongly focuses on the biological components of perceptual development. His concise and thoughtful discussion of this issue (1970, pp. 171–176) is very similar to that offered by Thomas & Chess (1980).

9. It is interesting that Brown is himself a cultural anthropologist, the intellectual heir to the great interactionist anthropologist Clyde Kluckhohn. What gives Brown's work its greater emphasis upon inherited psychic mechanisms is the ongoing refutation of cultural diversity data that had provided the (apparently inaccurate) basis for Kluckhohn's (1965) observations.

10. This criterion reflects the position taken by sociobiology (Wilson, 1975, 1982), evolutionary psychology (Brown, 1991), ethology (Tinbergen, 1951), physiological psychology (Dethier & Stellar, 1961; Ford & Beach, 1951), and the interactionist sociologists and anthropologists (Kluckhohn, 1965; Kluckhohn & Strodtbeck, 1961).

11. The traditional radical position of cultural anthropology is that universals are less impressive than cultural variation, a view that deemphasizes the probable biological basis for the need to address certain issues of human growth (Linton, 1959; Mead, 1935, 1949; Whiting & Child, 1953). The "chicken-or-egg" controversy has increasingly been resolved in favor of innate biological predispositions as the basis for universals in human nature (Barkow et al., 1992; Kluckhohn, 1953, 1965).

12. This, most stringent criterion, clearly met in the case of biological drives such as thirst and hunger, is that which was adopted by Linton (1959). As Bowlby (1973) has observed, while human social behavior is too complex to hope for simple functional explanations in biochemical terms, components of the behavior often have a known physiological basis. In his analysis of "natural clues to danger," for example, Bowlby (1973) describes responses related to innate fears (such as separation) and learned fears in terms of the physiology underlying fear responses. That humans are predisposed to perceive certain stimuli as dangerous is also a possibility (Rachman, 1990).

13. This is merely a restatement of phylogenetic continuity.

14. This point is often made by Montagu (1974b), who asserts that sociocultural factors, particularly child-rearing practices, frequently lead to "unnatural" behavior on the part of parenting persons. This position is not inconsistent with Montagu's emphasis on cultural determinants, rather confirming the potency of social influence. Montagu, incidentally, seems to have invented the word *sociobiology* (1961), although he is not, of course, an advocate of Wilson's genetic explanations.

15. The personality development of women has provided the exception to this emphasis. Erikson (1950), for example, argues that at stage IV, girls must regress to earlier stages of development, to become dependent and demanding, and, esssentially, halt their independence development.

16. Bowlby (1969), the theorist most connected to the concept of attachment, rejects the notion that *dependence* and *attachment* are synonymous. His major objection is that dependence appears most frequently in psychological literature as a "secondary drive"; affiliative needs, especially with a caregiver, are learned via association of the caregiver's presence with physiological changes after nurturance is provided. Bowlby's position, on the other hand, is that attachment behavior is innate and its maturation schedule is separate from dependence behavior. This technical distinction in terminology is a little too fine for the purposes of this book, and we use the terms interchangeably despite the fact that Bowlby's usage is probably more accurate. Bowlby's other objection with the term *dependence* is mainly "political"; he observes that *dependency* has become a disparaging word, while *attachment* is more neutral and sometimes (when equated to "love," for example) even positive. We agree, in this respect, with the majority opinion that attachment or homonomy also has negative connotations, especially in the motive repertoire of males (Angyal, 1965; Kagan & Moss, 1962; Spieler, 1986; Ullian, 1981.

17. Until recently "Passive-Dependent Personality" was an accepted diagnosis of psychiatric disturbance.

18. See Mahler (1952) and Horner (1975) for a psychoanalytic-developmental explanation of autistic children, and Ainsworth, Blehar, Waters, and Wall (1978) for a detailed description of the scheme.

19. B-type attachment resembles what in Bowlby's theory (1973) is a (normal) manifestation of separation anxiety. In Mahler's system behavioral responses similar to these will occur during the "practicing" subphase (Mahler, 1968) and at around fifteen months of age, the rapprochement subphase (Mahler, 1972; Mahler et al., 1975).

20. Although the research findings that underlie Ainsworth's "types" suggest that children with C-type attachment are not as severely or chronically disturbed as those in the other two categories, the symptoms of these children resemble those described by Mahler in her work on symbiotic psychosis (Mahler, 1952, 1965; Mahler & Furer, 1960). The observations of Mahler and her colleagues were arguably more in-depth than those of typical Ainsworth-style studies (Kemp, 1987).

21. Attachment, or bonding—the relationship with the parent or caregiver—in this work are different concepts from that discussed by Eyer (1993). As bonding became popularized in the 1970s, mothers were told that holding and touching their infants were absolutely necessary for the child's emotional well-being. Eyer's argument that the popularized "rules" went beyond the research data available is probably legitimate. Our sense of attachment and bonding, however, is not based on the number of minutes one holds a child but on the environment in which the child is raised and the amount of emotional support that the caregivers provide.

22. It should be noted that the children in this study who were separated briefly from their mothers shortly after birth did not show greater separation fears or acute distress during the very early separation (Klaus & Kennell, 1976). The deleterious effects of interference with bonding were manifested in the mothers' relative inability to provide nurturance and safety for their children thereafter.

23. A specific example of this process is the finding that rejected or abused mothers who are below average in intelligence or who suffer *general* cognitive deficiencies are more likely to become rejecting or abusive to a child (Kempe, Silverman, & Stule, 1962; Main & Goldwyn, 1984). Low general intelligence, thus, increases the probability that any mother who had been mistreated will mistreat her own offspring (DeLozier, 1982; Main & Goldwyn, 1984).

24. The cognitive problems of rejecting parents resemble those observed in studies of mistreated young children (the problems in emotional expressiveness do also, but to a lesser degree in parents). The intergenerational rejection findings thus give evidence of the persistence of this syndrome, with its related vulnerabilities and defects, throughout life.

25. The work of this group has thrown some doubt, however, on the stability of those temperament traits observed initially in very young children (Thomas & Chess, 1977). That temperament traits are somewhat malleable is also suggested by the findings of the longitudinal study of the Fels Research Institute (Kagan & Moss, 1962).

26. There is considerable discussion in feminist literature that gender differences are mere social constructions—that is, that differences in the behavior, attitudes, personality, etc., of men and women are artifacts of particular cultures. While this may lead to interesting philosophical discussions, there is considerable evidence in the data from anthropologists, psychologists, and sociologists that men and women perceive them-

selves to be different, that they are treated differently, and that biological susceptibilities are different. For the purposes of this discussion, we are going to assume that these differences are real, and that they have a very real impact on the lives of individuals.

27. In a 1968 article, Greenson noted similar problems with male gender identity. Working with transsexual and neurotic male patients, Greenson suggests that womb envy is quite common and intense. The stronger the male child identifies with mother, the more difficult time he has separating from her, and the more problematic his establishment of a strong and positive male identity becomes.

28. This is not to suggest that all developmental psychologists currently conducting research separate gender for data analysis—they appear not to.

29. Our informal survey of Mahler's published cases (e.g., in Mahler et al., 1975) suggests that Olesker is correct in this appraisal. Mahler and her associates (including Olesker) are more interactionist than most other psychoanalysts, and even they underplay the importance of gender differences in maternal attitudes as well as in biological maturation. This oversight is not true of Olesker or Bergman (1982).

30. There is considerable evidence that parents spend more time handling, stimulating, and attending to male infants than female infants (Chorodow, 1976; Korner, 1974; Maccoby & Jacklin, 1974; Moss, 1967, 1974; Mott, 1991). Infant boys receive more attention because they need and demand attention: they cry more, sleep poorer, toilet train later, and have poorer judgment than their same-aged sisters (Garai & Scheinfeld, 1968).

31. Although this finding is consistent with their own research, the conclusion of Maccoby and Jacklin (1974) is that mothers are no more likely to encourage boys to separate than girls. Their review cites a number of studies that show no differences, many of these published in the 1960s and 1970s.

7

The Umbilicus Complex: The Dread of Abandonment as a Life-Long Dynamic

Secure attachment, cohesive self-experience and object constancy all imply the capacity to tolerate rage toward the lost or depriving object. When there are sufficient positive feelings toward the separated figure to balance the negative feelings engendered by the loss, loss is less threatening and separation is facilitated.[1] But the less one is loved, the more rage and anger are produced; heightened rage originating from inadequate nurturance is inherently disturbing because internalized loving and soothing self- and object structures are fewer. (Bloom-Feshbach & Bloom-Feshbach, 1987, p. 43)

Socialized within a context where specific images of men and women, mother and son, guide and shape behaviors, biologically vulnerable male children are denied expression and fulfillment of dependency needs while pushed toward excessive independent behaviors. A core requirement of the socialization process is not merely to teach the child appropriate behaviors for his or her society, including appropriate gender roles, but to have the child internalize the society's values. The sense of self that the child develops thus reflects these values, since the self can only be perceived within a broader context of a society of individuals. The sense of self, in turn, influences the child's ability to competently deal with the autonomy-homonomy conflict during the early stages of the individuation process.

Male children are psychobiologically more vulnerable and their social environment more difficult; their early relationships with mother are strained, the standards to which they are held are more stringent, they are only accepted when they produce, and their gender role is narrow and limited in scope. Males are also more susceptible to physical disease and disorder and to psychological trauma. This situation leads men to seek nurturing relationships, usually with women, while at the same time to deny their need. The emotional conflict results, in some highly susceptible men, in what we have called the *Umbilicus Complex*.

Before we present examples of how the Umbilicus Complex may be manifested at different stages of development and an explanation of how the dynamic remains powerful for individuals, we thought a review of the basic theoretical notions would be useful.

1. Development of self-identity is a function of an innate psychobiological mechanism (Angyal, 1965); the process begins in the earliest differentiation of an infant from what is perceived as "not me" (James, 1890) and is part of the inevitable, invariable biological architecture.

2. Self-identity is influenced by the maturation of cognitive ability (Hartmann, 1964a). Before the infant is able to achieve even primitive object constancy in Piagetian terms, she or he will respond to the absence of a caregiver with a dread of abandonment (Mahler, 1968; Settlage, 1971). This dread occurs earlier than separation fears.

3. The fear of separation from a mothering person may also be innate (Bowlby, 1973; Wellman & Gelman, 1992). Experiences of separation throughout one's lifetime revitalize this fear, which is felt as anxiety (Bowlby, 1969).

4. Because "safe anchoring" (gratification of homonomy needs) is necessary for the maintenance of a stable self-identity, attempts at individuation require support and encouragement by the mothering person (Bowlby, 1973; Mahler et al., 1975).

5. Although the usual reaction to forced separation, particularly in sensitized individuals, is almost always unpleasant and often debilitating (Bowlby, 1973), there are even more disastrous consequences to self-esteem (Snyder & Ickes, 1985) and self-organization (Lecky, 1945). Not only is a loss perceived as a rejection, but the role of that person in providing input for the others' realistic evaluation of self is lost (Vallacher, 1980).

We take an interactionist view of the development of self-identity. Nevertheless, we tend to emphasize certain aspects of the developmental process, primarily because we wish to apply the more general self theory to a specific case: how the self-identity of particular adult males becomes conflict ridden, particularly when threatened with emotional abandonment. We assert that the same factors that may undermine the development of a cohesive, adequate self-identity in infancy lead to life-long patterns of difficulty in adjusting to experiences of separation. Toward these ends, we emphasize the importance of the interaction of three crucial factors in the development of self-identity: psychobiological determinants, including maturation; gender differences, particularly during developmental "stages"; and differential need for homonomy (attachment).

LIFE-LONG CONFLICT: AUTONOMY-HOMONOMY

We argue that among the most basic traumatic experiences, repeated frustration of the infant's needs for nurturance and secure attachment, particularly before object constancy is achieved, will lead to a dread of abandonment. Using repetition-compulsion as an explanatory concept, we suggest that traumatized individuals relive dependence-independence conflict experiences in an attempt to conquer their anxiety, fear, and dread of being abandoned. Some individuals become increasingly able to cope with the affective component (the dread) associated with threatened loss of attached, nurturing persons during their lifetime; this is especially true for those individuals, mostly men, who are able to form life-long attachments to women. Others, those less fortunate, however, try to cope with their feelings of dread by active "mastery" over the rejecting individual and/or over the abandonment experiences, such as divorce. These unsuccessful individuals often become violent or demonstrate other abnormal, self-defeating behaviors. At the very least, individuals who are sensitized and, therefore, compelled to overcome their dread will engage in exaggerated domination of and attempts to control nurturing persons (mothers, wives, etc.)—the behaviors that characterize the babe-pasha dynamic.

Adult males in this society inevitably must cope with a series of losses in the course of their life, some minor, some catastrophic (Vaillant, 1977). There is considerable evidence that in general males deal with the stress of loss of nurturance and security less effectively than females. Some, particularly vulnerable men, reveal almost complete helplessness in the face of such losses and, except for rapid replacement of a nurturing object relationship, can muster almost no adequate mechanisms to recover either self-esteem, a feeling of competence, or even mental health after confrontation with threatened abandonment.

Functional Continuity of Attachment Conflicts

Similar to other psychodynamic and social learning personality theories, the Umbilicus Complex accepts the functional continuity of autonomy-homonomy problems as highly probable (Ainsworth, Blehar,

Waters, & Wall, 1978; Bowlby, 1980; Cohler & Stott, 1987; Gewirtz, 1972; Mahler et al., 1975; Vaillant, 1977).[2] We assume that the separation experiences during the first two years, which are qualitatively different for boys and girls, influence all subsequent attempts to cope with loss or anticipated loss of nurturing persons. The specific events in infancy, combined with a unique psychobiological predisposition, produce varying degrees of vulnerability to the threat of abandonment. For some individuals loss of a nurturing person does not signal the apprehension referred to as "separation anxiety" but a more primitive "dread of abandonment."

Vulnerable individuals, especially those who exhibit excessive dependence, a desire to dominate and control nurturing persons, and clearly abnormal self-defeating reactions to actual or anticipated separation or loss, as enduring personality traits, are more likely to suffer from the Umbilicus Complex. To describe the process of life-long, repeated incidents of relative helplessness in the face of rejection and loss, which revitalize prototypical experiences of feeling the dread of the danger of loss, we have chosen, as an explanatory mechanism, the Freudian concept, repetition-compulsion. Abandoned, we believe prematurely, the compulsion to repeat provides the specifics by which the Umbilicus Complex becomes manifest.

Because gender differences have been ignored or underplayed in dynamic and developmental theories, a very plausible explanation for the genesis of psychopathology in males who suffer loss or threatened abandonment has been overlooked. It is well established that, except for special skill in aggressive or violent activities and in manipulating inanimate objects, where males are superior, females mature earlier and remain ahead of male age-mates at least until adolescence.

Among the more significant maturational stepping stones, for the psychology of separation, attachment, and loss, are maturational superiority in cognitive ability, individuation, and social skills. The advanced maturation rate of females reduces the likelihood that they will develop life-long primitive reactions to the threatened loss of nurturance.

Social interaction factors also contribute to the differences noted between individuals in the ability to cope successfully with loss of security and dependence gratification. Maternal handling discontinuity and sociocultural expectations almost guarantee that males will be more sensitive to the threat of abandonment, will be more likely to suffer dependency conflict, and will be relatively helpless to cope with loss of nurturance (except for the adaptive act of quickly establishing a new dependence-gratifying relationship).

Separation Anxiety vs. the Dread of Abandonment

General theories that describe parent-child interactions are relatively uncomplicated, usually including only a few variables and describing growth processes in simple, discrete, highlighted "stages." The diverse, research-based determinants have yet to be absorbed as mediating variables (Bowlby, 1973; Erikson, 1950; James, 1890; Mahler, 1968).[3] In 1968, Mahler suggested a distinction between "separation anxiety" and the "fear of the loss of the object" (Mahler, 1968; Settlage, 1971); the latter phenomenon we prefer to call the *dread of abandonment*. Chronologically, according to Mahler, the infant's fear that mother's absence will be permanent occurs early in normal emotional development—earlier than the anxiety-eliciting (temporary) absences of mother after the child achieves object constancy. Simply, before a child learns that anything, including mother, exists and persists outside his or her perceptual sphere. he or she could not know or anticipate that an absent mother might return.

The dread of abandonment appears very early and persists until object constancy is achieved. Before the child's cognitive development makes it possible to appreciate that mothers have an independent, enduring existence and can return, the infant likely perceives mother's absence as a potential "loss of the object" (Mahler, 1969, p. 221). The dread of abandonment is theoretically more likely in males because, as relatively less developed neonates, males are more helpless, are more demanding of maternal care, and develop a sense of separateness, the differentiation of "me" from "not me," much later than females (Olesker, 1990).

This distinction between a primitive, prebonding dread and separation anxiety is important for explanations of the etiology of severe disturbance in children, but was not given much attention in later work on the elaboration of the separation/individuation process (Mahler, 1968). This distinction did not receive adequate importance, we believe, for the same reason that most of Mahler's ideas are today so often questioned; she ignored gender differences. By her lack of attention to female-male differences, both in cognitive development and maternal care, Mahler evolved generalizations that obscured crucial differences in the timing of separation stages. In particular, as the research briefly noted in Chapter 6 indicates, boys are much more likely to experience the dread of abandonment and girls, more likely to exhibit true separation anxiety.

Both boys and girls encounter autonomy-homonomy conflict during what Mahler calls rapprochement (around age two and a half), but the conflict is very different for each gender. Girls, who are more socially aware, better differentiated, and more mature and potentially independent, are then encouraged to stay close to their mother. Capable of object constancy, two-year-old girls display signs of separation anxiety in exaggerated "shadowing" of mother, which is encouraged by the latter. The more aggressive, externally oriented boys of the same age, who may not yet have developed object constancy and have a strong, primitive dependence on mother, are, on the other hand, abruptly encouraged to be autonomous. Physically separated from mothers, young girls show anxiety, which is relieved by physical closeness, whereas young boys, who continually seek the sight of mothers "from a distance," become panicked.

The Revitalization Process

One shortcoming of psychodynamic theories is their failure to explain functional continuity in personality development. Except for a few simple concepts such as fixation, which states merely that a core conflict and character defenses persist, not much has been offered to explain how early experiences and their immediate sequelae might be revitalized in the life process. While case studies—for example, in psychoanalysis—regularly reveal that certain traumatic issues appear repeatedly, there is little interest in how or why persons tend to experience certain problems over and over again. In a number of publications, most notably in 1920, Freud described a process that he called repetition-compulsion (Freud, 1920, 1926, 1939).

The repetition-compulsion, an explanation for normal personality development (Freud, 1920) and "the most fundamental characteristic of the mind" (Freud, 1939, p. 178), provides a concept that facilitates the description of how early traumatic experiences influence later life.

The effects [of repetition-compulsion] can be incorporated into the so-called normal Ego and in the form of constant tendencies lend to it immutable character traits, although—or rather because—their real cause, their historical origin, has been forgotten. Thus a man who has spent his childhood in an excessive "mother-fixation" may all his life seek for a woman on whom he can be dependent, who will feed and keep him. (Freud, 1939, p. 95)

Freud considered the compulsion to repeat crucial experiences to be basic in normal as well as abnormal personality development.[4] However, as Spieler (1986) has observed, Freudian theory equates autonomy ("masculinity") with mental health, especially for males. Therefore, the man who engages in a life-long quest for mothering relationships would not be considered by traditional Freudian theoreticians as the best example of a paragon of mental health. A characteristic of prototypical experiences of anxiety is that the individual is in a state of relative helplessness. It was this quality that was emphasized, for example, in Rank's (1924) birth-trauma theory.

Clearly, the anticipation of the loss of a nurturing, protective person in the first few months of life can be said to impinge upon the consciousness of a person who is helpless, particularly helpless to prevent the absence of that other person. When mothering is undependable (Erikson, 1950) or the mothering person is neglectful or rejecting and the infant is particularly immature and helpless, the absence becomes traumatic and, according to this application of repetition-compulsion, the threat of loss of nurturance, protection, and security will revitalize the affective component of the trauma.

It is also consistent with the mechanism related to repetition-compulsion that an individual will unconsciously put himself or herself in situations that repeat the original traumatic situation. This tendency, which seems at first to be self-defeating and bleakly tragic for the course of life, provides, on the contrary, Freud's most "optimistic" explanatory concept. Although apparently willful repetitions seem, Freud noted, to be motivated by something other than drive reduction—the phenomena being thus "beyond the pleasure principle" (Freud, 1920), even instances of persons' putting themselves in positions unintentionally (or "unconsciously") where they will relive unpleasant (or traumatic) experiences needs to be explained.

Based upon reports of dreams and observations of children's play (Wälder, 1933), sources that provide evidence of the compulsion to repeat, Freud's later theoretical contributions include what might be called an innate "need to master" an early trauma. In *Beyond the Pleasure Principle*, for example, Freud (1920, p. 29) writes:

In the case of children's play we seemed to see that children repeat unpleasurable experiences for the additional reason that they can master a powerful impression far more thoroughly by being active than they could by merely experiencing it passively. Each fresh repetition seems to strengthen the mastery they are in search of.

Unfortunately, instead of developing the need-to-master idea[5] and making it a major motivational concept in personality development, Freud (p. 30) goes on to introduce the "death instinct" as the basic biological process underlying repetition-compulsion.

Table 7.1
Course of Separation in Life History

PHASE	APPROXIMATE AGE	DESCRIPTION	PATHOLOGICAL SYMPTOMS	INTERVENTIONS
I. Differentiation	"Psychological birth"	Earliest separation of self from environment. Primitive perception of mother. Establishment of core identity.	Autism, ritualistic behavior, bizarre responses. Failure to develop normal attachment behavior. Catastrophic reaction to minor changes in environment. Being oblivious to mother's presence may fluctuate with rage in her absence.	Physical, including chemotherapy. Institutional care in some cases. Organic etiology probable. Very rare incidence.
II. Individuation	6-24 months	Most significant events in adjustment to separation. Movement from psychological symbiosis to individuated self. Establishment of trust.	Symbiotic psychosis. Separation anxiety. Fear of strangers. Excessive timidity. Clinging behavior.	Parent education. Psychotherapy. Encourage emotional support for independent physical activity.
III. Primary Autonomy	2-3 years	Establishment need state as different from that of others. Toilet training primary avenue. Development of control.	Excessive shame. Oppositional behavior or overcompliance. Negativism. Encopresis and withholding of feces.	Psychotherapy. Behavior modification that emphasizes self-control. Support for decision-making.
IV. Oedipal	1-5 years	Rivalry and sharing. Perception of triadic relations. Confirmation of competence. Separation from "primal hearth."	Gender identity confusion. Possessive love for mother. Jealousy and overcompetitiveness. Fearfulness. Hostility toward same-sex parent.	Psychotherapy. Encourage sense of security in love of same-sex parent. Support normal competitiveness. Reward achievement.

PHASE	APPROXIMATE AGE	DESCRIPTION	PATHOLOGICAL SYMPTOMS	INTERVENTIONS
V. School Entrance	5-6 years	Socially prescribed separation from "primal hearth." Demands for performance. Adapt to strange surroundings, standards, and rules. Working relationships with strangers.	School refusal. Inability to share teacher. Phobias. Regressive behavior. Opposition to authority.	Psychotherapy. Home again becomes a secure, "safe harbor." Reward competence.
VI. Secondary Autonomy	Adolescence	Independence striving. Peer group substitutes for the family. Sexual "awareness." Practice adult role.	Defiance of authority. Independence-dependence conflict. Alcohol/drug use. Social isolation. Antisocial behavior.	Group psychotherapy. Encourage child to sever emotional ties to family.
VII. "Breaking away"	Legal Maturity	Physical separation from parental home. Accepting adult status.	Irresponsibility and immaturity. Separation anxiety. Depression and forms of neurosis.	All types of mental therapy. Treatment is usually not the responsibility of parents. Support groups to enhance security feelings necessary for movement into adulthood.
VIII. Catastrophic Loss A. Death of parent(s) B. Death of spouse C. Divorce D. Other	Maturity	Temporary period of grieving is necessary after serious loss. When available, a new love object is attached to, replacing the loss. Loss provides opportunity to increase self-sufficiency, establish a philosophical outlook, and develop new interests.	Revitalization of separation anxiety. Depression and grief. Rage. Disorientation and loss of self-esteem. Feeling abandoned, alienated. Increase in need for dependence.	Support groups. Encourage to engage in self-centered and narcissistic pursuits. Give time to "lick wounds" before pressing for establishing new relationships.

Ignoring the metaphysical conceptualization that suggests that the "goal" of repetitions of unpleasant experiences is a return to a state of stimulus-free–ness ("the aim of life is death" [Freud, 1920, p. 32]), Robert Wälder (1933, p. 216) presented a "psychoanalytic theory of play" that emphasized the mastery aspect of repetition.

The individual has been through a specific experience, which was too difficult or too large for him to assimilate immediately. This unabsolved, or incompletely absorbed experience weighs heavily upon his psychic organization and calls for a new effort at handling and for a reexperience. . . . [The repetition represents] the ego's attempt to assimilate the experience more completely through renewing and thereby gaining the mastery over it.

The Frustration-Aggression Hypothesis

"Children who hate" are children who lack ego-controls and who perceive almost any experience as unpleasant and frustrating. These children, especially when frustrated by external forces, become anxious or angry (Redl & Wineman, 1952).

Their [delinquent children] frustration tolerance is so low, their ability to remain reasonable under the impact of unpleasant experiences is so undeveloped, that any experiences of punishment would hit them without any ability to cope with them. This means, for instance, that the withdrawal of a privilege, even when it is considered fair and deserved, would expose them to the untenable situation of suffering frustration, to which they would react with the usual display of increased pathology. (Redl & Wineman, 1952, pp. 234–235)

In trying to bridge the gap between Freud's motivation theory and Hull's learning theory, behaviorist-leaning theoreticians postulated the frustration-aggression hypothesis: the notion that frustration always leads to some form of aggression. In spite of the fact that the original notion was overstated and that much of the subsequent research and observational data do not confirm the invariability of the relationship (Baron, 1977), the postulate is useful to explain, in non-Freudian terms, how anger functions as a secondary drive.[6]

The frustration-aggression hypothesis suggests that "normal" persons become angry when they do not get what they want, when their needs are not met, or when they are insecure (Dollard & Miller, 1950). However, in normal individuals the repertoire of behaviors is far more varied and more socially acceptable than that exhibited by Redl and Wineman's delinquents.

Parental rejection or desertion may likewise produce anger in the child. If the child feels secure only when the parents are present, it may react with fear when the parents leave or when they threaten to leave again. When the parents return, the child may make excessive claims, want unusual favors, "be clingy." To these demanding and possesive gestures on the part of the child the parent may react with unintelligent punishment, thus again teaching the child to fear. (Dollard & Miller, 1950, p. 150)

These observations of how children are likely to react to situations of frustration may be generalized to adult males. Every male in this society "knows" that he "ought not" feel apprehension, confusion, endangered, or intensely angry when faced with or threatened by the loss of security and nurturance. The older he is, the more likely that the negative reinforcement will come from an internalized source, his self-identity. Thus, the understanding of a person afflicted with a dread of abandonment that his feelings of dread and anger are "inappropriate and unacceptable" may increase his anxiety in the current situation, increase the likelihood that a future repetition will occur, and interfere with his ability to master the dread and other affective components of the threatened abandonment.

The idea of repetition is not only a concept in Freudian theory. Life-long repetitions of behavior sequences are a function of "habit," in learning theories, which are mediated by "generalization."

There are always small but specifiable changes between any two stimulus presentations separated in time. The cues presented on the second occasion are always slightly different than those that appeared on the first occasion. The concept of generalization is given the important function of accounting for the tendency on the part of the individual to display the same response even though there has been variation in the cue situation. In simple terms, this concept implies that habits learned in one situation will tend to be transferred or generalized to other situations to the extent that the new situations are similar to the original situations. (Hall & Lindzey, 1957, p. 434)

Whether a child's fear of being alone and tendency to "overact" when frustrated and deprived is due to primarily genetic predispositions or to learned habits, it is well established that in the life of some individuals who have been traumatized in early childhood the threat of abandonment persistently triggers "overreaction," "excessive demands," and self-defeating attempts at mastery, including aggression against the person or persons perceived to be the source of frustration or anticipated frustration.

LIFE-LONG PROBLEMS

The dread of abandonment does not wait until an individual is an adult to find manifestations in disordered or dysfunctional behaviors. For the susceptible individual, there will be signs throughout life of the autonomy-homonomy struggle. For example, during the first phase of the individuation process—the stage of differentiation, at approximately two months—a child for whom separation may be a continuing problem will exhibit catastrophic reactions to even minor changes in the environment. Table 7.1 presents our delineation of the phases of the separation process and our ideas about what symptoms are likely to occur at each phase.

RECAPITULATION

The human neonate is notably helpless, almost completely unable to survive without the ministration of others. Male infants, who are arguably more highly valued in this society, are typically pampered and receive more attention than their sisters; this may indicate that parents recognize that male infants are biologically less mature and develop more slowly than females. In this regard, an important gender difference is the advanced cognitive maturity of girls, which results in their differentiating earlier and appreciating that maternal separations are temporary. Boys of the same age are less able to appreciate that the absence of the nurturing person will end and are more likely to perceive temporary separations as devastating abandonment.

At about age two, a discontinuity in maternal handling occurs that has immensely significant consequences. The paradox is that males, with the explicit encouragement of their mothers, are supposed to become increasingly independent and unattached from home and hearth. Whereas the natural inferiority of male children had earned them a greater amount of handling and conscientious care for most of their first two years, mothers feel constrained, because of social expectations, to push their babes away so that they can grow into self-sufficient men—men who "don't need anyone."

In males the prototypical experience of early separation trauma is the perceived abandonment of the young infant. It can and often does become a complex that is repeated many times in a male's life, a dread of possible annihilation accompanied by irrational anger and a strong, learned drive to master anxiety by controlling the nurture provider. Females learn that safety is with mother, with whom they identify, and they may develop true separation anxiety because the prototypical (learned) anxiety situation occurs after object constancy is established.

What we call the Umbilicus Complex is, thus, more substantive than the term *mother fixating* suggests. It involves panic, helplessness, and rage, when, later in his life, a man is faced with another repetition of the abandonment thema.

NOTES

1. *Separation* in this context refers to the sense of autonomy, a somewhat different usage of the word from that in attachment theory (Bowlby, 1973). In most psychoanalytic theories influenced by Mahler autonomy is presented, at least implicitly, as the positive goal of maturity.

2. That personality development theory does not require the assumption of relatively unchanged "dynamics" that originate in infancy has been forcefully maintained by Allport (1937, 1960, 1961). His emphasis on the determining influence of contemporaneous social factors is supported in some well-known longitudinal studies (Kagan & Moss, 1962; Thomas & Chess, 1980).

3. There are several reviews of literature on parent-child interaction—for example, Appleton, Clifton, and Goldberg (1975), Collins and Gunnar (1990), and Martin (1975).

4. This is one of the rare occasions when Freud was to deal, if briefly, with "normal" personality development. In the context of repetition-compulsion, he defined *normal* as "without symptoms" (Freud, 1920). It should be noted that in his most expansive theorizing Freud connected repetition-compulsion to a more metaphysical concept; when he explained the universal tendency to repeat in terms of the death instinct (Freud, 1933), he sounded its death knell. When his followers rejected the death instinct, they abandoned repetition-compulsion as well.

5. White (1959) is usually credited with the most satisfactory elaboration of this concept. Recently, child development researchers have begun to conduct studies on the evolution of a sense of competence in young children inspired by White's comments (Donovan, Leavitt, and Walsh, 1990; Donovan and Leavitt, 1992; Ross, 1992; and Trad, 1987).

6. When the social scientists of Yale's Institute for Human Relations, who were interested in forming a bridge between Freud's motivation theory and Hull's learning theory, introduced the notion that frustration always leads to some form of aggression, they made the error, later corrected, of overstating their case. Despite the fact that much of the subsequent research and observational data do not confirm the invariability of the relationship, the frustration-aggression hypothesis has proved to be an influential explanation for the development of anger as a secondary drive.

It is not fair to accuse the Yale group of ignoring primary aggression, since the instinctive nature of aggression is included, although not emphasized, in later works (Dollard & Miller, 1950; Miller & Dollard, 1941). It is interesting, in this regard, that Miller and Dollard have also been accused of misstating Freud's biological orientation toward motives. Yet, the secondary-drive notion of aggression is explicit in Freud's later writing (Freud, 1926, 1933), which was pointed out by Bowlby (1973).

Some of the controversy about the hypothesis was due to the original definition of *frustration*. The authors were interested in psychological and social psychological research, and the operational definition of frustration—the impeding or thwarting of goal-directed behavior—although indirectly related, seems to ignore the more basic deprivation of needs implied by the term, important in particular to infants and young children.

8

Marriage and Divorce

So ancient is the desire of one another which is implanted in us, reuniting our original nature, making one of two, and healing the state of man. (Plato, c. 500 B.C./1971, p. 159)

Although it is comforting to think that early humans were just like us, it is unlikely that our ancestors would have had "marriages" similar to current-day marriages any more than they would have had similar tastes in food, music, or clothes. Since the family structure at its most basic is a mother-child dyad,[1] it is most likely that during the primal stage of human development, females, traveling with their children, and males, traveling alone, would meet and mate and then each would have continued on her or his separate way (deWaal, 1989; Hardy, 1981).[2] It is likely that sexual attachments would have been casual; individual possessiveness and jealousy would not have been problematic.

Some writers and theoreticians try to impose current mores and values onto early humans and suggest that families have always been nuclear and females monogamous (males, it is argued, have always found it difficult to maintain a singular, stable sexual relationship) (Ardrey, 1966; Morris, 1967). An alternative perspective theorizes that pair-bonding began during the Pleistocine era, not because sexual intercourse was problematic or that early humans developed moral codes which would limit sexual promiscuity, as the Tarzan theorists suggest, but because people, especially males, realized that group membership provides certain positive benefits (Hardy,

1960; Morgan, 1972); hunting and living together assures that there will be more food and that the food store will be protected from animals. The division of labor, which can occur in a heterosexual group with women gathering grains and catching small animals and men hunting, makes sense, as it would be convenient for mothers to stay with the younger children. It was during this time that women developed skills in sewing, fire making, cooking, pottery, and agriculture.

From the point of view of the female, males would add an extra element of protection for her and the children; children would be taken care of by everyone.[3] Males, on the other hand, would gain a lot. By establishing a place among the group of women and children, males gained emotional security, companionship, and a stable food supply. Within the family, *Homo sapien* males also learned to temper their aggression toward other males; the incentive to obtain nurturance motivating them to adapt their behaviors.[4]

It is most likely that our style of marriage developed with the advent of farming and the concomitant recognition of paternity, but even though marriage has been around for years and years, marriage styles have not been consistent. For example, preliterate cultures, such as the Todas, have been known to have practiced polyandry (one woman and several men) (Kephart, 1966), while other groups, including early Mormons in this country, have practiced polygyny (one man and several women, often sisters). Monogamy (one man and one woman) is the standard that we are most familiar with.[5]

The nuclear family—the family that most individuals in the United States have experienced (a mother, father, and children living in a separate dwelling)—is relatively recent. Prior to the industrial revolution, in the United States and Western Europe, the extended family (several generations of relatives living together) was more common. Often in the extended-family model, marriage was an economic or political alliance between families rather than a culmination of romance between individuals; the emotional needs of family members were not considered important.[6] With the rise of individualism, the ever-growing transient nature of the workforce, and the belief in personal happiness, the nuclear family has replaced the extended family (Murstein, 1974).

In the extended family, relatives were available for emotional support. In the nuclear family, however, there is greater emphasis on obtaining emotional support from the intimate partners, and there is now a greater burden on women who are assigned the expressive role and given total responsibility for nurturance and love. Interestingly, the intensity of this specialized relationship leaves men even more vulnerable than before to trauma, less sure of their ability to withstand daily or job-related stress.

While marriage has been around for eons, only recently have we explored what marriage is like for the participants—what the role demands are. In a now-classic study, Jessie Bernard (1972) documented that marriage was different for men and women. Bernard made the point that, while men disparage marriage, probably as a defensive reaction guarding against awareness of dependency needs, it is demonstrably a good deal for men, a bad deal for women.

MARRIAGE AND ITS BENEFITS TO MEN

> The special woman helps him to shape and live out the Dream: She shares it, believes in him as its hero, gives it her blessing, joins him on the journey and creates a "boundary space" within which his aspirations can be imagined and his hopes nourished. (Levinson et al., 1979)

The hormonal changes at puberty inform the male child that he is becoming an adult and as an adult that he should seek out a person with whom to mate. Historically, males and females were considered adults when they reached sexual maturity; however, recently adolescence has emerged as a transitional period between childhood and adulthood. Modern adolescence, which is a product of social evolution and definition, denies the reality of biological maturation and has become a most stressful period. The *Sturm und Drang* idea of adolescence obfuscates the most important battle that is "refought" during adolescence—separation. The challenge of autonomy-striving is excited by pubescent cravings, evoked by the individuation process of which it is a phase, and made conflicted by the dread of abandonment that is revitalized.[7]

One could look at the motives for mate seeking in three different ways: biological, social, and emotional. The biological need for sex is a powerful motive. Men unsure of themselves and uncomfortable with women can find release of sexual needs with prostitutes or through a series of one-night stands. To meet the social needs of adulthood, men often seek marriage; status is often denied unattached men, men who are perceived as undependable, immature, irresponsible, and nonproductive (Gilder, 1986). Adolescent males and young single men who have not been successful in mating are the expendable elements in all recorded societies.

Single men are not in general very good at life. Often they know little about the most important parts of it. But they are sometimes fiercely ingenious at death. If you want a troop of killers, the military has learned, it is best to stick with singles. Whether you are a Maoist who wants Red Guards to terrorize the land, an Indonesian general intent on massacring Chinese, a Ugandan out to banish Indians, a Nazi recruiting storm troopers, or an American officer looking for men equal to a Mylai, you stay away from the securely married. You want your lieutenants callow and womanless. (Gilder, 1974, p. 25)

In addition to satisfying the well-recognized needs for a sexual partner and establishing himself as a normal adult,[8] marriage is a man's way to find a replacement for mother. By attaching himself to an adult woman, a man unconsciously and symbolically returns to the family, its protection, its nurturance (Bernard, 1972; Cantor, 1982; Gilder, 1974, 1986; Levinson et al., 1979; Myers, 1989).

The father [husband], like the children, is presumed to be entitled to the mother's love, nurturance, and care. In fact, his dependent needs actually supersede those of the children, for if the mother fails to provide the accustomed attentions, it is taken for granted that some other female must be found to take her place. (Herman, 1981, p. 46)

Males have a traditional view of the wife's role (Bernard, 1972; Komarovsky, 1967); she is supposed to be the housekeeper, making sure that the daily chores of living, cooking, cleaning, washing clothes, bill payment, and so on, are taken care of, freeing males from the cares of the everyday world. A recent study (Ganong & Coleman, 1992) of unmarried college students reported that their expectations of the characteristics of future marriage partners has not changed significantly. While almost all of the subjects, both men and women, responded that they expected to be successful in educational and professional attainment, the women said they expected their husbands to be superior to them in intelligence, income, success, ability, and education. The male subjects, while expecting that their potential spouse would be equal in intelligence, ability, and education, also expected to be more successful and earn a much higher income. Being a competent, primary breadwinner is, thus, still an important, perhaps the exclusive, function of men in marriage (Dowling, 1981; Peplau, 1983).

Marriage provides a situation for the male, at least on the surface, where he is safe from the vicissitudes of life, protected, comforted, needed, wanted, valued, desired, and in charge.[9] More importantly, marriage protects the male from his deep-seated feelings of separation anxiety.

Being emotionally tied to other individuals is important for all humans, but men who typically deny homonomy needs find solace in marriage because, as a social institution, it allows dependency behavior without the stigma of being dependent.

Men need women—far more than women need men—for their very survival. Men need a biological and sexual tie of the sort uniquely provided by marriage and children. Otherwise they are relegated to the optional fringes of life; and, like single warriors, they know they are dispensable. The struggle for marriage and family is a struggle for life itself. (Gilder, 1974, p. 28)

How Good Is Marriage?

How good a deal marriage is for men is clear from the demographic data: married men have significantly lower rates of severe depression and incidence of phobic symptoms than married women (Knupfer, Clark, & Room, 1966); findings that never-married women are healthier, physically and mentally, than married women (Knupfer et al., 1966; National Center for Health Statistics [NCHS], 1970) are fairly consistent indicators that the advantages of marriage are differentially bestowed on males. But the best evidence comes from comparisons of married men with never-married and divorced men, where the data suggest that marriage is needed by men for success, longevity, health, and happiness (Bernard, 1972; Gilder, 1974, 1986; Gove, Hughes, & Style, 1983).[10] Compared to never-married and divorced men, married men have relatively higher earned income (Carter & Glick, 1970), live longer (Gove et al., 1983; Kitagawa & Hauser, 1973; NCHS, 1970), are healthier and happier (Bernard, 1972; Gove et al., 1983; Levinson et al., 1979; Riessman & Gerstel, 1985), and are less likely to suffer a major affective disorder (Clark-Stewart & Bailey, 1989; Durkheim, 1951; Knupfer et al., 1966; Kramer, 1966). Generally, Gilder's (1974) thesis that marriage keeps men safe, sane, and civilized seems reasonable—single men are particularly apt to do violence to themselves and to others, and both their suicide and homicide rates are the highest for any demographic classification and they also suffer the greatest number of accidents and injuries. Consistent with earlier demographic findings, Riessman and Gerstel (1985) present data that indicate married persons enjoy better physical and psychological health than the unmarried.[11]

When a man gets married, the changes in his life go far beyond his immediate relationship. Statistically, his college grades summarily climb above those of more talented singles, his crime rate plummets, he pays his bills, and qualifies for credit. He drives more carefully and qualifies for cheaper insurance. His income as much as doubles. He becomes more psychologically stable. Contrary to the theory that breadwinning duties account for high male mortality, he lives much longer than his counterpart who stays single. (Gilder, 1974, p. 152)[12]

Perhaps the best evidence that men need (or want) to be married is that almost all divorced men remarry; more than 80 percent of men remarry, 50 percent remarry within the first three years after the divorce (Cherlin, 1981; Weingarten, 1985). There is some evidence, in addition, that men who remarry attain the same high level of "marital happiness" of men who are in their first marriage (Ganong & Coleman, 1991; Glen & Weaver, 1977).[13]

Attachment Needs and Marriage

For both men and women marriage furnishes an opportunity for the reestablishment (or repetition) of attachment relationships that were experienced in early childhood (Kiecolt-Glaser, Fisher, Ogrocki, & Stout, 1987; Weiss, 1975). Marital bonds, thus, satisfy important emotional needs for men and women, but his marriage is different from her marriage. He has experienced pampering and then continuing support and encouragement for achievement outside the home (Levinson et al., 1979; Ullian, 1981). While his socialization generally requires that he suppress his homonomy needs and disparage dependency upon others, the male in this society can legitimately obtain gratification of his needs for nurturance and support within a marital relationship where he enjoys power over a woman with inferior status. Marriage replicates a man's attachment experience in a way that is generally very satisfying for him (Kiecolt-Glaser et al., 1987; Kitson, 1982; Rhyne, 1981; Weiss, 1975). The satisfaction of attachment needs becomes so compelling that for many men the anticipation of the dissolution of marriage evokes "separation distress" (Kiecolt-Glaser et al., 1987; Weiss, 1975) and may precipitate emotional suffering and abnormal rage (Halle, 1982; Myers, 1989).

As Nancy Chodorow (1978) has pointed out, in marriage a woman is the nurturer, caregiver, and homemaker. (Rhyne's [1981] data indicate that women are far less satisfied with these functions than are their husbands.) Encouraged to identify with their own mothers and subordinate autonomy needs in favor of homonomy needs (Spieler, 1986), women are rewarded for skill in homemaking and child care (Chodorow, 1978) and obtain special gratification in intimate friendship relationships (Fox, Gibbs, & Auerbach, 1985). Although many women remain resentful over their role of giver rather than receiver in marriage (Bernard, 1972), they also suffer "separation distress" (Kiecolt-Glaser et al., 1987) and, of course, about 75 percent of divorced women eventually remarry (Cherlin, 1981).

Married men, biologically less able to deal with stress and more vulnerable to illness than women generally, remain healthy because living with a "wife-mother" reduces stress. Marriage benefits men, not only because they can demand physical care but because the reproduction of the attachment relationship in marriage provides a multitude of positive-need gratifications. A man finds security and attachment in a setting where he generally is in control of a mother substitute. As we shall see, for some men made particularly vulnerable through early experiences, the benefits of marriage are easily discernible when they are rescinded by divorce.

DIVORCE AND THE DREAD OF ABANDONMENT

Increasingly the best psychological theories of the marital satisfaction–divorce distress of adult males make use of attachment theory (Bowlby, 1980; Kitson, 1982; Weiss, 1975) or separation-individuation concepts from Mahler (Cantor, 1982; Levinson et al., 1979; Myers, 1989). A developmental theory that considers divorce to be a highly significant threat to an adult male's homonomy needs is, thus, increasingly relevant for an understanding of the accumulating actuarial and clinical data in relation to marriage and divorce.

I know of no medicine fit to diminish the violent natural inclinations you mention and if I did, I think I should not communicate it to you. Marriage is the proper remedy, the natural state of a man. A single man has not nearly the value he would have in the State of Union. He is an incomplete man, the odd half of a pair of scissors. (Benjamin Franklin, *A Letter to a Young Man on Taking a Mistress*, cited in Gilder, 1974, p. 8)

For more than four decades, social scientists have presented statistical data that confirm what most divorced individuals already know: divorce can be an unmitigated psychological catastrophe (Holmes & Rahe, 1967; Vaillant, 1977; Wallerstein & Blakeslee, 1990).[14]

Next to the death of a loved one, divorce is the most severe trauma an adult can experience. Every emotional reaction is possible: anger, despair, guilt, depression, anxiety, fear, loneliness, euphoria. What often goes unrecognized is that the emotional toll on men is equal to and perhaps greater than the effect on women. (Cassidy, 1977, p. 35)

What is not so evident, however, is that divorce is even more catastrophic for men; some men, their dramatic suicides and even more
frequent homicidal violence being impossible to ignore, cannot cope at all
with divorce (Bloom, Asher & White, 1978; Clarke-Stewart & Bailey,
1989; Riessman & Gerstel, 1985). Not only is the effect of divorce on men
not as evident, except to mental health workers, but the data suggesting
that for certain men divorce has worse emotional consequences than it
does for women and children, are not widely appreciated.[15] The reason,
of course, for a divorce's greater devastation on males is that marriage is
very good for men—much better than it appears to be for women (Bernard,
1972). Marriage keeps men healthy; divorce makes men sick, sometimes
fatally.

Unlike death, divorce involves choice, and the long-lasting changes it effects
carry the promise of positive outcomes. . . . Divorce is also unique in that it gives
rise to the central passions of human life. Feelings of loss and grief commingle
with those of love and hate. Sexual jealousy is triggered and reinforced by a sense
of betrayal. Relief is tinged with guilt. Narcissistic rage is precipitated by
humiliation. Acute depression rides on the heels of rejection. When long-lasting
marriages break up, a person's very identity may be threatened. (Wallerstein &
Blakeslee, 1990, p. 6)

While there is continuing debate about who is most damaged by divorce,
the rationale for the increasing number of authors who suggest that men
suffer more greatly psychologically rests with the severity of their reactions (Clarke-Stewart & Bailey, 1989). Evidence sugggests that divorce
affects men and women differently and that, while women suffer adjustment problems early in the process, men are more likely to develop longer
lasting, more severe, and sometimes dangerous reactions later in the
divorce process (Pledge, 1992).

The following behaviors [are] characteristic [of divorcing men]: violent behavior
directed against their wives (especially battering and sexual assault); violence
toward their children and strangers; decreased work efficiency and productivity
including absenteeism from work; compulsive and frenetic dating; indiscriminate
sexual behavior including first-time involvement with prostitutes and first-time
engagement in homosexual behavior; isolation from family and friends; limited
and superficial relationships with other men; and early entry into new relationships with women. (Myers, 1989, p. 13)

Demographic statistics and questionnaire research tend to confirm
clinical observations. The most commonly encountered diagnosis for

divorced men and women is depression[16] (Bloom et al., 1978; Briscoe et al., 1973; Riessman & Gerstel, 1985). Most studies agree that affective disorders in divorced males tend to be more severe (Clarke-Stewart & Bailey, 1989; Knupfer, 1966; Riessman & Gerstel, 1985; Spanier & Thompson, 1983; Weiss, 1975); divorced men are, in fact, the group with the highest rate of admission to psychiatric hospitals (Bloom et al., 1978; Briscoe, et al., 1973; Goode, 1956; Gove et al., 1983; Reissman & Gerstel, 1985).

Divorced men may feel angry and resentful long after the marriage is disrupted (Myers, 1989; Price & McKenry, 1988; Weiss, 1975). In fact, Wallerstein and Blakeslee (1990) found that anger and retaliation were still present in divorced fathers ten years later. Sometimes the anger is turned inward and suicide occurs; divorced men have the highest rate of successful suicides (Kitagawa & Hauser, 1973; NCHS, 1970; Price & McKenry, 1988; Stack, 1980), although single, white males under the age of twenty-five are closing the gap. It is rare for divorced males to physically attack another adult. Wallerstein and Blakeslee, however, report that divorced men are likely to be aggressive toward children or toward their ex-spouse. Briscoe et al. (1973) also found a large number of diagnosed sociopathic personalities among divorced men (none of the divorced women were so diagnosed), which may explain why they have such a high rate of prison incarcerations and are both victims and perpetrators of violent crimes (Gilder, 1974). Kiecolt-Glaser et al. (1987) suggest that the type of depression during the divorcing process may be gender specific, with males more likely to suffer an agitated depression with associated anxiety, aggression, and/or volatility.

Stages of Divorce Coping

Consistent with a number of studies that suggest that being "abandoned" is far more debilitating psychologically than being the initiator of marital disruption—and men are usually not the initiator and do not want the divorce—Myers (1989) has described the (mainly pathological) reactions to abandonment in five subgroups.[17] His types of "abandoned husbands" are the Overtly Aggressive, the Passive-Aggressive, the Depressed, the Sexist, and the Passive-Dependent. The Overtly Aggressive male is one who has resisted the divorce and is openly furious at his wife's uppitiness; their wives are often afraid of them.

Some of these husbands are verbally aggressive—they shout, yell, scream, swear, or fly into rages. . . . Other men are psychological bullies—they intimidate and control their wives with their talk. . . . Some . . . are wife batterers who use physical violence in response to threats of abandonment or actual abandonment. (Myers, 1989, p. 115)

The Passive-Aggressive ex-husband expresses his emotional reaction more subtly; he may be "detached, pouty, sulky, or sarcastic." At the divorce situation these men often become resistant, do nothing, suggest that their wives have "thrown them out," and play the victim with family and friends. The Depressed husband is often hospitalized for clinical depression; successful suicides are more likely to come from this group as revitalized feelings of abandonment overwhelm the individual. At the other extreme, a depressed divorcing male may have homicidal fantasies, imagining how he might do away with an unfaithful wife, imagined or real boyfriends, and/or himself in a murder-suicide. Myers's fourth type, the Sexist, when told about his wife's impending divorce action, reacts with outrage and disbelief. These men, traditional in their beliefs about gender roles, typically have dismissed their wives' complaints and worries, have denied their own emotional involvement in the marriage, and find seeking help during and/or after the divorce extremely difficult. The Passive-Dependent husbands—those who have been overdependent on wives—perhaps feel the most abandoned. Their dependency needs have been so great that they have failed to learn how to make decisions, and they often suffer depression at the onset of divorce proceedings.

Myers's data suggest that a large number of men undergo serious, pathological changes as a result of "abandonment." The disturbance in functioning Myers describes is by its nature pervasive and long-lasting, and in many cases can be explained (as Myers does) as a reaction consistent with a revitalization of a disrupted attachment experience with roots in childhood.

We have no argument with the position of Clarke-Stewart and Bailey (1989) and Briscoe et al. (1973) that, although the incidence of severe pathology is extremely high for divorced men in comparison with married men, mental illness, suicide, violence, and hospitalization are still rare occurrences. In 1970, for example, "only" 2,167.6 divorced men per 100,000 population were admitted to state and county hospitals for psychiatric illness (Riessman & Gerstel, 1985); this may reflect a relatively low number (!) of individuals, but this rate is about twenty times higher than that of married men and close to three times the rate for divorced women for that year.

The most dramatic, extreme cases—where an "abandoned" man returns to murder his estranged wife or his family[18]—make the headlines, but thankfully are relatively rare in this civilized society. The rage, resentment, and hurt that abandoned men feel are almost universal in men who are convinced that the psychological benefits of being married (or possessing a wife) are denied them.

Marriage is good for men and they know it (Vaillant, 1977). The results of a number of studies indicate that men are satisfied with their marriage, believe that marriage is forever, and are highly resistant to the disruption of marriage. It is the legally (and religiously) sanctioned vehicle for meeting a man's sexual, security, and dependency needs. Marriage replicates the family of his childhood with, in most cases, the man effectively in control.

Almost every adult male has severed his ties with his mother in order to establish his own family. This is so much a social imperative that separation has been made the "normal" (Spieler, 1986) or "natural" (Levinson et al., 1979) process to describe the development of males. Divorce threatens men, not merely because they must deal with quasi-conscious dependency needs, but because they must adjust to a separation loss that rekindles the dread of a loss of attachment.

Perhaps a large minority of men, for whom childhood separation was traumatic and being abandoned by divorce is equivalent to annihilation, cannot adjust to the loss of a wife-mother by anything more adaptive than remarriage. Pushed to the extreme by inner distress, men whom we call suffering an Umbilicus Complex are particularly likely to act out the ultimate autonomy-homonomy conflict by extreme self-destructive acts or irrational, catastrophic behavior.

NOTES

1. For a discussion of family life for other primate groups lower on the philogenetic scale, see Dethier & Stellar (1961), Fossey (1983), Galdikas (1975), Kevles (1976), Kummer (1971), Strum (1987), van Lawick-Goodall (1967, 1971), or Washburn, 1963).

2. To avoid aggressive confrontation and announce that one is not a threat, many species of animals developed a method of presenting the jugular. All primate females (and some human ones) solicit sex from aggressive males to reduce hostility; in primates this is done by presenting the genitalia to the male.

3. In some preliterate societies, children are seen as an asset, appreciated and loved and cared for by all members of the society.

4. Lower-order female primates are reported to more willingly share meat with males who are nonaggressive, nurturant, and "kind" (Strum, 1987).

5. The term *serial monogamy* has been used to describe the current situation when men and women marry, divorce, remarry, and so on.

6. Arranged marriage is still common in countries outside of the United States. For example, in the 1980s the prime minister of Pakistan had her husband selected for her

and the prime minister of Japan had to have parental approval of the woman he wanted to marry.

7. We know from cross-cultural studies that this separation phase of adolescence can be ameliorated by close bonding with adult males. When an adolescent is indoctrinated at sexual maturity into the society through a *rite de passage*, the family of men is substituted for the family dominated by women.

Lower-order primate males mature sexually later than females, yet they are encouraged to leave the family earlier than females; male monkeys, in fact, are frequently bitten and battered to encourage them to leave the mother's nest. Whatever the primate juvenile period is, it is not strictly sexual, since only 10 to 25 percent of mature males mate, the remaining males being relegated to low status among the group or being ostracized. There is some evidence, however, that suggests that the culture of these lower-order primates provides a "cushion" for the males during the difficult time prior to being accepted as a sexual partner.

8. Recently, two writers on the condition of the family, Gilder (1974, 1986) and Bloom (1987), have suggested that another important function of marriage is to control male aggression. They both suggest that without women's commitment to men, men will become more and more aggressive and out of control.

9. Research typically reports that men are more satisfied with marriage than are women (Rhyne, 1981); women become more satisfied with marriage after the children are grown.

10. Both Bernard (1972) and Gilder (1974, 1986) observe that there are other interpretations of these data, in particular that marital state might not "cause" the differences. It is possible, for example, that severely disturbed men are less likely to marry and that the observed higher rates of mental illness and antisocial behavior as well as lower income and occupational achievement of never-married men are the results of "marital selection factors." The study by Gross (1968), for example, indicated that "depression-prone" men are less likely to marry. The same argument can be made for noted differences between married and divorced men; it is possible that men who are divorced were inferior to those who remain married in some important characteristics.

11. In the research they cite, including their own, Reissman and Gerstel (1985) suggest that the most important differences are primarily between marital statuses. Married women seem to be enjoying better health than, as reported in the early seventies, they had in comparison to never-married and divorced women. While they attribute the greater health and longevity to advantages of being married, they also consider (and do not reject) the alternative hypothesis (1985, p. 627) that being ill decreases the likelihood of being married and illness, particularly mental disorders, may contribute to dissolution of marriage.

12. Gilder has become *persona non grata* with feminists because of his advocacy of traditional marriage, specifically his suggestion that women, by virtue of their genetic endowment, should be caretakers providing support and nurturance to their husband as much as their offspring. Generally his books are well documented and he provides a good, journalistic explanation of (selected) research evidence on marriage and divorce. Like Freud, Gilder inspires special hostility because his convincing writing style makes his ideas accessible to the general public.

13. Remarried women reported significantly lower marital satisfaction than women in their first marriage, especially women who are thrust into the role of stepmother (Ganong & Coleman, 1991).

14. In their article, which purports to demonstrate that men adjust "easier" to divorce than women, Clarke-Stewart and Bailey (1989) make the important point that those men who do not adjust quickly are apt to demonstrate severe psychopathology. Their own research, which used a checklist, yielded inconsistencies with Cherlin's (1981) demographic data as well as Bernard's (1972) predictions.

15. We believe, as do others, that the trauma males suffer owing to a divorce, especially divorce instigated by the wife, or separation from a significant other, has been ignored because males are perceived as the villain. We are not denying that divorce has serious consequences for women and children, particularly economic consequences. However, we believe that it is not only good for men but also good for women, children, and all of society to recognize that males also suffer emotionally owing to divorce. If nothing else, this information should be useful for women who are thinking about divorcing their husbands.

16. In one of the few studies using a control group for comparison (Briscoe et al., 1973), divorced men had a very high incidence of severe depressive symptoms (68 percent), but women had even a higher incidence (75 percent). Briscoe and his associates entertain the notion that the depression may have contributed to the *cause* of the marital dissolution; apparently half of the depressed divorced men had suffered an episode of depression some months before the divorce. Kraus (1979), however, argues that the "mental disease" like that diagnosed in Briscoe et al. is really a temporary maladjustment to the specific stressors associated with the divorcing process.

17. Recently, other theoreticians have also developed theories to explain the emotional turmoil of divorce (Bohannan, 1980; Ponzetti & Cate, 1986; Chiriboga & Krystal, 1985).

18. As we write this, the local newspaper is running the story of a merchant who shot his mother- and father-in-law and then himself (a successful suicide in his case). His estranged wife had been living with her parents and speculation is that she was the target of the merchant's rage.

9

The Violent Pasha

Wife beating has taken on the dimensions of an indoor sport, being played by a growing number of men. . . . Psychodynamically its purpose appears to be the punishment of the symbolically loved-hated mother. Sociodynamically its purpose is to punish symbolically the usurper of his "god-given" economic and social rights. (Lesse, 1979, p. 198)

Men who perceive divorce as abandonment are frequently filled with a persisting rage (Myers, 1989; Wallerstein & Blakeslee, 1990; Weiss, 1975). The effects of this rage, fused with irrational and primitive fears in many cases, is sometimes expressed directly toward the ex-spouse, with elements of revenge and retaliation motives. However, it is more often displaced to others, especially the children (Myers, 1989; Wallerstein & Blakeslee, 1990), or "turned inward," precipitating episodes of depression and acts of suicide (Kitagawa & Hauser, 1973; NCHS, 1970; Stack, 1980).

Retaliation against a person who deprives and rejects is, however, only one of a number of causes of aggression toward women perpetrated by men. A pasha may reserve the power to punish acts of betrayal and disobedience, but the essence of the pasha-babe is his wish and need to control the sources of nurturance and security. He asserts control often by intimidation and force and when these become obsessive, the pasha plays out his fantasies, sometimes in dangerous games called physical abuse, domestic violence, rape, and murder.

There is still controversy concerning whether aggression is an inborn or learned drive for humans, but there is little doubt that some of its manifestations are adaptive and normal and that, throughout the animal kingdom, the male is usually more aggressive than the female.

In very global terms . . . it seems that aggression is often so well integrated into otherwise positive relationships that it begins to contribute to their strength. Aggressive behavior has its dangers and needs to be contained, yet it also serves to achieve solutions and compromises when there are conflicts of interest. . . . Aggression and subsequent appeasement, as we are learning, have an intensifying effect on relationships that, paradoxically, some forms of abuse may tighten the social bond. (deWaal, 1989, p. 16)

Violence, on the other hand, is often adaptive (in the sense that it brings about an objective desired by the perpetrator), but is usually abnormal. Theories of violence toward women, particularly relevant to the psychology of men proposed in this book, include two root sources that explain generally irrational acts of men who cannot deal with the dread of abandonment: violence motivated by sexual jealousy and by the acting out of matricide fantasies.

AGGRESSION AND VIOLENCE

Despite some evidence from ethology of a considerably higher incidence of violent behavior in such species as hyenas, lions, and langur monkeys (Wilson, 1982),[1] *Homo sapiens* is reputed to be a particularly bloodthirsty species. Humans apparently kill, maim, and attack without concern for the survival needs of the species; theories that propound a unique propensity for violence in men, such as that of Lorenz (1963), Ardrey (1966), and Fromm (1973), almost always assume that violence and aggression are innate, probably instincts. The nativist position is, however, not universally adopted. Although aggression is increasingly given the status of a biological drive, such as thirst and hunger, a majority of social scientists in the United States prefer to consider aggression to be a secondary or learned motive (Brown, 1991; Geertz, 1973; Tooby & Cosmides, 1992; Wilson, 1982).[2]

We have discussed the nature-nurture controversy and also both the nativist position and the environmentalist position in earlier chapters. It should be noted that the battleground for the conflict has often been in descriptions of aggression and violence, most likely because social scientists who believe that aggressive behavior is learned also cherish the hope that human violence can be reduced if not eliminated. However, it is clear that there has not been much success in the attempt to eradicate violence in this society; between 1985 and 1990 there was a 16.5 percent increase in violent crime in the United States (U.S. Federal Bureau of Investigation, 1990).[3]

The position of psychoanalysis on aggression is interesting. While sadistic urges are considered to be innate, the overall approach is interactionist; experiences and culture modify the expression and aim of the sadistic instincts.

During the oral stage of organization of the libido, the act of obtaining erotic mastery over an object coincides with that object's destruction; later, the sadistic instinct separates off, and finally, at the stage of genital primacy, it takes on, for the purposes of reproduction, the function of overpowering the sexual object to the extent necessary for carrying out the sexual act. (Freud, 1920, p. 48)

This (innate) merging of Eros and sadism, which may be the source of ambivalent feelings toward mothers (during the oral stage) and wives (during the genital stage), does not, in Freud's original conceptualization, lead invariably to violent encounters between males and females. He suggested that a number of defense mechanisms, including sublimation, displacement, and reaction formation, could modify the expression of aggression and socially acceptable, civilized behavior is possible. A less optimistic view was presented by Gregory Zilboorg (1944, p. 288), one of Freud's followers: "Let me then reduce to their simplest terms the psychological reactions of the human male to the female: the male who first overcame the woman by means of rape was hostile and murderous toward the female; he hated her."

The social-learning approach might also predict that aggression and violence by males against females are probable. In the famous conceptualization of aggression as a secondary drive, which was nevertheless influenced by psychoanalytic thinking—for example, the frustration-aggression hypothesis (Dollard, Doob, Miller, Mowrer, & Sears, 1939)—one observes that in a majority of cases the frustrating agent is a woman. Mothers provide nurturance, but they also deny nurturance; women reject men; women divorce men.

The tendency to aggress is an innate human characteristic tied to testosterone level (but undoubtedly normally distributed in men). This is suggested by the fact that males, in all cultures, commit more acts of aggression and violence than do females (Dobash & Dobash, 1979; Toch, 1992; Weiner & Wolfgang, 1989).[4] However, we also contend that early experiences, unlearned emotional control mechanisms, and society's reinforcement of certain aggressive behaviors lead some males to act on their aggressive urges to a greater extent than other males. Specifically within the area of crimes against women, where the statistics are increasing, we assert that these crimes are committed predominately by men who have failed to properly individuate and, therefore, have ambivalent feelings toward their mother.[5] This ambivalence is transferred to women in general and, in periods of frustration or reactivation of separation anxiety, reemerges. To regain control or to punish "mother," men lash out at the closest woman around.

In our extension of the babe-pasha metaphor, the explanation of violence toward women focuses on the need to control and master women—mothers and wives. We are especially interested in the work on sexual jealousy and spousal homicide of contemporary psychologists associated with evolutionary psychology.

In studies of spousal homicide motives . . . the leading substantive issue identified by police and psychiatrists is invariably "jealousy," and more specifically jealousy on the part of the man, regardless of which partner ends up dead. . . . The major source of [domestic] conflict in the great majority of spouse-killings is the husband's knowledge or suspicion that his wife is either unfaithful or intending to leave him. (Wilson & Daly, 1992, p. 305)

VIOLENCE AS SYMBOLIC MATRICIDE

The abuse of females by males is an exclusively human virtue. (Ward, 1916, p. 347)[6]

A growing segment of victims of violent crimes are women both inside and outside of marriage relationships.[7] The increase of violence toward women might have been expected because of the women's liberation movement, which by increasing women's position in the marketplace led to women's direct competition with men, or because of the sexual revolution, which by eroding women's position on the pedestal made them more vulnerable to sexual violence and perversion. However, this would only explain violence toward working women, women in direct competition with men, and/or women between twenty and forty, those who are involved in the process of mate seeking. While violence toward this group has increased, violence toward elderly women, women who do not compete, women who do not have valuables worth stealing, and women who are unlikely to sexually provoke a borderline rapist, has also increased and this violence cannot be explained easily: "From June 1962, to January 1964, the city of Boston was beset by a killer who strangled and stabbed eleven women, many of them elderly, and left their sexually mutilated bodies in garish postures with a nylon stocking knotted about the neck" (Brownmiller, 1975, p. 200).[8]

That this incident is not unusual is suggested by evidence in newspaper reports that, taken together, suggest that men are serious about ridding the world of women. For example, the *New York Times* reported that the body of a fourth elderly black woman,[9] slain by Richard L. Hunter, was found in Atlanta; a fifteen-year-old, Ivan Mendoza, was held for killing two elderly women; Ronald Steele of Cannonburg, Pennsylvania, was convicted of the murder of three elderly women; and the *Los Angeles Times* reported that Brandon Tholmer was convicted of raping and killing four elderly women.[10] During the same period, the *Wall Street Journal* noted that Aloysius Jay Garrow murdered two Soviet nuns at a Russian Orthodox convent in Jerusalem and, in Salvador, five national guardsmen stood trial for the 1980 murder of four U.S. churchwomen.[11]

Nuns and elderly women are symbolic representations that elicit irrational, fantasy-driven acts—in this case homicidal acts displaced from the mother experienced in early childhood. Nurses and waitresses, whose occupational role requires providing nurturance and thus facilitates their becoming mother symbols through stimulus generalization (Miller & Dollard, 1941), are even more likely to become victims of serial violence based upon matricide fantasies. Melanie Klein (1933, pp. 252–253) presented a historic psychoanalytic theory of the origin of such fantasies:

As we proceed to analyze the content of [child analytic patients'] anxiety, we see the aggressive tendencies and phantasies which give rise to it come forward more and more, and grow to huge proportions, both in amount and intensity. . . . As the analysis of every grown-up person demonstrates, in the oral-sadistic stage which follows upon the oral sucking one, the small child goes through a cannibalistic phase with which are associated a wealth of cannibalistic phantasies. These phantasies, although they are still centered on eating up the mother's breast or her whole person, are not solely concerned with the gratification of a primitive desire for nourishment. They also serve to gratify the child's destructive impulses.

In his recent reconceptualization of the frustration-aggression hypothesis, made necessary by accumulated negative evidence for its traditional wording, Russell Green (1990, p. 34) suggests that "aggression is a reflexive and innate reaction to being thwarted . . . evidence of such a reflexive response to frustration in humans is difficult to obtain, however, because learned behavior may overshadow and obscure innate ones."

Children who fantasize a great deal are more aggressive than those who do not. A reason for this may be that fantasizing causes rehearsal of existing schemata for behavior; children who fantasize about violence may thereby be increasing the likelihood of retrieving an aggressive schema on occasions of future interpersonal conflict. (Green, 1990, p. 167)

According to psychoanalytic research, children's fantasies typically involve murder of the mother (Freud, 1920; Klein, 1933), fantasies which persist and lead to compulsively repeated acts. In a person with extremely poor ego controls (persons who are most likely insane), these fantasies may be acted out, in a displaced form, against mother figures. The alarming increase in violent crimes perpetrated against elderly women, nuns, nurses, and waitresses can be explained as symbolic retaliation. The victims were selected because they possess various characteristics of motherhood.

MASS MURDER

While the same distortions of psychobiological mechanisms that lead to violence toward elderly women and nuns may motivate the mass murderer, most self-reports of these men include justifications that are bizarre, trivial, even ridiculous. The victims are usually similar to each other in some way, according to the usual modus operandi of the serial killer, but each killer seems to have his own compulsion in the selection of characteristics. Almost all serial killers are men; very often the victims are women (or weak, helpless persons, such as children).

In Philadelphia, Harrison Graham confessed to killing seven women in a manner similar to that of Gary Heidnik, who was charged with kidnapping, raping, and torturing four young women—killing one in his dungeonlike basement.[12] Thirty-seven women were slain by (it is presumed) a single male, called the "Green River Killer," around Seattle; seventeen (if not more) women were murdered in Los Angeles by, it is thought, one individual; and seventeen, perhaps more, have been killed by Robert Hansen in Alaska.[13] Mass murders of women have also been reported in Fort Worth, Paris, Illinois, and Southeastern Connecticut.[14] Christopher Welder, captured in 1984, was accused of torturing and murdering a large number of young women; Douglas Clark was convicted of killing six women and sentenced to death; Caral Eugene Watts confessed to killing thirteen women; Henry Lee Lucas boasted of slaying between 100 and 150 women; and Michael B. Ross, a Cornell University graduate, was a suspect in the rape-murders of six women.[15]

More recently, William Lester Suff was charged with the murder of fourteen prostitutes; Arthur J. Shawcross was convicted of killing ten women; and five women in San Diego have been murdered, it is believed, by a new serial killer.[16] Perhaps the most notorious mass killer of women in recent times, in part because he appeared so charming to many women, was Ted Bundy, who is thought to have killed fifty women.[17]

In what are perhaps the best examples of the problem we discuss were the siege held in a Utah hospital's maternity ward by Richard Worthington because his wife threatened to leave him and Marc Lepine's mass murder of fourteen women at the University of Montreal because, he said, feminists were the cause of all of his troubles.[18]

In almost every one of these cases the victim posed no threat to the killer and often was not even known to him. This suggests that the motive for the crime lies in deep, generalized hatred of women. The intensity of the hatred is attested to by the frequency of rape[19] and torture, which is common to many of these examples. Very often, particularly with the mass murders, the perpetrator is an unattached, socially unconnected man who plays out some unthinkable, perverted fantasy on women selected at random.

DOMESTIC VIOLENCE: LOSS OF ATTACHMENT AND SEXUAL JEALOUSY

> Today, Mother's Day, look at your watch. Every 18 seconds a woman will be beaten. Every six minutes a woman will be raped. (Stillman, 1993)[20]

Although violence toward all women is increasing, domestic violence is the most common type of violence perpetrated against women (U.S. Department of Justice, 1980).[21] While there is some female-on-male aggression within the home, the vast majority of violence in the home is male on female; "ninety-five percent of assaults on spouses or ex-spouses are committed by men against women" (U.S. Bureau of the Census, 1992), with the number of murders of wives by husbands rising.[22] It has been suggested that 6 million women are victims of violence in their home, while Amnesty International lists abuse of women throughout the world as a leading human rights problem.[23] Gelles and Straus (1979) maintain that "physical violence between family members is a normal part of family life in most societies . . . and in American society in particular," and Okun

(1986) asserts that there are "cultural norms that permit conjugal violence, especially woman abuse."

Besides the "regular" wife battering and general forms of both physical and psychological abuse, there are any number of grisly and bizarre murders of female family members. Memorable cases include Robert Cohn, who beat his mother to death with an iron pipe when she refused to serve him spaghetti and meatballs for Thanksgiving dinner, and Joseph M. Lyons of New London, Connecticut, who bludgeoned his wife to death with a sewing machine.[24] In Dallas, David Martin Long received the death penalty for killing three women, whom he said he hacked to death after he tired of hearing them quarrel.[25]

From his earliest experiences with women, the pasha-babe develops an insatiable need to control, master, manipulate, and exploit those who supply nurturance. Domestic violence often results from a feeling of frustration and rejection, its roots stemming from oral-stage disturbance.

The symptoms of separation distress in adults are very similar to those exhibited by young children who have lost attachment figures. One list of reactions among children to loss of a parent includes, among others, rage and protest over desertion, maintenance of an intense fantasy relationship with the lost parent, persistent efforts at reunion, anxiety, and a strong sense of narcissistic injury. (Weiss, 1979, p. 205)

While battering is less frequent when the marriage is intact and the incidence of violence escalates dramatically after separation and divorce in the case of oral-stage violence, the opposite is generally true in the case of genital-stage domestic violence. Fidelity and control of reproduction, which reveal the origin of the disturbance in adolescent sexual identity confusion, are important issues in marriage. Evolutionary psychologists such as Wilson and Daly (1992) are in agreement with sociologists who argue that there are sexual bases for the domestic violence toward women. The evolutionary psychologist adds sexual jealousy to other suggested underlying reasons for male violence toward women: psychobiological mechanisms and the need to control women sexually. The evolutionists suggest that sexual jealousy and other controls over the wife's sexual behavior serve the adaptive function of reducing doubts about true paternity and that violence and intimidation are their instruments.

It is the thesis . . . that there have evolved in *Homo sapiens* certain psychological propensities that function to defend paternity confidence. Manifestations include the emotion of sexual jealousy, the dogged inclination of men to possess and control women, and the use or threat of violence to achieve sexual exclusivity and control. (Daly, Wilson, & Weghorst, 1982, p. 11)

OTHER EXAMPLES OF SEXUALIZED VIOLENCE

While abuse within rather long-standing relationships, both legal and common law, has been recognized historically,[26] violence in dating relationships is a newer but increasingly problematic area. It has been estimated that violence occurs in 50 percent of dating relationships (Lloyd, 1991) and of those relationships, between 39 and 54 percent of the participants, primarily women, continue the relationship (Bird, Stith, & Schladale, 1991). Several explanations have been offered for the increased violence. Waller (1951) notes that there has been a decline in etiquette and the monitoring of the dating couples by the family. Lloyd (1991) suggests that peer influence is partly responsible for the increase in abuse. Since the male is expected by his peers to be emotionally more distant than the woman and in control of the dating relationship, she argues, when the woman becomes too assertive, he is likely to become aggressive. In spite of the data suggesting that women most often end a dating relationship (the same way they end most marriages), men, because their peers expect them to be emotionally distant, act as if "she trapped me, so I broke it off." Lashing out against the woman who is about to abandon him is "socially acceptable" behavior, and, interestingly, convinces some women that the man "really cares for me." Another suggestion is that when conflict affects an individual's sense of well-being, he is likely to lash out to reduce the threat (Folkman, 1984).

While in date rape the initial motivation of the man is arguably sexual and the violence is seen as an instrumental act to force a partner's compliance with sexual intercourse, there has been a tendency to view rape generally, since 1970, as a crime of violence rather than a sex crime (Giacopassi & Wilkinson, 1985). The latter position, which was implicit in the rape reform laws of the past two decades, denies the special trauma suffered by victims and of the fusion of sexual and aggressive impulses that is the root cause of rape.

It has been argued that rape is the nonsexual use of sex and should be seen as a crime of violence since the dominant motive in many rapes is not sexual gratification but the humiliation and domination of the female victim. This orientation toward rape obviously takes the perspective of the offender, for female victims react to rape as a sexual offense as well as a crime of violence (Giacopossi & Wilkinson, 1985, p. 379)

Between 1960 and 1975, "the number of reported rapes increased dramatically by 378%" (Giacopassi & Wilkinson, 1985). Because so many rapes go unreported, it is likely that rape is the most common crime of violence in the United States (Griffin, 1971); the rate of reported rape, for example, increased at a much higher rate (47 percent) than "Type One" violent crimes (such as murder, aggravated assault, and robbery), which increased on an average of 30 percent for the years between 1970 and 1975 (MacNamara & Sagarin, 1977).

Women also have been subjugated to infibulation, clitoridectomy, chastity belts, prostitution, rape, forced pregnancies, incest, bondage and torture, battering, and general denigration in a large number of cultures.[27] Clitoridectomy and infibulation, while suggested by some anthropologists to be similar to male *rite de passage* circumcision, are usually not carried out in public and do nothing but assure a total lack of pleasure and/or interest in sex for women. Like chastity belts, these surgeries are men's way to control women's sexual behavior; what better way to guard against maternal incorporation than to sew up the passage back to the "uterine paradise"?

At the same time men prevent women from enjoying sexual relations or assuring themselves that women have no sexual impulse, several thousand women, world wide, have been sold into a life of prostitution, usually by males who aver that they have no other recourse in their quest to earn a living.

Female sexual slavery is a highly profitable business that merchandises women's bodies to brothels and harems around the world. Practiced individually . . . it is carried out by pimps. . . . The private practice . . . is carried out by husbands and fathers who use battery and sexual abuse as a personal measure of their power over their wives and/or daughters. (Barry, 1979, p. 33)

VIOLENCE TOWARD AND DENIGRATION OF WOMEN

Although rape in particular has been called the "all-American crime," even the briefest of surveys reveals that violence toward women is universal. A recent issue of the *Utne Reader* (Nov.-Dec. 1989) reported that in Thailand 50 percent of married women are beaten regularly, in Ecuador 80 percent of women have been physically abused, and in Nicaragua 44 percent of men admit to beating their wives and girlfriends. The *New York Times* reports that 150 Muslim women have been raped by Serbians, the trafficking of women still continues in China, and extreme brutality against women occurs daily in Brazil.[28] Indicating gross disregard for women, David Hoffman reported, Arab men killed four Israeli women merely to provoke a response by the U.S. Secretary of State, James A. Baker.[29] And perhaps in one of the more bizarre reports, the *Los Angeles Times* noted that in Africa, women were attacked because men blamed the women's immoral behavior for a drought.[30]

A review of the statistics suggests the obvious: hatred of women has become more naked and more virulent. The increased disregard for women cannot be explained sociologically, at least not in terms of socioeconomic factors,[31] nor psychologically as merely the result of the sexual frustration of a majority of young men who are, nevertheless, overrepresented as perpetrators of all violent crimes. The motivation for the denigration of women has as its source primitive rage; its roots precede genital interest in women.

The denigration of women in which men participate is, we suggest, a way to avenge early rejection by the mother. Individual males begin to denigrate women during their adolescent rebellion against authority. Many male psychiatric patients reveal an intense envy and hatred toward women that is, in the final analysis, symbolic of generalized devaluation of mother as a primary object of dependency (Horney, 1932; Kernberg, 1972; Lerner, 1974).

Thus, battering of women results from the defensive denial by men of their own powerlessness. The physical abuse of women occurs not only in marriage relationships where the wife becomes a direct mother substitute and sons can "safely" beat mom but, indicative of the pervasiveness of the anxiety that denial of their powerlessness has, violence also occurs in dating relationships where the tie to mother is less direct.

DEPENDENCE, DENIAL, AND REACTION FORMATION

Mother is the giver of life, the giver of nourishment, the giver of nurturance, and the denier of all of these also.[32] Whether or not it reproduces the womb experience, for which there may or may not be memory traces (Rank, 1924), the earliest infant-mother period is one of unqualified love, perfect security, and complete protection.[33] The natural and imperative separation/individuation process, however, curtails this perfect relationship and, as Klein has suggested, the infant's frustrated wishes result in anger and resentment toward the mother who is both provider and frustrator (Klein & Rivere, 1937).

Journalists, commentators on popular culture, and "pop" psychology writers assert that it is a special type of mother, one who is narcissistic, overwhelming, and ungiving, who produces a most unnatural hostile attitude in sons. Klein and other clinicians who have treated either young children or schizophrenics, however, tend to present a view of the "primordial" mother as all-powerful and controlling in the eyes of the infant. To Zilboorg (1944) and Rank (1924) this perception is a natural result of the differential power between mother and helpless child.

The adult harbors a life-long, mainly unconscious wish to reunite with an all-powerful, all-giving person, a wish manifested frequently in a secondary nostalgia for the primal hearth. Unlike many of their fellow-animals, human infants cannot do anything for themselves; they cannot eat, drink, keep themselves clean, or transport themselves. It is within the context of the symbiotic relationship with the mother that individuation takes place. Maturity and good mental health require that sufficient and appropriate dependence needs have been gratified during this period and that the boy feels secure in his separation from mother.

A FEMINIST VIEW OF THE SUBJUGATION OF WOMEN

Wife batterers and rapists are often not noticeably different from other men. They are not psychopathic brutes and in most other areas of their lives they are generally not violent (Walker, 1979): violence for these men has become particularized. Their violence is motivated by a desire to dominate women, by intimidation and injury; for some, their sex drive has become fused with a primitive urge to master women.

As early as 1916, Lester Ward recognized that the wish to dominate women was the principal motive of men and that rape was the vehicle for the subjugation of physically weaker women. Ward suggests that in "primordial" times, congruent with what we currently recognize about nonhuman primate groups, the human female selected her mate and defined kinship units. In his view the female-dominant society was "natural" and was subverted by the unnatural "discovery" of rape.

It thus appears that, whatever the family may be to-day in civilized lands, in its origin it was simply an institution for the more complete subjugation and enslavement of women and children, for the subversion of nature's method in which the mother is the queen, dictates who shall be fathers, and guards her offspring by the instinct of maternal affection planted in her for that express purpose. The primitive family was an unnatural androcratic excrescence upon society. (Ward, 1916, p. 353)

Susan Brownmiller (1975, p. 14–15) suggests that "man's discovery that his genitalia could serve as a weapon to generate fear must rank as one of the most important discoveries of prehistoric times, along with the use of fire and the first crude axe."

The wish to dominate women, to force women to serve, to play out a master-slave fantasy, is thus the mechanism underlying the contemporary denigrator of women, whether he be a rapist, batterer, pimp, or murderer. To force a woman to yield to one's will is a residual of the Umbilicus Complex, an unconscious motive that can too easily combine with violence.

Adding a psychoanalytic perspective to the sociology of Ward, one may suggest that the early development of infant males is an ontogenic replication of prehistory. The infant, after all, reexperiences the situation where woman is queen, the ultimate provider or frustrator of need satisfiers and the co-partner in a one-sided power relationship (Horney, 1932; Rank, 1924; Zilboorg, 1940). The human male, long before there is an Oedipus conflict, would have no more understanding of paternity than did our prehistoric ancestors. He would, however, appreciate the power of the mother. Hate and envy are the natural by-products of males who have been frustrated, who have not learned how to successfully control and manipulate mother.[34] The male who experiences a disturbed mother-child relationship, who has not achieved successful individuation, who suffers from the Umbilicus Complex, and who harbors resentment toward women, is pathologically motivated to exert control over them, and in times when the primitive dread of abandonment and maternal rejection is reactivated, as with the threat of divorce, often lashes back in violence.

NOTES

1. For a discussion of the psychology of violence in humans, see, for example, Feshbach (1990). A few species of rodents also participate in wanton destruction of other members of their group (Aronson, 1992). While our primate heritage is often blamed for human aggression, recent work by primatologists suggest that successful male primates are conciliatory rather than aggressive (deWaal, 1989). The infanticide practiced by cats and primate groups is currently considered to be functional; when the new male-line dominant animal destroys the previous male's relatives to establish his own offspring, the female estrus cycle resumes immediately; thus the continuance of his gene pool is assured.

2. Brown's (1991, p. 144) assessment of current thinking on biological influences— that is, that "behaviorism and the tabula rasa view of the mind are dead in the water," while representing the goals of evolutionary psychology, may be premature.

3. Indications of the basic human "need" to aggress come also from the tribal violence that erupted as the USSR was replaced by the CCS in 1992.

4. It was extremely popular, especially at the beginning of the newest wave of feminism, to suggest that women would be as violent as men if they had the "proper"

socialization experiences. More contemporary writers are quite persuasive in their dismissing of this position (Dobach et al., 1992; Maccoby & Jacklin, 1974; Miller & Simpson, 1991; Munroe, Munroe, & Whiting, 1981).

5. Also debated is whether criminals, especially those who commit violent acts, are mentally disturbed (Monahan, 1992). We, however, suggest that the vast number of men who perpetrate violent acts against women would not qualify for traditional diagnosis. For the most part, the men we describe—those with the Umbilicus Complex—are in good mental health except when faced with reactivation of separation dread.

6. The use of the word *virtue* is, of course, ironic. Lester Ward was an important pioneer, a nonandrocentric sociologist, who coined the term *gynocentric*,—that is, women centered, in 1888, as an explanatory concept for the world prior to the first rape.

7. Of all violent crime, domestic violence is considered the most common. It has been estimated that in 30 percent of all marriages abuse is a sometime event and in 13 percent, spousal abuse occurs frequently (Strauss, Gelles, & Steinmetz, 1980). While there has been some discussion of symmetry in marital violence, Dobash et al. (1992) present a complete argument dismissing this proposal.

8. Although Brownmiller (1975) and most experts seem willing to accept a "sexual" motive for deSalvo's crimes, it should be noted that the Boston Strangler usually murdered his victims *before* he raped them. His first five victims were fifty-five, sixty-eight, sixty-five, seventy-five, and sixty-seven years old, respectively.

9. The *Wall Street Journal* reported, August 7, 1992, that homicide had become the number one killer of black women.

10. *New York Times*, April 13, 1986; April 18, 1982; and January 23, 1986, respectively; *Los Angeles Times*, July 16, 1986.

11. *Wall Street Journal*, July 28, 1983; February 15, 1984, respectively.

12. *New York Times*, August 18, 1987; March 27, 1987, respectively.

13. *New York Times*, July 7, 1987; August 18, 1987; February 24, 1984, respectively.

14. *New York Times*, January 27, 1985; July 7, 1986; June 30, 1984.

15. *Cosmopolitan*, April 1985; *New York Times*, February 16, 1983; September 4, 1982; October 13, 1983; June 30, 1984, respectively.

16. *New York Times*, July 30, 1992; December 14, 1990; October 16, 1990, respectively.

17. *New York Times*, January 26, 1989.

18. *Los Angeles Times*, October 6, 1991; *Christian Science Monitor*, December 21, 1989, respectively.

19. From 1980 to 1990 there has been a 12 percent increase in the rate of forcible rape (U.S. Federal Bureau of Investigation, 1990). Of course this statistic is for reported forcible rape only; date rape, acquaintance rape, and rape in marriage are not included in this category. However, even the statistic for forcible rape is thought to be under-reported (*New York Times*, April 24, 1991), and figures for date rape are undoubtedly higher.

20. Andrea L. Stillman, *The Day*, New London, Connecticut, May 9, 1993.

21. Child abuse is certainly a domestic violence problem. While it is likely that the Umbilicus Complex could be used as an explanatory concept for the occurrence of child abuse, where immature men take advantage of little girls because of an inability to relate to adult women in an adult manner, a discussion of this problem is beyond the scope of this current work.

We also recognize that sexual harassment is a form of abuse perpetrated by men upon women; a discussion of this topic and the characteristics of men who continue to harass women will, also, have to wait for another place.

22. *Christian Science Monitor*, February 6, 1990. A year later, January 1, 1991, the *New York Times* noted that there had been a decline in violent crime against men.

23. *New York Times*, March 18, 1992; *Christian Science Monitor*, March 8, 1991, respectively.

24. *New York Times*, August 11, 1986; August 19, 1987, respectively.

25. *New York Times*, February 11, 1987.

26. For an interesting discussion of American social policy against family violence, see Pleck (1987).

27. Pornography is interesting in this regard. Certainly pornography denigrates women and is indicative of generalized disregard for and depersonalization of women. However, it is also devoid of emotion and separated from real-world relationships. Pornography may be useful to some males, in that they could "safely" exert their hostility toward women without injuring particular women.

28. *New York Times*, October 3, 1992; January 7, 1992; November 17, 1991, respectively.

29. David Hoffman, *Washington Post*, March 13, 1991.

30. *Los Angeles Times*, July 19, 1992.

31. See Walker (1979), for example, whose observations counter the myth that battering and abuse are restricted to the poor and socially bereft.

32. The individuation process is also frustrating to little girls, but the problems are neither as severe nor do they usually result in violence or emotional problems.

33. There are some mothers who violate this idealic relationship by abusing even the smallest infant. For the most part, mothers, at least at our youngest ages, tend to fulfill our collective unconscious beliefs about what mothers should be like.

34. We cannot accept the notion that the origin of envy in males is rooted in an awareness that they cannot reproduce. Although Zilboorg, Horney, and Rank (and also Ward) make this cognition an essential part of their theories, it is unlikely that infants appreciate gender differences related to reproduction. By "envy" we refer to an understanding that mother is the agent of control over (and possessor of) nurturance supplies and has the power to meet the infant's needs for care. "The first object to be envied is the feeding breast, for the infant feels that it posseses everything he desires and that it has an unlimited flow of milk and love which the breast keeps for its own gratification" (Klein, 1957, p. 10).

10

Making Boys into Men: Preventing and Treating the Umbilicus Complex

It's becoming clear to us that manhood does not happen by itself; it does not happen just because we eat Wheaties. (Bly, 1990, p. 15)

Individuation, a life-long, inevitable, and necessary process whereby human infants come to recognize their own ego, is motivated by psycho-biological mechanisms. Individuation begins with the earliest differentiation from mother and becomes a focus of personality development at various critical periods in one's life.

The Umbilicus Complex develops in a biologically vulnerable individual who experiences a disturbed mother-child relationship. Most critical for the development of symptoms associated with the Umbilicus Complex, which are relatively nonspecific and vary from individual to individual, are events that occur within the first two years of the child's life. The disturbance can be the result of a severe situation, such as inadequate parenting, or a simple mismatch between the personality of the child and the personality of the mother.

As a result of this disturbed relationship, the child fails to complete individuation and develops a morbid dread of abandonment. Males are more likely to develop symptoms of the Umbilicus Complex because they suffer both a relative biological and a psychological maturational retardation and because there is social pressure for earlier separation from mother and what she represents. A life-long pattern of the disorder ensues, exacerbated by the male social role that precludes awareness of emotionality and discourages the development of a social support network.

There are situations in the life of individual males, not inherently traumatic nor necessarily occurring at periods critical for individuation, that evoke the dread of abandonment. Among the most common, for adult males, are divorce, separation, or death of a wife or significant other. Separation situations provoke a revitalization of earlier abandonment fears and are more pathogenic when the separation is instigated by a woman. When this situation arises in the life of a vulnerable man, those most susceptible to the Umbilicus Complex, pathological reactions occur. Common symptoms include emotional distress, alcohol abuse, suicide ideation and/or behaviors, and the physical and/or emotional abuse of women, including homicide.

The impossible bind is that [an adult male] cannot let go of his need to control and dominate because it threatens his masculinity, yet holding on to it eliminates the possibility of having a flowing experience, one in which he can move easily and comfortably between active and passive behavior . . . his early conditioning has severely impaired or destroyed most of what is required for sustained pleasure in the area of sexual involvement in a relationship. (Goldberg, 1979, pp. 223–224)

Personality development is inherently complicated and the determining factors leading to the formation of an Umbilicus Complex arise from a variety of sources. It is incumbent upon us, however, to suggest possible treatment and prevention strategies. Our suggested prevention strategies focus on modifying the education and training of boys, as well as the social milieu. It is our belief that these modifications will arrest the spread of abandonment dread and prevent further generations of emotionally crippled men. For the treatment of those already afflicted, we suggest modified traditional therapy with the addition of all-male groups that provide a nurturing atmosphere of male bonding for men otherwise deprived of homonomy-need gratification.

The objectives of a prevention program are:

1. to alter the sense of identity and expectations of males by restructuring the gender role;
2. to educate parents, teachers, and other socialization agents concerning genuine sex differences;
3. to modify child-rearing practices that traditionally perpetuate the production of babe-pashas who are vulnerable to a perceived loss of security, support, and nurturance; and

4. to develop emotionally healthy males who can live full and productive lives harmoniously coexisting with women.

The objectives of a treatment program are:

1. to reduce the level of anxiety experienced by men when separation from a nurturing female occurs or is imminent;
2. to help men recognize and accept as normal their dependency needs and passivity;
3. to facilitate the formation of social support systems for men dealing with crises involving the threat of abandonment;
4. to provide opportunities for men to learn to communicate feelings; and
5. to encourage improved relationships with females, without mastery and dominance or resentment and violence.

PREVENTION STRATEGIES

"Natural" Child Care

> All cultures have rules not only for behavior but for breaking rules for behavior. (Harris, 1988, p. 30)

For personality development the most potent "rules for behavior" are socialization practices. Certain psychobiological processes, such as the trends toward autonomy and homonomy and the maturation of ego-identity, and unlearned dynamics related to the overidealization and fear of mother, are of crucial importance in the formation of persons. The advocacy of "natural" child care—that is, socialization practices that offer the least influence over biology, which has led to zealous attempts to change the social structure—is perhaps too radical a position for a preventive program. On the other hand, some changes in the rules provide the only plausible means to break the pattern that makes men vulnerable "robots" (Goldberg, 1979).

The leading spokesperson for the less extreme position is Ashley Montagu (1961, p. 65). In his essay on the development of love, which he believes is a reflection of an "innate need for love, with a need to respond to love," he states,

The biological basis of love consists in the organism's drive to satisfy its basic needs in a manner which causes it to feel secure. Love is security. Mere satisfaction of basic needs is not enough. Needs must be satisfied in a particular manner, in a manner which is emotionally as well as physically satisfying. Babies as well as adults cannot live by bread alone.

Implicit in a program designed to prevent abnormalities in the adult male's reaction to dependency needs is that males in this society must learn how to love and how to be loved (Montagu, 1961; Goldberg, 1979).

One reason why "manhood doesn't happen by itself" is that human infants cannot survive without the care and protection of others. The psychobiological mechanisms that provide that chronology of maturation are influenced at each stage by the attitudes and behaviors of ministering adults, who control the essential social learning of the developing child. In most cases, what is complexly "normal" in child care will supersede what is simply "natural." Psychobiological determinants cannot be understood outside the social context and the social structure is demonstrably resistant to change.

On the other hand, biology—which is clearly immutable, at least in terms of our immediate efforts—may itself be incompatible with normal, well-adjusted behavioral demands. Natural developmental processes might be inherently problematic and require the modulation and influence of socializing experiences.

Males' evolutionary adaptations to the roles of competitor, hunter, and protector result in pressures and responses ill suited to modern life, with its emphasis on relatively sedate endeavors and on only polite and verbal (rather than physical) acts of violence and territory claiming. (Heesacker & Prichard, 1992, p. 282)

Physical maturation is affected by the reactions of others, who observe, evaluate, and selectively praise and punish its behavioral manifestations. On a social-structural level, expectations (sometimes in the form of "norms"; almost always in terms of gender stereotypes), role definitions, and cultural values may support, discourage, or, in some cases, distort innate predispositions and their expression. Socialization, in other words, is "adaptive" in that it molds individuals into a predetermined cast, but the finished product and the developmental processing procedures may be "unnatural."

If role behavior is based entirely on cultural stylization, it ought to be possible to recast the male role despite the resistance of traditional mores. The problem would be then one of education and re-education. But if role behavior is instinctual, educational measures could only create a superficial facade and a false consciousness. (Bednarik, 1970, pp. 22–23)[1]

Individualism and Emasculation: Social Change and Prevention

Should the traditional male role and the patterns of behavior associated with it be discarded and revised to fit existing conditions? Or is it possible to retain the role and change the condition? To what extent would the roles or the conditions, or both, have to be changed to eliminate the great discrepancies between them? (Bednarik, 1970, pp. 21–22)

We contend that the most effective prevention program—that is, one which has some probability of success—will focus on modification of child-rearing practices by educating parents. Evidence of the wisdom of this choice is indicated by sociological analyses of the effects of the social and political changes of the past few decades, which suggest that even though there have been political and social changes that have had a direct influence on the position and conduct of adult males, there has been little notable change in the male-role stereotype or in child-rearing practices.

Despite the fear that conservative sociologists, psychologists, and social historians had that the women's movement would make passive and emasculated men, there has been little change in the position or power of men in this society. Like other civil rights movements, the women's movement emphasized fairness (or equity), elimination of institutionalized discrimination, and greater social and political participation of persons previously excluded. This political and economic agenda has been somewhat successful without any noticeable change in the political participation of men. A major objective of the social agenda of the women's movement was to modify gender-role definitions; in some cases its leaders' espoused androgyny as a goal of child-rearing. Notwithstanding the rhetoric that was scary to conservatives, there is little evidence that the male gender-role definitions or child-rearing practices have changed (Chodorow, 1971, 1978; Doyle, 1989; Meth & Pasick, 1990; Stevens, Gardner, & Barton, 1984).

In reanalyzing the men involved in Whyte's (1956) classic study, the *Organization Man*, and extending their analysis to include the children of these men, Leinberger and Tucker note that while there has been in the United States, a "hip" generation, with its dedication to self-expression and personal freedom, and a "me" generation, dedicated to self-fulfillment and hedonism, there has been a *continuing erosion of individualism*.[2] The traits revealed by middle-class adult males in their occupational life are more consistent with conformist "organizationalism" than the traditional gender role.

In pursuing the ideal of the authentic self, the offspring [have] produced the most radical version of the American individual in history—totally psychologized and isolated, who has difficulty "communicating" and "making commitments," never mind achieving community. But by clinging to the artist ideal, the organization offspring try to escape the authentic self and simultaneously to maintain it as the ultimate value. (Leinberger & Tucker, 1991, p. 15)

Leinberger and Tucker suggest that in their vocational pursuits the modern, middle-class male is a conformist, influenced by homonomy needs, while in his avocations—for example, hobbies and recreation— he maintains ideals consistent with the traditional male role. These results point out a paradox: current child-rearing practices, which evidence suggests are designed to create domineering, demanding, macho males, who are individualistic and self-reliant, are maladaptive for modern males. As we have noted earlier, socialization has, as its primary function, the production of individuals who "fit in" to the society. The demands of their adult life may emphasize homonomy, as Leinberger and Tucker (1991) indicate, but the goals of the socialization of males are the opposite.

Clearly, socialization practices will not change to meet the reality requirements of the modern era or to prevent the perpetuation of the emotional crippling of males without a frontal attack. It has been demonstrated that a change in "existing conditions"—for example, a modification in male occupational role requirements—may not affect the goals of the socialization of boys (Leinberger & Tucker, 1991). Even more ironically, traditional role definitions may persist because of (and be reinforced by) incorrect notions about sex differences. Child-rearing practices that include abrupt demands for separation from mother, for example, appear to depend on notions that males are inherently power-driven, independent, self-sufficient, and biologically superior.

Consequently, a prevention program must focus on child-rearing practices. Parents will have to understand the data concerning the physical and emotional vulnerability of young males, will have to be educated to help males accept dependency needs, and will have to concentrate their efforts on teaching their sons coping skills to deal with rejection by and resentment toward females, encouraging alternatives to violence and control, if babe-pashas are to become whole men.

Mother-Anxiety: A Tradition of Western Civilization

> The recurrent experiences of gratification and frustration are powerful
> stimuli for libidinal and destructive impulses, for love and hatred. As a
> result, the breast, inasmuch as it is gratifying, is loved and felt to be "good";
> in so far as it is the source of frustration, it is hated and felt to be "bad." (Klein,
> 1933, p. 62)

While a modification of child-rearing practices, where the actual gender
differences are acknowledged, may bring about the changes in self-identity
that will make men less vulnerable, less apt to dread abandonment, there
exists a strong, irrational emotional component to the mother-son relationship that may be impervious to change. There is, at least, a tradition, based
in cultural myths and archetypes, that the overidealization of mother and
fear of an all-powerful mother-figure are instinctual and thus relatively
uninfluenced by experience, if not immutable.

> The virgin Mother Goddess with her divine child long procedes Christianity,
> was worshipped from Egypt to China, and constitutes the closest human bond
> of all, the truly nuclear family. [A typical mythic goddess] was the Celtic
> Five-fold Goddess Danie, whose son was born to her, initiated by her, became
> her lover, was lulled to sleep by her, and finally killed by her. (Lederer, 1968,
> pp. 119–120)

Klein's (1957, 1933; Klein & Rivere, 1937) theory of the mental
development of infants offers an explanation of how an irrational fear of
mother can arise from mother-child interactions; there is an implicit
invariability in the driving force, however, suggesting an instinctual or
archetypal, to use Jung's term, basis for the anxiety. As the possessor of
the good or bad breast, to expand Klein's reconceptualization of Freud's
developmental theory, the mother becomes the recipient of idealized love
and intense hatred. When the infant is capable of projection, a transforma-
tion of perception occurs: rather than hatred localized internally and
directed toward the mother, the child externalizes the hatred so that it
emanates from the mother and is directed toward the child. To some
degree, therefore, the persecutory anxiety toward mother figures is
learned, a point which is central to psychologists who emphasize social
learning theory (Goldberg, 1979).

Klein does not emphasize gender differences in her theory (although
most of her illustrative cases are boys). There is reason to suppose, how-

ever, that boys are more likely to exhibit residual primitive rage than girls. As Hartmann (1939) has noted, ego defenses, including projection, require some element of perceptual maturity, most particularly object constancy. Since boys are more likely to suffer frustration of the need for nurturance before object constancy develops (later than it does for girls), life-long hatred of mother figures may result. The same logic would lead to a prediction that girls and early-maturing boys would be more prone to suffer mother anxiety.

The infantile origin of emotions toward mother figures explains the irrationality and potency of the anger and fear and the contempt men feel toward women. In a similar conceptualization, Ruth Mack Brunswick (1969) and Janie Chasseguet-Smirgel (1971) observe that the standard outcome for the Oedipus complex is contempt for women.

Superstitions and irrational ideas about mother images are also found in preliterate societies. However, in these societies, the men have institutionalized customs to cope with mother anxieties; in many such social groups there are menstruation taboos, restrictions in living arrangements, avoidance patterns (particularly in regard to mothers-in-law), and adolescent *rites de passage* (which in some societies involve being reborn to men). What is common to preliterate solutions is gender segregation; by entrance into the world of men, literally as well as symbolically, males are freed from the fear and awe of the life-giving and death-taking mother.

Our modern post-industrial-revolution culture, on the other hand, leaves men with little training in how to cope with mother anxiety. The increasingly transient nature of families, the social isolation of the nuclear family, the virtual elimination of men from the life of boy children, and the overemphasis on a rigid and narrow stereotype for men, for example, create a situation where emotional support comes only from a small family unit, usually dominated by a (feared) woman.

Patterns that exacerbate and reinforce a possibly innate predisposition to overvalue and to develop anxiety and hatred of nurturing women have themselves proved to be almost intractable. The social systems that encourage irrational and excessive feelings toward mother figures have often been the target of social reformers, but attempts to alter social patterns at this level have been usually unsuccessful, at best have effected short-lived results. While we would like to see changes in society so that gender-role definitions are modified to reflect biology and not myth, it is unlikely that such changes are imminent. Therefore, our suggestions focus on other areas, where change is perhaps a bit more likely.

Participation of Fathers as a Preventive Agency

Women, it is true, make human being, but only men can make men. (Mead, 1949, p. 84)

Life-long contempt for women and paradoxically the overidealization of women, as well as the need to dominate, control, and appease mother figures, is impelled and propelled by mother anxiety and mother hatred. Although the motive force may be psychobiological in origin, a number of thinkers, including Dorothy Dinnerstein (1977), Nancy Chodorow (1978), and Kyle Pruett (1987) have suggested that an increased role for men in the life of children can mitigate the derivative behavior.

Until recently, only minimal energy has been spent attempting to understand the role of the father within the family. While evidence of the importance of the father-son relationship has been noted since 1927, when Thrasher (1927) reported that boys in delinquent gangs had poor relationships with their fathers, the dearth of research investigating the impact that fathers can have on children, or within the family in general, is in itself interesting. It is almost as if the predominantly male researchers have repressed their own urges for paternal involvement, denied their feelings of isolation from their children, and, in what could only be called "mother-bashing" research, found a methodology by which they could put a sense of legitimacy on their hostility toward mothers.

However, what little research there is all points in the same direction: fathers are important to the development of both children but especially to the development of little boys (Johnson, 1963; Lisak, 1991). Boys who have been deprived of a nurturant father have been noted to be more aggressive (Biller, 1974; Reuter & Biller, 1973) and hypermasculine (Lisak, 1991) than are non-father–deprived boys. Little boys who have missed out on positive relationships with their fathers have also been reported to be more hyperactive and destructive (Popplewell & Sheikh, 1979; Trunnell, 1968) and to suffer more from cognitive, behavioral, and emotional problems (Garmezy, Clarke, & Stockner, 1961; Mussen & Distler, 1961; Popplewell & Sheikh, 1979). As father-deprived boys reach adolescence, they are more likely to have distorted assumptions regarding women (Miller, 1958) and adult sexuality (Nash, 1965; Winch, 1950). Research also reports that rapists have poor relationships with their fathers, whom they accuse of being distant and uncaring (Lisak, 1991); this finding is similar to earlier research analyzing the etiology of male delinquents (Andry, 1960; Bandura & Walters, 1959; Medinnus, 1965; Miller, 1958).

In a society such as ours, where the father is often absent or whose participation in child-rearing is minimal and there are rather rigid boundaries between what is accepted as male and female, it is difficult for a male to include in his ego-identity such traits as emotionality, sensitiveness, and dependence. Little boys are reared by mothers and take on some feminine characteristics. The transition to adult male, therefore, requires a form of self-mutilation (Lisak, 1991) owing to the fact that these feminine characteristics must be excised.

In most traditional families, because the mother is alone in child-rearing, it is inevitable that she is cast as both the good mother-goddess and the bad mother-goddess: she gives nurturance but she can also be a threat. Adult male social-role identification, therefore, demands rejection of any personality characteristics that are similar to mother's and rebellion toward her and her wishes. "It will be a problem for those boys who have formed a strong identification with women only if the people in the[ir] world make it clear that being a man is very different from being a woman and that men are more important and powerful" (Whiting, 1965, p. 135).

In order for the Oedipal conflict to be successfully resolved, for boys to renounce their wish for a baby and repudiate the feminine, without the concomitant feelings of rage, jealousy, rivalry, impotence, and helplessness when confronted with mother, fathers must be present in an active and caring manner. It is not enough for men to be only occasional fathers; they must be full members of the family and clearly share parenting responsibilities.

SUMMARY OF PREVENTION STRATEGIES

The major thrust of a program designed to decrease the dread of abandonment in men is in modifying child-rearing practices. Socialization agents must be made aware of sex differences, particularly differences in the rate of maturation of young children, and also of the deleterious practices that make males deny their dependency needs.

The particular modifications in child-rearing practices, to make later separations less threatening, involve:

1. minimalizing maternal absences from the male infant until he has developed object constancy;
2. providing security assurances to boys during autonomy training;
3. encouraging boys to be aware of dependency needs and to accept such needs as normal and natural; and

4. devaluing dominance and violence in the behavioral repertoire of boys.

To augment these modifications, change should also be encouraged to various aspects of society, most importantly the role expectations associated with societal perceptions of gender. Boys and men need a broader definition of gender role so that some passivity, dependence, communication of feelings, and moodiness are considered normal for males. In addition, fathers should be encouraged to become more involved in the child-rearing process. For boys, the greater participation by fathers may lead to identification with the world of men and to gender segregation at an age earlier than adolescence.

In another context we (Gardner & Stevens, 1992) have described a similar situation where psychologists and sociologists attempted to effect change in a social, political, and economic system because they believed that the system was inhumane. In interbellum Vienna, young, radical psychologists were interested in creating a "new" individual, a person who was humane, civilized, and interested in the general welfare of humankind. These psychologists sought changes in society generally, often with vitriolic attacks against the affluent and politically entrenched. They quickly turned their major efforts, perhaps because they were successful in making sociopolitical changes only in Vienna, to modifying the family structure and, in particular, child-rearing practices.

Perhaps because of the experiences in this country over the past three decades, we are somewhat less optimistic about effecting long-lasting changes in the social structure, or in socialization practices, than our Viennese colleagues had been. Yet, recognizing the obvious causal relationship between socialization and its goals, and later personality structure, and notwithstanding that social systems are conservative and resistant to change, the reeducation of parents is a crucial aspect of a preventive program. We therefore suggest that the following ideas need to be included in any program whose aim is decreasing the incidence of abandonment dread:

1. the actual gender differences in temperament and cognitive development, which justify the pampering of male infants;

2. the gender differences in rate of maturation, which justify the continuing of pampering of male infants and indicate the need for a revision of developmental stages based upon chronological age norms (and thus lower the expectations for autonomy-striving in boys under two years of age);

3. postponement of separation training until there is evidence that object constancy has developed;

4. encouragement of boys to have a longer period of attachment to mothers; and

5. gradual separation training and less abrupt discontinuity.

SPECIFIC TREATMENT STRATEGIES

The "orthopsychiatric" position suggests that successful treatment of children who exhibit neurotic symptoms may prevent the occurrence of severe mental disorders later in life. The "interventions" listed in Table 7.1 provide, thus, individual psychotherapy for the manifestations of the Dread of Abandonment at all the infantile "phases" of development. It should be noted that the earlier the manifestation, the more severe the pathology and the poorer the prognosis.

What we are concerned with here, however, is the treatment of adult males who exhibit signs of the dread of abandonment, and for them the orthopsychiatric interventions may be classified as preventive methods. In adults the treatment involves individual psychotherapy, group therapy, or a combination of both, supplemented in most cases with psychoactive medications that treat the panic and/or depression that accompany an episode of abandonment dread or an actual separation.

Men in Therapy

Establishing a psychological treatment program for adult males presents special problems (Wilcox & Forrest, 1992). First, research suggests that men are reluctant to enter or remain in therapy (Nadler, Maler, & Friedman, 1984; Robertson, 1988; Russo & Sobel, 1981; Scher, 1979). The reason usually offered for this reluctance is that seeking and receiving help is inconsistent with the male gender-role stereotype that includes self-reliance, toughness, and control over emotions (Wilcox & Forrest, 1992): "Most men have a great investment in their ability to control feelings with a concomitant fear of letting go emotionally" (Goldberg, 1976, p. 60).

Second, the content of much traditional psychotherapy emphasizes a man's becoming a "whole" person" that is, becoming aware of aspects of his personality that he has submerged. He will be encouraged to recognize his passivity, softness, and dependency, all of which he has labeled feminine, and to question his need to dominate others and be in control. Such changes in his self-perception probably need to precede formal therapy if it is to be successful (Wilcox & Forrest, 1992). Therapy, in other words, needs to question traits that a male patient does not believe are maladaptive—traits he believes are, in fact, necessary for success outside the context of the therapy situation. The feeling of being superior to women has negative consequences for men's social relationships, yet they maintain notions of superiority because of an early learned fear of their own femininity.

Overall, the masculine mystique implies that men are superior to women and masculinity is superior to femininity; power, control, and dominance are essential to prove masculinity; emotions, feelings, vulnerability, and intimacy are to be avoided because they are feminine; and career success and sexual potency are measures of masculinity. (O'Neil, 1990, p. 20)

An interesting further complication is the conventional practice of having the patient and therapist sit facing each other (usually across a desk), which maximizes intimacy and presents the opportunity for eliciting the patient's feeling of shame (Williams & Myer, 1992). In addition to making the male patient uncomfortable and defensive, this arrangement might stimulate a "competition for power" between patient and therapist (Osherson & Krugman, 1990). It was Bly (1990) who noted that this face-to-face, possibly confrontational positioning is not natural for men; in men's gatherings, particularly where working side-by-side or participating in a ritual process is involved, he observes, men sit as equals, usually in a circle, within an arrangement or gesture of cooperation and teaching. In any event, in traditional therapy men do not learn the value of being in a dependent, vulnerable position, and there is much in traditional individual psychotherapy that revitalizes the parent-child situation.

Strategies for Therapy

Because of the problematic nature of individual psychotherapy for adult males, bibliotherapy and/or group therapy or support groups are likely adjuncts to and may even need to be substituted for individual treatment. One might expect that the reluctance and resistance noted above will be intensified when, as in the case of the man whose dread of abandonment has been revitalized, the relationship issues that make men so uncomfortable and defensive in therapy are the focal content of the therapy.

Psychotherapy for adult males who exhibit an inability to cope with existing or anticipated loss of a mother figure should include the following:

1. acceptance of the patient as an adult;
2. emphasis on personality strengths and on the history of successful coping behaviors;

3. didactic sessions dealing with development, gender differences, and gender stereotypes; and

4. delineation of ways for adults to satisfy homonomy needs (e.g., participation in men's organizations).

In treating a patient with an investment in appearing strong and independent, one would avoid the structure usually employed in forms of therapy that encourage a childish dependence. One would not, for example, have the patient lie on a couch or refer to him by his first name. An important issue, in this regard, is how it is that an individual who generally sees himself, often with good justification, as competent, successful, and self-reliant, comes to an expert to "tell him how to live." This source of initial resistance to the therapeutic process must be dealt with early in the therapy, with the patient's understanding that it is not shameful or an admission of weakness for an individual to consult an expert with special information. In our experience, if an adult male patient does not conceptualize therapy as a cooperative effort at problem solving—a professional consultation, where he is treated as a generally competent adult—he does not commit himself to the therapeutic endeavor and the therapy is very brief and unsuccessful.

While treatment will necessarily challenge the patient's *need* to be always in control, to secure care and nurturance by dominance and intimidation, this must be done without putting down the patient or otherwise engaging in a power struggle with him. In a defensive way men who have established neurotic or disordered patterns of behavior as a *reaction formation* to unconscious needs to be submissive, dependent, infantile, and feminine are likely to be pugnacious and argumentative in therapy.

Confrontations, such as those typical of Gestalt therapy, the establishment of a transference neurosis (which is common in traditional psychoanalysis), and other therapeutic gambits that use the patient-therapist relationship as the instrument of change will usually lead a vulnerable male patient to become defensive and terminate therapy. In a sense, any therapeutic approach that is manipulative and elicits regression and resistance is to be avoided in a therapy that is egalitarian, cooperative, primarily didactic, and probably brief in duration.

Men who suffer an Umbilicus Complex have learned to fear their dependency needs, a fear that is manifested paradoxically in episodes of separation anxiety. While cognitive insight into the primitive sources of the fear—mother anxiety and projected mother hatred—and the history of separation experiences is helpful (especially if a complete cure is the goal of the therapy), learning new ways to cope with abandonment and temporary loss of self-esteem are the main objectives of treatment for the disorganization and disorder of abandonment. In this endeavor the therapist is a teacher, a guide, and a role model who suggests alternative behaviors and encourages greater flexibility in reactions. In addition, the therapist will invite the patient to participate in and identify with the world of real men, whole men.

The therapeutic process, thus, is a learning process—a learning process that focuses on the maturity and competence of men and provides a cooperative, didactic situation that facilitates an understanding of personality development. Additionally, the therapeutic process should elaborate on the exaggerations within gender stereotypes that make men victims of their unaccepted instinctive needs. The therapy, finally, encourages participation in all-male organizations as an important adjunct to the healing process.

Support Groups

The men's movement has received predominantly bad press for its creation of radical consciousness-raising groups. Based upon anachronistic, gestalt-therapy notions of the 1970s, the weekend marathons in the woods with tom-tom beatings and the like appeal to the emotional component of masculinity and male bonding. While such group experiences serve a ritual purpose and may initiate some men into masculine identification, they appear to have no more sustaining effect that the brief emotional experience encountered in the crowd at a football game that one attends with buddies. To sustain the feeling state of participation in and identification with the world of men, which are necessary but secondary considerations in an effective support group, there must be an external purpose to the group. The group must be a continuing, almost permanent one, and what is learned in the group about relationships must be able to be integrated into the individual's everyday life. The group experience, in short, should have a sustaining supportive influence rather than be merely a peak experience.

Current literature abounds with new, experimental support groups for men. One such example, selected because it was conducted by our friends in the local community, is the use of parent education workshops for noncustodial divorced fathers (Devlin, Brown, Beebe, & Parulla, 1992). The small-group workshops in this study were focused in content; only one of the topics included an exploration of the feelings of the subjects relative to the emotional and practical problems of the divorced father. The success of the program—even in a brief, experimentally constrained format—was that the fathers did not merely *feel* more competent as fathers at the conclusion, they *were* more competent.

A support group provides participation and opportunity for direct satisfaction of homonomy needs through group identification. To be maximally effective for the specific problems of adult males who suffer the dread of abandonment, support groups should:

1. have a serious purpose, preferably an educational one;
2. have a focus that is external to relationship issues or the group process per se;
3. be open-ended, as to the number of sessions; and
4. encourage social interaction but not as the primary objective (tom-tom beating is okay but not isolated from reality issues).

THE UMBILICUS COMPLEX AS A DSM DISORDER

Description

The disorder known as the Umbilicus Complex is characterized by excessive apprehension concerning abandonment. It is diagnosed in adults; its source, however, begins in infantile separation experiences that are traumatic to individuals who exhibit the symptoms of the disorder. The presenting symptoms are:

1. Distress
2. Subjective feelings of anxiety
3. Dysphoria, often accompanied by feelings of guilt and unworthiness
4. Rage
5. Revenge fantasies, sometimes leading to violence toward women
6. Unconscious death wishes, usually directed toward mother figures

Types

There are two separate manifestations of this disorder, differentiated according to severity. The milder form, *Separation Anxiety Syndrome* (SAS), typically includes symptoms 1, 2, and 6 although some cases also show mild depressive symptoms. It is theorized that SAS originates in traumatic separation experiences that occur after a child develops object constancy, in most cases around twelve months of age (earlier for females).

The more severe form, *Dread of Abandonment Syndrome* (DAS), begins before object constancy, when an infant is not able to understand that an absent mother can return. The expectations that the loss of a nurturing person will be a permanent condition persists throughout the life of the individual. DAS will include five or six of the presenting symptoms, and since the potential for violence toward others and for suicide is elevated, persons experiencing an episode must be considered a danger to self and others.

Prevalence by Gender

There is evidence that females are more likely to develop the milder form of the disorder than males. A preponderance of those who develop Dread of Abandonment Syndrome are males.

Course

The early separation trauma makes individuals specifically vulnerable to later experiences of separation from nurturance providers. These include temporary absence of a mother from an infant, separation training of toddlers, attendance at school, and loss through death or divorce. The symptoms of the disorder are thus episodic and their severity is determined by the amount of success or failure in learning coping skills relevant to independent living, by the amount of anxiety and/or trauma involved in a particular incident, and by the degree to which an individual is able to accept his own dependency needs.

SUMMARY

While the prevention of the widespread disorder we call Dread of Abandonment Syndrome may require social changes that are difficult to effect, since relevant aspects of the social system have proved to be intractable in past attempts at reformation, there is reason to hope that modifications in child-rearing practices can reduce the incidence of the disorder in males. Reeducation of parents in a program that provides information on gender differences in maturation and encourages changes in autonomy training should make males in general less vulnerable to breakdown when reality considerations impel a loss of a nurturance provider.

The treatment of adult males already inflicted with the disorder is complicated by factors that demonstrably restrict their ability and willingness to become engaged in a therapeutic process. The usual problems of reluctance and resistance to seeking and receiving help are compounded when the forces that result in resistance are the core issues that perpetuate the specific disorder to be treated. If a fear of entering a dependency relationship with a therapist is, for example, a major obstacle to obtaining help in most adult males, a treatment program that specifically addresses the normality or better the instinctual or natural character of dependency or homonomy becomes uniquely problematic. Treatment strategies that are egalitarian, emphasize cooperation, and discourage regression are suggested.

NOTES

1. Karl Bednarik, a Viennese journalist and sociologist, writes about the "emasculation" of the European male. His conclusions, which affirm significant similarities to this society, are based primarily on American data.

2. While their generalizations pertain primarily to middle-class men, Leinberger and Tucker describe conditions and consequent conflicts that have significance for all males in this society. It is likely that neither the trend toward homonomy (organizationalism) nor the idealization of autonomy goals (self-fulfillment) have had as much impact on working-class men.

References

Adler, A. (1927). *Understanding Human Nature*. New York: Greenberg.
——— . (1935). The Fundamental Views of Individual Psychology. *International Journal of Individual Psychology, 1*, 5–8.
Adorno, T. W., Frenkel-Brunswik, Else, Levinson, P. J., & Sanford, R. N. (1950). *The Authoritarian Personality*. New York: Harper.
Ainsworth, Mary D. S. (1973). The Development of Infant-Mother Attachment. In B. M. Caldwell & H. R. Ricciuti (Eds.), *Review of Child Development Research* (pp. 1–94). Chicago: University of Chicago Press.
Ainsworth, Mary D. S., Blehar, M. C., Waters, E., & Wall, S. (1978). *Patterns of Attachment: A Psychological Study of the Strange Situation*. Hillsdale, NJ: Erlbaum.
Ainsworth, Mary D. S., & Wittig, Barbara. (1969). Attachment and Exploratory Behavior of One-Year-Olds in a Strange Situation. In B. M. Foss (Ed.), *Determinants of Infant Behavior* (Vol. 4, pp. 111–136). London: Methuen.
Allport, G. W. (1937). *Personality: A Psychological Interpretation*. New York: Henry Holt.
——— . (1960). *Personality and Social Encounter*. Boston: Beacon.
——— . (1961). *Pattern and Growth in Personality*. New York: Holt, Rinehart and Winston.
——— . (1985). The Historical Background of Social Psychology. In G. Lindzey & E. Aronson (Eds.), *Handbook of Social Psychology* (3rd ed., Vol. 1, pp. 1–46). New York: Random House.
Alvis, G. R., Ward, Jeannette P., Dodson, Deanna L., & Pusakulich, R. L. (1990). Inverse Pattern in Successful Finger-Maze Acquisition Performance by Right Handed Males and Left Handed Females. *Bulletin of the Psychonomic Society, 28* (5), 421–423.
Anastasi, Anne. (1958). *Differential Psychology*. New York: Macmillan.
Andry, R. G. (1960). Faulty Paternal and Maternal Child-Relationships, Affection and Delinquency. *British Journal of Delinquency, 97*, 329–340.

Angyal, A. (1941). *Foundations for a Science of Personality*. New York: Commonwealth Fund.

————. (1951). A Theoretical Model for Personality Studies. *Journal of Personality, 20*, 131–142.

————. (1965). *Neurosis and Treatment: A Holistic Theory*. New York: John Wiley.

Anshen, Ruth Nanda. (1959). *The Family: Its Function and Destiny*. New York: Harper.

Antill, J. K. (1988). Parents' Beliefs and Values About Sex Roles, Sex Differences, and Sexuality: Their Sources and Implications. In P. Shaver & C. Hendrick (Eds.), *Sex and Gender* (pp. 294–328), Newbury Park, CA: Sage.

Appleton, Tina, Clifton, Rachel, & Goldberg, Susan. (1975). The Development of Behavioral Competence in Infancy. In Frances D. Horowitz (Ed.), *Review of Child Development Research* (Vol. 4, pp. 101–186). Chicago: University of Chicago Press.

Ardrey, R. (1966). *The Territorial Imperative*. New York: Atheneum.

Aronson, E. (1992). *The Social Animal* (6th ed.). New York: W. H. Freeman.

Bachofen, J. J. (1861). *Das Mutterrecht: Eine Untersuhung über die Gynaikikritie der alten Welt nach ihrer religiosen und rechtlichen Natur.* Stuttgart: Krais & Hoffman.

Bakan. D. (1979). *And They Took Themselves Wives*. New York: Harper & Row.

Baker, Mary Anne. (1987). Sensory Functioning. In Mary Anne Baker (Ed.), *Sex Differences in Human Performance* (pp. 5–36). Chichester, England: John Wiley.

Bandura, A. (1986). *Social Foundations of Thought and Action*. Englewood Cliffs, NJ: Prentice-Hall.

Bandura, A., & Walters, R. H. (1959). *Adolescent Aggression*. New York: Ronald.

Bardwick, Judith. (1971). *Psychology of Women*. New York: Harper.

Barfield, A. (1976). Biological Influences on Sex Differences in Behavior. In M. S. Teitelbaum (Ed.), *Sex Differences: Social and Biological Perspectives* (pp. 62–122). Garden City, NJ: Anchor Books.

Barkow, J., Cosmides, Leda, & Tooby, J. (Eds.). (1992). *The Adapted Mind: Evolutionary psychology and the generation of culture*. New York: Oxford University Press.

Baron, R. A. (1977). *Human Aggression*. New York: Plenum.

Barrett, D. E. (1979). A Naturalistic Study of Sex Differences in Children's Aggression. *Merrill-Palmer Quarterly, 25* (3), 193–203.

Barry, Kathleen. (1979). *Female Sexual Slavery*. Englewood Cliffs, NJ: Prentice-Hall.

Basow, Susan A. (1980). *Sex-Role Stereotypes: Traditions and Alternatives*. Monterey, CA: Brooks/Cole.

Baum, A., & Grunberg, N. E. (1991). Gender, Stress, and Health. *Health Psychology, 10* (2), 80–85.

Beck, S. L., & Rosenblith, Judy F. (1973). Constitutional Factors in Behavior. In Judy F. Rosenblith, W. Allinsmith, & Joanna P. Williams (Eds.), *Readings in Child Development* (pp. 36–43). Boston: Allyn and Bacon.

Bednarik, K. (1970). *The Male in Crisis*. New York: Knopf. (Original in German)

Bell, R., & Harper, L. (1977). *Child Effects on Adults*. Lincoln: University of Nebraska Press.

Beller, E. K. (1955). Dependency and Independence in Young Children. *Journal of Genetic Psychology, 87*, 23–25.

Bem, Sandra L. (1974). The Measurement of Psychological Androgyny. *Journal of Consulting and Clinical Psychology, 42*, 155–162.

Benedict, Ruth. (1938). Continuities and Discontinuities in Cultural Conditioning. *Psychiatry, 1*, 161–167.

Bergman, Anni. (1982). Considerations about the Development of the Girl During the Separation-Individuation Process. In D. Mendell (Ed.), *Early Female Development: Current psychoanalytic views* (pp. 61–80). New York: S. P. Medical and Science Books.

Bergman, S. J. (1990). Men's Psychological Development: A Relational Perspective. Work in Progress, No. 48. Wellesley, MA: Stone Center Working Paper Series.

Bernard, Jessie. (1972). *The Future of Marriage*. New York: World Publishing.

Bettelheim, B. (1962). *Symbolic Wounds*. New York: Collier.

Biller, H. B. (1974). *Paternal Deprivation*. Lexington, MA: Lexington.

Biller, H. B., & Borstelmann, L. J. (1967). Masculine Development: An Integrative Review. *Merrill-Palmer Quarterly, 13*, 253–294.

Bird, Gloria W., Stith, Sandra M., & Schladale, Joann. (1991). Psychological Resources, Coping Strategies, and Negotiation Styles as Discriminators of Violence in Dating Relationships. *Family Relations, 40*, 45–50.

Birdsell, J. B. (1975). *Human Evolution*. Chicago: Rand-McNally.

Björnberg, Ulla (Ed.). (1992). *European Parents in the 1990s*. New Brunswick, NJ: Transaction.

Bloom, A. (1987). *The Closing of the American Mind*. New York: Simon & Schuster.

Bloom, B. L., Asher, Shirley J., & White, S. W. (1978). Marital Disruption as a Stressor: A Review and Analysis. *Psychological Bulletin, 85* (4), 867–894.

Bloom-Feshbach, J., & Bloom-Feshbach, Sally. (1987). Introduction: Psychological separateness and experience of loss. In J. Bloom-Feshbach & Sally Bloom-Feshbach (Eds.), *The Psychology of Separation and Loss* (pp. 1–61). San Francisco, CA: Jossey-Bass.

Bly, R. (1990). *Iron John: A Book about Men*. New York: Vintage Books.

Bohannan, P. (1980). Marriage and Divorce. In H. I. Kaplan, A. M. Freedman, & B. J. Sadock (Eds.), *Comprehensive Textbook of Psychiatry* (3rd ed., Vol. 3, pp. 3258–3268). Baltimore, MD: Williams & Wilkins.

Bouchard, T. J., Jr., Lykken, D. T., & McGue, M. (1990). Sources of Human Psychological Differences: The Minnesota Study of Twins Reared Apart. *Science, 250*, 223.

Bowlby, J. (1969). *Attachment and Loss: Vol 1. Attachment*. New York: Basic Books.

———. (1973). *Attachment and Loss: Vol. 2. Separation*. New York: Basic Books.

———. (1980). *Attachment and Loss: Vol. 3. Loss: Sadness and Depression*. New York: Basic Books.

Brenner, A. (1950). The Great Mother Goddess: Puberty Initiation Rites and the Covenant of Abraham. *Psychoanalytic Review, 37*, 320–340.

Briffault, R. (1927/1977). *The Mothers*. New York: Atheneum. (Original in 3 volumes)

Brisco, Anne. (1978). Hormones and Gender. In Ethel Tobach & Betty Rosoff (Eds.), *Genes and Gender* (pp. 31–50). New York: Gordion Press.

Briscoe, C. W., Smith, J. B., Robbins, E., Marten, Sue, & Gaskin, F. (1973). Divorce and Psychiatric Disease. *Archives of General Psychiatry, 29*, 119–125.

Bronson, W. C. (1971). *Exploratory Behavior of 15-month-old Infants in a Novel Situation*. Paper presented at the meeting of the Society for Research in Child Development, Minneapolis, MN.

Brookover, W. B., Thomas, S., & Paterson, A. (1964). Self-Concept of Ability and School Achievement. *Sociology of Education, 37*, 271–278.

Broverman, Inge, Broverman, D. M., Clarkson, F. E., Rosenkrantz, P. S., & Vogel, Susan R. (1970). Sex-Role Stereotypes and Clinical Judgments of Mental Health. *Journal of Consulting and Clinical Psychology, 34*, 1–7.

Broverman, Inge, Vogel, Susan R., Broverman, D. M., Clarkson, F. E., & Rosenkrantz, P. S. (1972). Sex Role Stereotypes: A Current Appraisal. *Journal of Social Issues, 28* (2), 59–78.

Brown, D. E. (1991). *Human Universals.* Philadelphia, PA: Temple University Press.

Brownmiller, Susan. (1975). *Against Our Will.* New York: Simon & Schuster.

Brunswick, Ruth Mack. (1969). The Preoedipal Phase of the Libido Development. In R. Fliess (Ed.), *The Psychoanalytic Reader* (pp. 231–253). New York: International Universities Press. (Original published in 1940)

Buffery, A. W., & Gray, J. A. (1972). Sex Differences in the Development of Spatial and Linguistic Skills. In C. Ounsted & D. C. Taylor (Eds.), *Gender Differences: Their Ontogeny and Significance* (pp. 123–158). Edinburgh, Scotland: Churchill Livingstone.

Burns, G. W. (1976). *The Science of Genetics: An Introduction to Heredity* (3rd ed.). New York: Macmillan.

Cahill, S. (1986). Childhood Socialization as Recruitment Process: Some Lessons from the Study of Gender Development. In Patricia Adler & P. Adler (Eds.), *Sociological Studies of Child Development* (Vol. 1, pp. 163–186). Greenwich, CT: JAI Press.

Calkins, Mary W. (1896). Community of Ideas of Men and Women. *Psychological Review, 3*, 426–430.

Campbell, J. (1949). *The Hero with a Thousand Faces.* Princeton, NJ: Princeton University Press.

———. (1962). *The Masks of God: Oriental Mythology.* New York: Viking.

———. (1988). *Myths to Live By.* New York: Bantam Books.

Cantor, D. W. (1982). Divorce: Separation or Separation-Individuation? *American Journal of Psychoanalysis, 42*, 307–313.

Carter, C. O. (1972). Sex-Linkage and Sex-Limitation. In C. Ounsted & D. Taylor (Eds.), *Gender Differences: Their Ontogeny and Significance* (pp. 1–12). Edinburgh, Scotland: Churchill Livingstone.

Carter, H., & Glick, P. (1970). *Marriage and Divorce: A Social and Economic Study.* Cambridge, MA: Harvard University Press.

Cassidy, R. (1977). *What Every Man Should Know About Divorce.* Washington, DC: New Republic Books.

Chasseguet-Smirgel, Janine. (1971). Feminine Guilt and the Oedipus Complex. In Janine Chasseguet-Smirgel (Ed.), *Female Sexuality* (pp. 94–134). Ann Arbor, MI: University of Michigan Press.

Chavetz, J. S. (1978). *Masculine/Feminine or Human?* (2nd ed.). Itasca, IL: Peacock.

Cherlin, A. J. (1981). *Marriage, Divorce, Remarriage.* Cambridge, MA: Harvard University Press.

Child, I. L. (1954). Socialization. In G. Lindzey (Ed.), *Handbook of Social Psychology* (Vol. 2, pp. 655–692). Cambridge, MA: Addison-Wesley.

Chiriboga, D. A., & Krystal, S. (1985). An Empirical Taxonomy of Symptom Types Among Divorcing Persons. *Journal of Clinical Psychology, 41* (5), 601–613.

Chodorow, Nancy. (1971). Being and Doing: A Cross-Cultural Examination of the Socialization of Males and Females. In Vivian Gornick & Barbara K. Moran

(Eds.), *Women in a Sexist Society: Studies in Power and Powerlessness* (pp. 173–197). New York: Basic.

———. (1976). Oedipal Asymmetries and Heterosexual Knots. *Social Problems, 23,* 454–468.

———. (1978). *The Reproduction of Mothering: Psychoanalysis and the Sociology of Gender.* Berkeley: University of California Press.

Clarke-Stewart, K. Alison, & Bailey, Bonnie L. (1989). Adjusting to Divorce: Why Do Men Have it Easier? *Journal of Divorce, 13,* 75–94.

Clausen, J. A. (1966). Family Structure, Socialization, and Personality. In Lois W. Hoffman & M. L. Hoffman (Eds.), *Review of Child Development* (Vol. 2, pp. 1–54). New York: Russell Sage Foundation.

Clausen, J. A., & Williams, Judith R. (1963). Sociological Correlates of Child Behavior. In H. W. Stevenson (Ed.), *Child Behavior* (pp. 62–107). Chicago: University of Chicago Press.

Cohen, H., & Levy, J. J. (1986). Sex Differences in Categorization of Tactile Stimuli. *Perceptual and Motor Skills, 63,* 83–86.

Cohler, B. J., & Stott, Frances M. (1987). Separation Interdependence, and Social Relations Across the Second Half of Life. In J. Bloom-Feshbach & Sally Bloom-Feshbach (Eds.), *The Psychology of Separation and Loss* (pp. 165–204). San Francisco: Jossey-Bass.

Colby, E. (1925). *The Life of Thomas Holcroft, Continued by William Hazlett* (Vol. 2). London: Constable & Co.

Collins, W. A., & Gunnar, M. R. (1990). Social and Personality Development. *Annual Review of Psychology, 41,* 387–416.

Collum, U.C.C. (1939). Die schöpferische Mutter-Göttin der Völker keltischer Sprache. In V.C.C. Collum (Ed.), *Eranos Jahrbuch 1938* (pp. 221–324). Zurich: Rhein Verlag.

Cossette, Louise, Malcuit, G., & Pomerleau, A. (1991). Sex Differences in Motor Activity During Early Infancy. *Infant Behavior and Development, 14,* 175–186.

Cowan, Caralyn P. (1992). *When Partners Become Parents.* New York: Basic Books.

Cronk, Lee. (1991). Preferential Parental Investment in Daughters over Sons. *Human Nature, 2* (4), 387–417.

Curtiss, S. (1977). *Genie: A Psycholinguistic Study of a Modern-Day Wild Child.* New York: Academic Press.

d'Aguili, E. G., & Laughlin, C. D. (1979). The Neurobiology of Myth and Ritual. In E. G. d'Aguili, C. D. Laughlin, Jr., & J. McManus (Eds.), *The Spectrum of Ritual: A Bio-Genetic Structural Analysis* (pp. 152–182). New York: Columbia University Press.

Daly, M., Wilson, Margo, & Weghorst, S. J. (1982). Male Sexual Jealousy. *Ethology and Sociobiology, 3,* 11–27.

Davis, A. (1943). Child Training and Social Class. In R. G. Barker, J. S. Koumen, & H. F. Wright (Eds.), *Child Behavior and Development* (pp. 607–620). New York: McGraw-Hill.

Dawkins, R. (1986). *The Blind Watchmaker.* New York: W. W. Norton.

Delaney, Janet, Lupton, Mary Jane, & Toth, Emily. (1976). *The Curse.* New York: Dutton.

DeLisi, Lynn E., Dauphinais, I. Deborah, & Hauser, P. (1989). Gender Differences in the Brain: Are They Relevant to the Pathogenesis of Schizophrenia? *Comprehensive Psychiatry, 30* (3), 197–208.

DeLozier, Paulene P. (1982). Attachment Theory and Child Abuse. In C. M. Parkes & J. Stevenson-Hinde (Eds.), *The Place of Attachment in Human Behavior* (pp. 95–117). New York: Basic Books.

Dennis, W. (1941). The Significance of Feral Man. *American Journal of Psychology, 54*, 425–432.

Dennis, W., & Najarian, P. (Eds.). (1957). *Infant Development under Environmental Handicap. Psychological Monographs, 71* (7).

Department of Health and Human Services. (1982). *Prevention '82.* DHHS (PHS), Publication #82-50157.

Dethier, V. G., & Stellar, E. (1961). *Animal Behavior: Its Evolution and Neurological Basis.* Englewood Cliffs, NJ: Prentice-Hall.

Devlin, Ann S., Brown, Elizabeth H., Beebe, Josephine, & Parulla, Elaine. (1992). Parent Education for Divorced Fathers. *Family Relations, 41*, 290–296.

deWaal, F. (1989). *Peacemaking Among Primates.* Cambridge, MA: Harvard University Press.

Dinnerstein, Dorothy. (1977). *The Mermaid and the Minotaur.* New York: Harper.

Dobash, R. E., & Dobash, R. P. (1979). *Violence Against Wives: A Case against the Patriarchy.* New York: Free Press.

Dobash, R. P., Dobash, R. E., Wilson, Margo, & Daly, M. (1992). The Myth of Sexual Symmetry in Marital Violence. *Social Problems, 39* (1), 71–91.

Dollard, J., Doob, L. W., Miller, N. E., Mowrer, O. H., & Sears, R. R. (1939). *Frustration and Aggression.* New Haven: Yale University Press.

Dollard, J., & Miller, N. E. (1950). *Personality and Psychotherapy.* New York: McGraw-Hill.

Donovan, Wilberta L., & Leavitt, L. A. (1985). Simulating Conditions of Learned Helplessness: The Effects of Interventions and Attributions. *Child Development, 56*, 594–603.

———. (1992). Maternal Self-Efficacy and Response to Stress: Laboratory Studies of Coping with a Crying Infant. In Tiffany M. Field, P. M. McCabe, & N. Schneiderman (Eds.), *Stress and Coping in Infancy and Childhood* (pp. 47–68). Hillsdale, NJ: Erlbaum.

Donovan, Wilberta, Leavitt, L. A., & Walsh, R. O. (1990). Maternal Self-Efficacy: Illusory Control and Its Effect on Susceptibility to Learned Helplessness. *Child Development, 61*, 1638–1647.

Dowling, C. (1981). *The Cinderella Syndrome.* New York: Pocket Books.

Doyle, J. A. (1989). *The Male Experience.* Dubuque, IA: Wm. C. Brown.

Drake, Angela I., Hannay, H. Julia, & Gam, J. (1990). Effects of Chronic Alcoholism on Hemispheric Functioning: An Examination of Gender Differences for Cognitive and Dichotic Listening Tasks. *Journal of Chronic Alcoholism, 12* (5), 781–797.

Draper, Patricia. (1985). Two Views of Sex Differences in Socialization. In Roberta L. Hall (Ed.), *Male-Female Differences* (pp. 5–25). New York: Praeger.

Dubbert, J. L. (1979). *A Man's Place: Masculinity in Transition.* Englewood Cliffs, NJ: Prentice-Hall.

Durkheim, E. (1951). *Suicide.* New York: Free Press.

Eaker, E. D., Packard, B., Wenger, N. K., Clarkson, T. B., & Tyroler, H. A. (1988). Coronary Artery Disease in Women. *American Journal of Cardiology, 61*, 641–644.

Earls, F., & Jung, K. G. (1988). Temperament and Home Environment Characteristics as Causal Factors in the Early Development of Childhood Psychopathology. In Stella Chess, A. Thomas, & Margaret E. Hertzig (Eds.), *Annual Progress in Child Psychiatry and Child Development* (pp. 373–393). New York: Brunner/Mazel.

Egeland, B., & Sroufe, L. A. (1981). Attachment and Early Maltreatment. *Child Development, 52,* 44–52.

Elkin, F. (1960). *The Child and Society: The Process of Socialization.* New York: Random House.

Ellis, H. (1930). *Man and Woman.* London: A. & C. Black.

Eme, R. F. (1979). Sex Differences in Childhood Psychopathology: A Review. *Psychological Bulletin, 86,* 574–595.

Erikson, E. H. (1950). *Childhood and Society.* New York: W. W. Norton.

————. (1968). *Identity: Youth and crisis.* New York: W. W. Norton.

Escalona, Sibylle K. (1949). A Commentary upon Some Recent Changes in Child Rearing Practices. *Child Development, 20,* 157–163.

Estes, Clarissa P. (1992). *Women who Run with the Wolves.* New York: Ballatine Books.

Eyer, Diane E. (1993). *Mother-Infant Bonding: A Scientific Fiction.* New Haven, CT: Yale University Press.

Fairbairn, W.R.D. (1941). Schizoid Factors in the Personality. In W.R.D. Fairbairn (Ed.), *An Object-Relations Theory of the Personality* (pp. 3–27). New York: Basic Books.

Farrand, L. (1902). Traditions of the Quinault Indians. *Memoirs of the American Museum of Natural History, 4.*

Farrell, W. (1986). *Why Are Men the Way They Are?* New York: Berkeley Books.

Fast, I. (1984). *Gender Identity: A Differentiation Model.* Hillsdale, NJ: Erlbaum.

Feinberg, M. R., Smith, M., & Schmidt, R. (1958). An Analysis of Expressions used by Adolescents at Varying Economic Levels to Describe Accepted and Rejected Peers. *Journal of Genetic Psychology, 93,* 133–148.

Feinman, S. (1974). Approval of Cross-Sex Role Behaviour. *Psychological Reports, 35,* 643–648.

Ferenczi, S. (1950). *Sex and Psychoanalysis.* New York: Basic Books. (Original title: *Contributions to Psychoanalysis*)

Ferree, M. M. (1987). She Works Hard for a Living: Gender and Class on the Job. In B. B. Hess & M. M. Ferree (Eds.), *Analyzing Gender: A Handbook of Social Science Research* (pp. 322–347). Newbury Park, CA: Sage.

Feshbach, S. (1990). Psychology, Human Violence, and the Search for Peace: Issues in Science and Social Values. *Journal of Social Issues, 46* (1), 183–198.

Field, Tiffany M. (1977). Effect of Early Separation, Interactive Deficits, and Experimental Manipulations on Infant-Mother Face-to-Face Interaction. *Child Development, 48,* 763–771.

Flaum, M., Arndt, S., & Andreasen, Nancy C. (1990). The Role of Gender in Studies of Ventricle Enlargement in Schizophrenia: A Predominantly Male Effect. *American Journal of Psychiatry, 147* (10), 1327–1332.

Fling, S., & Manosevitz, M. (1972). Sex Typing in Nursery School Children's Play Interests. *Developmental Psychology, 7,* 146–152.

Floody, O. R., & Pfaff, D. W. (1977). Aggressive Behavior in Female Hamsters: The Hormonal Basis for Fluctuations in Female Aggressiveness Correlated with

Estrous State. *Journal of Comparative and Physiological Psychology, 91,* 443–464.

Flor-Henry, P. (1985). Schizophrenia: Sex Differences. *Canadian Journal of Psychiatry, 30,* 319–322.

Folkman, S. (1984). Personal Control and Stress and Coping Processes: A Theoretical Analysis. *Journal of Personality and Social Psychology, 46,* 839–852.

Ford, C. S., & Beach, F. A. (1951). *Patterns of Sexual Behavior.* New York: Harper.

Fossey, Dian. (1983). *Gorrillas in the Mist.* Boston: Houghton-Mifflin.

Fox, Margery, Gibbs, Margaret, & Auerbach, Doris. (1985). Age and Gender Dimensions of Friendship. *Psychology of Women Quarterly, 9,* 489–485.

Frankenhaeuser, Marianne. (1991). The Psychophysiology of Sex Differences as Related to Occupational Status. In Marianne Frankenhaeuser, U. Lundberg, & Margaret Chesney (Eds.), *Women, Work and Health* (pp. 39–61). New York: Plenum.

Franklin, C. W. (1984). *The Changing Definition of Masculinity.* New York: Plenum.

Frazer, J. G. (1922/1950). *The Golden Bough* (abridged edition). London: Macmillan & Co.

Fredrick, W. N., Tyler, J. D., & Clark, J. A. (1985). Personality and Psychophysiological Variables in Abusive, Neglectful, and Low-Income Control Mothers. *Journal of Nervous and Mental Disease, 173,* 449–460.

Freud, S. (1905/1965). *Three Essays on the Theory of Sexuality.* New York: Avon Books. (Original in German)

——— . (1909/1959). Analysis of a Phobia in a Five Year Old Boy. In S. Freud (Ed.), *Collected Papers* (pp. 149–295). New York: Basic Books. (Original in German)

——— . (1913/1950). *Totem and Taboo.* New York: W. W. Norton. (Original in German)

——— . (1920/1961). *Beyond the Pleasure Principle.* New York: W. W. Norton. (Original in German)

——— . (1925/1964). Some Psychological Consequences of the Anatomical Distinction Between the Sexes. In *Standard Edition* (Vol. 5). London: Hogarth Press.

——— . (1926/1959). *Inhibitions, Symptoms and Anxiety.* New York: W. W. Norton. (Original in German)

——— . (1930/1961). *Civilization and Its Discontents.* New York: W. W. Norton. (Original in German)

——— . (1933). *New Introductory Lectures on Psycho-Analysis.* New York: W. W. Norton. (Original in German)

——— . (1939). *Moses and Monotheism.* New York: Vintage Books. (Original in German)

Friedman, R. M., & Lerner, Lelia (Eds.). (1986). *Toward a New Psychology of Men.* New York: Guilford Press.

Fries, Margaret E., & Woolf, P. J. (1971). The Influence of Constitutional Complex on Developmental Phases. In J. B. McDevitt & C. F. Settlage (Eds.), *Separation-Individuation: Essays in Honor of Margaret S. Mahler* (pp. 274–296). Madison, CT: International Universities Press.

Frisch, H. (1977). Sex Stereotypes in Adult-Infancy Play. *Child Development, 48,* 1671–1675.

Frodi, Ann, Bridges, Lisa, & Shonk, Susan. (1989). Maternal Correlates of Infant Temperament Ratings and of Infant-Mother Attachment: A Longitudinal Study. *Infant Mental Health Journal, 10,* 273–289.

Fromkin, V., Krashen, S., Curtiss, S., Rigler, D., & Rigler, M. (1974). The Development of Language in Genie: Acquisition beyond the "Critical Period." *Brain and Language, 1*, 81–107.

Fromm, E. (1973). *The Anatomy of Human Destructiveness*. New York: Holt, Rinehart and Winston.

Gaensbauer, T. J., & Sands, K. (1979). Distorted Affective Communications in Abused/Neglected Infants and Their Potential Impact on Caregivers. *Journal of the American Academy of Child Psychiatry, 18*, 236–250.

Galdikas, Biruté F. (1975). Orangutans: Indonesia's People of the Forest. *National Geographic, 148* (4), 444–474.

Ganong, L. H., & Coleman, Marilyn. (1991). Remarriage and Health. *Research in Nursing & Health, 14*, 205–211.

————. (1992). Gender Differences in Expectations of Self and Future Partner. *Journal of Family Issues, 13*, 55–64.

Garai, J. E., & Scheinfeld, A. (1968). Sex Differences in Mental Health and Behavioral Traits. *Genetic Psychology Monograph, 77*, 169–299.

Gardner, S., & Stevens, Gwendolyn. (1992). *Red Vienna and the Golden Age of Psychology: 1918–1939*. New York: Praeger.

Garmezy, N., Clarke, A., & Stockner, C. (1961). Child Rearing Attitudes of Mothers and Fathers as Reported by Schizophrenic and Normal Patients. *Journal of Abnormal and Social Psychology, 63* (1), 176–182.

Garrett, H. E. (1971). *Heredity: The Cause of Racial Differences in Intelligence*. Kilmarnak, VA: Patrick Henry.

Geertz, C. (1973). *The Interpretations of Cultures*. New York: Basic Books.

Gelles, R. J., & Straus, M. A. (1979). Determinants of Violence in the Family: Toward a Theoretical Integration. In W. R. Burr, R. Hill, F. I. Nye, & I. L. Reiss (Eds.), *Contemporary Theories About the Family: Research-Based Theories* (pp. 549–581). New York: Free Press.

George, C., & Main, M. (1979). Social Interactions of Young Abused Children: Approach, Avoidance and Aggression. *Child Development, 50*, 306–318.

Geschwind, N., & Behan, P. (1982). Left Handedness: Association with Immune Disease, Migraine, and Developmental Learning Disorder. *Proceedings of the National Academy of Science, USA, 79*, 5097–5100.

Gewertz, Deborah. (1981). A Historical Reconsideration of Female Dominance Among the Chambri of Papua New Guinea. *American Ethnologist, 8*, 94–106.

Gewirtz, J. L. (1972). Attachment, Dependence, and a Distinction in Terms of Stimulus Control. In J. L. Gewirtz (Ed.), *Attachment and Dependency* (pp. 139–178). Washington, DC: Winston.

Giacopossi, D. J., & Wilkinson, Karen R. (1985). Rape and the Devalued Victim. *Law and Human Behavior, 9*, 367–383.

Gilder, G. (1974). *Naked Nomads: Unmarried Men in America*. New York: Quandrangle.

————. (1986). *Men and Marriage*. Gretna, LA: Pelican Publishing.

Gilligan, Carol. (1977). In a Different Voice: Women's Concepts of Self and Morality. *Harvard Educational Review, 47*, 481–517.

Gimbutas, Marija. (1989). *The Language of the Goddess*. New York: Harper & Row.

Gjerde, P. F., & Block, Jeanne. (1991). Preadolescent Antecedents of Depressive Symptomatology at Age 18: A Prospective Study. *Journal of Youth and Adolescence, 20* (2), 217–232.

Glen, N., & Weaver, C. (1977). The Marital Happiness of Remarried Divorced Persons. *Journal of Marriage and the Family*, *39*, 331–337.

Goldberg, H. (1976). *The Hazards of Being Male*. New York: New American Library.

———. (1979). *The New Male*. New York: New American Library.

Goldberg, Susan, & Lewis, M. (1969). Play Behavior in the Year Old Infant: Early Sex Differences. *Child Development*, *40* (1), 21–31.

Goode, W. J. (1956). *After Divorce*. New York: Free Press.

Goodheart, Carol D. (1992). Introduction: Young Adult Phase. In Barbara Rubin Wainrib (Ed.), *Gender Issues Across the Life Cycle* (pp. 25–27). New York: Springer.

Gough, Kathleen. (1953). Female Initiation Rites on the Malabar Coast. *Journal of the Royal Anthropological Institute*, *85*, 45–80.

———. (1979). The Origin of the Family. In Jo Freeman (Ed.), *Women: A Feminist Perspective* (pp. 83–105). Palo Alto, CA: Mayfield.

Gove, W. R., Hughes, M., & Style, Carolyn B. (1983). Does Marriage have Positive Effects on the Psychological Well-being of the Individual? *Journal of Health and Social Behavior*, *24*, 122–131.

Grady, K. E. (1977). *Sex as a Social Label: The Illustration of Sex Differences*. Doctoral dissertation, City University of New York, New York.

Graves, R. (1948/1958). *The White Goddess*. New York: Vintage.

Green, R. (1980). Patterns of Sexual Identity in Childhood. In J. Marmor (Ed.), *Homosexual Behavior: A Modern Reappraisal*. New York: Basic Books.

Green, R. G. (1990). *Human Aggression*. Pacific Grove, CA: Brooks/Cole.

Green, T. C., & Bell, P. A. (1987). Environmental Stress. In Mary Anne Baker (Ed.), *Sex Differences in Human Performance* (pp. 81–106). Chichester, England: John Wiley.

Greenson, R. R. (1968). Dis-Identifying from Mother: Its Special Importance for the Boy. *International Journal of Psycho-Analysis*, *49*, 370–372.

Griffin, S. (1971). Rape: The All-American Crime. *Ramparts*, *10*, 26–35.

Gross, H. J. (1968). The Depression-Prone and the Depression-Resistant Sibling: A Study of 650 Three-Sibling Families. *British Journal of Psychiatry*, *144*, 1559–1565.

Guilford, J. P. (1959). *Personality*. New York: McGraw-Hill.

Habib, M., Gayraud, D., Oliva, A., Regis, J., Salamon, G., & Khalil, R. (1991). Effects of Handedness and Sex on the Morphology of the Corpus Callosum: A Study with Brain Magnetic Resonance Imaging. *Brain and Cognition*, *16*, 41–61.

Hall, C. S., & Lindzey, G. (1957). *Theories of Personality*. New York: John Wiley.

Hall, Roberta. (1985). The Question of Size. In Roberta L. Hall, Patricia Draper, Margaret E. Hamilton, Diane McGuinness, Charlotte M. Otten, & E. A. Roth (Eds.), *Male-Female Differences: A Bio-Cultural Perspective* (pp. 127–154). New York: Praeger.

Halle, E. (1982). The "Abandoned Husband": When Wives Leave. In K. Solomon & N. B. Levy (Eds.), *Men in Transition: Theory and Therapy* (pp. 191–197). New York: Plenum Press.

Hamilton, J. B., Hamilton, R. S., & Mestler, G. E. (1969). Duration of Life and Causes of Death in Domestic Cats: Influence of Sex, Gonadectomy, and Inbreeding. *Journal of Gerontology*, *24*, 427–437.

Hamilton, J. B., & Mestler, G. E. (1969). Mortality and Survival: Comparison of Eunuchs with Intact Men and Women in a Mentally Retarded Population. *Journal of Gerontology*, *24*, 395–411.

Hardy, A. C. (1960). Was Man More Aquatic in the Past? *The New Scientist, 7*, 642–645.

Harlow, H. F. (1962). The Heterosexual Affectional System in Monkeys. *American Psychologist, 17*, 1–9.

Harmon, R. J., Wagonfield, S., & Emde, R. N. (1982). Anaclitic Depression: A Follow-up from Infancy to Puberty. *The Psychoanalytic Study of the Child, 37*, 67–94.

Harris, M. (1974). *Cows, Pigs, Wars, and Witches.* New York: Vintage Books.

———. (1988). *Culture, People, Nature: An Introduction to General Anthropology.* New York: Harper & Row.

Hartley, Ruth. (1959). Sex Role Pressures and the Socialization of the Male Child. *Psychological Reports, 5*, 457–468.

Hartmann, H. (1939/1958). *Ego Psychology and the Problem of Adaptation.* New York: International Universities Press. (Original in German)

———. (1964a). The Mutual Influences in the Development of the Ego and the Id. In H. Hartmann (Ed.), *Essays on Ego Psychology* (pp. 155–181). New York: International Universities Press. (Original publication 1952)

———. (1964b). On the Metapsychology of Schizophrenia. In H. Hartmann (Ed.), *Essays on Ego Psychology* (pp. 182–206). New York: International Universities Press. (Original publication 1953)

Hartup, W. W. (1963). Dependence and Independence. In H. W. Stevenson, J. Kagan, & C. Spiker (Eds.), *Child Psychology* (Part 1, pp. 333–363). Chicago: National Society for the Study of Education.

Hartup, W. W., Moore, S. G., & Sager, G. (1963). Avoidance of Inappropriate Sex-Typing by Young Children. *Journal of Consulting Psychology, 27*, 467–473.

Haussler, S. (1976). *Arztlicher Ratgeber für werdende Mutter.* Munich, Germany: Krankenkassenbrochure.

Heathers, G. (1955). Acquiring Dependence and Independence: A Theoretical Orientation. *Journal of Genetic Psychology, 87*, 277–91.

Heesacker, M., & Prichard, S. (1992). In a Different Voice, Revisited: Men, Women, and Emotion. *Journal of Mental Health Counseling, 14*, 274–290.

Herman, Judith. (1981). *Father-Daughter Incest.* Cambridge, MA: Harvard University Press.

Hess, R. D. (1970). Social Class and Ethnic Influences Upon Socialization. In P. H. Mussen (Ed.), *Carmichael's Manual of Child Psychology* (3rd ed., Vol. 2). New York: John Wiley.

Hickman, C. P. (1970). *Integrated Principles of Zoology* (4th ed.). St. Louis, MO: C. V. Mosby.

Hirsch, J. (1975). Jensenism: The Bankruptcy of "Science" Without Scholarship. *Educational Theory, 25*, 3–27.

Hochschild, A. (1989). *The Second Shift.* New York: Avon.

Hollingworth, Leta S. (1914). Variability as Related to Sex Differences in Achievement. *American Journal of Sociology, 19*, 510–530.

Holmes, T. H., & Rahe, R. H. (1967). The Social Readjustment Rating Scale. *Journal of Psychosomatic Research, 11*, 213–218.

Horner, Althea J. (1975). States and Processes in the Development of Early Object Relations and Their Associated Pathologies. *International Review of Psycho-Analysis, 2*, 95–105.

Horney, Karen. (1932/1967). The Dread of Women. In H. Kellerman (Ed.), *Feminine Psychology* (pp. 133–146). New York: Norton.

————. (1934/1967). The Overvaluation of Love. In H. Kellermann (Ed.), *Feminine Psychology* (pp. 182–213). New York: Norton.

Houser, Betsy Bosak. (1979). An Investigation of the Correlation Between Hormonal Levels in Males and Mood, Behavior, and Physical Discomfort. *Hormones and Behavior*, *12*, 185–197.

Hoyenga, Katherine B., & Hoyenga, K. T. (1979). *The Question of Sex Differences*. Boston: Little, Brown.

Hrdy, Sarah B. (1981). *The Woman that Never Evolved*. Cambridge, MA: Harvard University Press.

Hubbard, Ruth, & Lowe, Marian (Eds.). (1979). *Genes & Gender* (Vol. 2). New York: Gordian Press.

Hull, J. G., Van Treuren, R. R., Ashford, S. J., Propsom, P., & Andrus, B. W. (1988). Self-Consciousness and the Processing of Self-Relevant Information. *Journal of Personality and Social Psychology*, *54*, 452–465.

Hunt, M., & Hunt, Bernice. (1977). *The Divorce Experience*. New York: McGraw-Hill.

Hurlock, Elizabeth B. (1964). *Child Development* (4th ed.). New York: McGraw-Hill.

Hutt, C. (1972). *Males and Females*. Middlesex, England: Penguin.

Jahoda, Marie. (1977). *Freud and the Dilemmas of Psychology*. New York: Basic Books.

James, W. (1890). *The Principles of Psychology*. New York: Henry Holt.

Jastrow, J. (1896). Note on Calkins' "Community of Ideas of Men and Women." *Psychological Review*, *3*, 430–431.

Jensen, A. R. (1980). *Bias in Mental Testing*. New York: Free Press.

Jersild, A. T., & Holmes, F. B. (1935). *Children's Fears. Child Development Monographs*, *20*.

Johnson, M. (1963). Sex-role Learning in the Nuclear Family. *Child Development*, *34*, 319–333.

Johnson, S. M. (1977). *First Person Singular*. New York: Harper & Row.

Joseph, A. B. (1990). Non-Right-Handedness and Maleness Correlate with Tardive Dyskinesia Among Patients Taking Neuroleptics. *Acta Psychiatria Scandinaveca*, *8* (6), 530–533.

Jung, C. J. (1954). *Von den Wurzein des Bewusstseins*. Zurich: Rascher.

————. (1958). *Psychology and Religion*. Princeton, NJ: Princeton University Press.

————. (1968). *Psychology and Alchemy* (Translated by R.F.C. Hull). Princeton, NJ: Princeton University Press.

Kagan, J., & Moss, H. A. (1962). *Birth to Maturity*. New York: John Wiley.

Kardiner, A. (1945). *The Psychological Frontiers of Society*. New York: Columbia University Press.

Kellerhals, Jean, & Montandon, Cleopatre. (1992). Social Stratification and the Parent-Child Relationship. In Ulla Björnberg (Ed.), *European Parents in the 1990s* (pp. 10–119). New Brunswick, NJ: Transaction.

Kemp, Virginia. (1987). Mother's Perceptions of Children's Temperament and Mother-Child Attachment. *Scholarly Inquiry for Nursing Practice*, *1*, 51–68.

Kempe, R. S., & Kempe, C. H. (1978). *Child Abuse*. Cambridge, MA: Harvard University Press.

Kempe, R. S., Silverman, F. N., & Stule, B. F. (1962). The Battered Child Syndrome. *Journal of the American Medical Association*, *181*, 17–240.

Kephart, W. M. (1966). *The Family, Society and the Individual*. Boston: Houghton-Mifflin.

Kernberg, O. (1972). *Barriers to Being in Love* (Unpublished manuscript). The Menninger Foundation.

Kertesz, A., Polk, Marsha, Black, Sandra E., & Howell, Janice. (1990). Sex, Handedness, and the Morphometry of Cerebral Asymmetries on Magnetic Resonance Imaging. *Brain Research, 530*, 40–48.

Kessler, Jane. (1966). *Psychopathology of Childhood.* Englewood Cliffs, NJ: Prentice-Hall.

Kevles, Bettyann. (1976). *Watching the Wild Apes.* New York: E. P. Dutton.

Kiecolt-Glaser, J. K., Fisher, L. D., Ogrocki, P., & Stout, J. C. (1987). Marital Quality, Marital Disruption, and Immune Function. *Psychosomatic Medicine, 49*, 13–34.

Kierkegaard, S. (1844/1941). *Sickness Unto Death.* Princeton, NJ: Princeton University Press. (Original in Swedish)

Kitagawa, E. M., & Hauser, P. M. (1973). *Differential Mortality in the United States.* Cambridge, MA: Harvard University Press.

Kitson, G. C. (1982). Attachment to the Spouse in Divorce: A Scale and its Application. *Journal of Marriage and the Family, 44*, 379–393.

Kitzinger, Sheila. (1978). *Women as Mothers. How They See Themselves in Different Cultures.* New York: Random House.

Klaus, M. H., & Kennell, J. H. (1976). *Mother-Infant Bonding.* St. Louis, MO: Mosby.

Klein, Melanie. (1933/1975). The Early Development of Conscience in the Child. In *Love, Guilt and Reparation and Other Works, 1921–1945* (pp. 248–257). New York: Delta.

———. (1957). *Envy and Gratitude.* New York: Basic Books.

———. (1975). Some Theoretical Conclusions Regarding the Emotional Life of the Infant. In *Envy and Gratitude and Other Works 1946–1963* (pp. 61–93). New York: Delta. (Original published in 1952)

Klein, Melanie, & Rivere, Joan (Eds.). (1937). *Love, Hate and Reparation.* London: Woolf and Hogarth.

Kluckhohn, C. (1953). Universal Categories of Culture. In A. L. Kroeber (Ed.), *Anthropology Today* (pp. 507–524). Chicago: University of Chicago Press.

———. (1965). *Mirror for Man.* New York: Fawcett.

Kluckhohn, C., & Murray, H. A. (1962). Personality Formation: The Determinants. In C. Kluckhohn, H. A. Murray, & D. M. Schneider (Eds.), *Personality in Nature, Society, and Culture* (pp. 53–70). New York: Knopf.

Kluckhohn, Florence R. (1962). Dominant and Variant Value Orientations. In C. Kluckhohn, H. A. Murray, & D. M. Schneider (Eds.), *Personality in Nature, Society, and Culture* (pp. 342–357). New York: Knopf.

Kluckhohn, Florence R., & Strodtbeck, F. L. (1961). *Varieties in Value Orientations.* Evanston, IL: Row, Peterson.

Knupfer, Genevieve, Clark, W., & Room, R. (1966). The Mental Health of the Unmarried. *American Journal of Psychiatry, 122*, 842–844.

Kohlberg, L. A. (1966). A Cognitive-Developmental Analysis of Children's Sex-Role Concepts and Attitudes. In Eleanor Maccoby (Ed.), *The Development of Sex Differences* (pp. 82–172). Stanford University Press.

Kohut, H. (1971). *The Analysis of the Self.* New York: International Universities Press.

———. (1977). *The Restoration of the Self.* New York: International Universities Press.

———. (1980). From a Letter to a Colleague. In A. Goldberg (Ed.), *Advances in Self-Psychology* (pp. 456–469). New York: International Universities Press.

Komarovsky, Mirra. (1967). *Blue Collar Marriage*. New York: Vintage Books.

Korner, A. F. (1974). Methodological Considerations in Studying Sex Differences in the Behavioral Functioning of Newborns. In R. C. Friedman, R. M. Richard, & R. L. Vander Wiele (Eds.), *Sex Differences in Behavior* (pp. 197–208). New York: John Wiley.

Kramer, M. (1966). *Some Implications of Trends in the Usage of Psychiatric Facilities for Community Mental Health Progress and Related Research* (Public Health Service Publication, No. 1434). Washington, DC: U.S. Government Printing Office.

Kraus, S. (1979). The Crisis of Divorce: Growth Promoting or Pathogenic? *Journal of Divorce, 3,* 107–119.

Kubler-Ross, Elisabeth. (1969). *On Death and Dying*. New York: Macmillan.

Kummer, H. (1971). *Primate Societies*. New York: Aldine.

Kutner, L. (1992). Parent and Child. *New York Times*, November 12.

Lacan, J. (1968). *The Language of the Self*. Baltimore, MD: Johns Hopkins Press.

Lackey, Pat N. (1989). Adults' Attitudes About Assignments of Household Chores to Male and Female Children. *Sex Roles, 20,* 271–281.

Landreth, Catherine. (1967). *Early Childhood* (2nd. ed.). New York: Knopf.

Lang, P. J., Rice, D. G., & Sternbach, R. A. (1972). The Psychophysiology of Emotion. In N. S. Greenfield & R. A. Sternback (Eds.), *Handbook of Psychophysiology* (pp. 623–644). New York: Holt, Rinehart and Winston.

Lansky, L. M. (1967). The Family Structure also Affects the Model: Sex Role Attitudes in Parents of Pre-School Children. *Merrill-Palmer Quarterly, 13,* 139–145.

Lea, H. C. (1887/1961). *The Inquisition of the Middle Ages*. New York: Macmillan.

Lecky, P. (1945). *Self-Consistency: A Theory of Personality*. New York: Island Press.

Lederer, W. (1968). *The Fear of Women*. New York: Harcourt Brace.

Leinberger, P., & Tucker, B. (1991). *The New Individualists*. New York: HarperCollins.

Lerner, Harriet. (1974). Early Origins of Envy and Devaluation of Women. *Bulletin of the Menninger Clinic, 38,* 535–553.

Lesse, S. (1979). The Status of Violence Against Women: Past, Present and Future Factors. *American Journal of Psychotherapy, 33,* 190–200.

Lester, D. (1990). The Sex Distribution of Suicides by Age in Nations of the World. *Social Psychiatry and Psychiatric Epidemiology, 25,* 87–88.

Levinson, D. J., Darrow, Charlotte N., Klein, E. B., Levinson, Maria H., & McKee, B. (1979). *The Seasons of a Man's Life*. New York: Knopf.

Lewis, M. (1986). Origins of Self-Knowledge and Individual Differences in Early Self-Recognition. In J. Suls & A. G. Greenwald (Eds.), *Psychological Perspectives on the Self* (Vol. 3, pp. 55–78). Hillsdale, NJ: Erlbaum.

Lewis, M., Brooks-Gunn, Jeanne, & Jaskir, J. (1985). Individual Differences in Visual Recognition as a Function of Mother-Infant Attachment Relationship. *Developmental Psychology, 21,* 1181–1187.

Lewis, M., Feiring, C., McGuffog, C., & Jaskir, J. (1984). Predicting Psychopathology in Six-Year-Olds from Early Social Relations. *Child Development, 55,* 123–136.

Lewontin, R. C., Rose, S., & Kamin, L. J. (1984). *Not in Our Genes. Biology, Ideology, and Human Nature*. New York: Pantheon Books.

Lieberman, E. J. (1983). *Acts of Will: The Life and Work of Otto Rank*. New York: Free Press.

Linton, R. (1952). Universal Ethical Principles: An Anthropological View. In Ruth N. Anshen (Ed.), *Moral Principles of Action: Man's Ethical Imperative* (pp. 645–669). New York: Harper.

———. (1959). *The Tree of Culture.* New York: Vintage Books.

Lisak, D. (1991). Sexual Aggression, Masculinity, and Fathers. *Signs: Journal of Women in Culture and Society, 16* (21), 238–262.

Lloyd, Sally A. (1991). The Darkside of Courtship: Violence and Sexual Exploitation. *Family Relations, 40,* 14–20.

Lorenz, K. Z. (1952). *King Solomon's Ring.* New York: Thomas Y. Crowell.

———. (1963). *On Aggression.* New York: Harcourt, Brace & World.

Lynn, D. (1969). *Parental and Sex Role Identification.* Berkeley: McCutchan.

Maccoby, Eleanor E. (Ed.). (1966). *The Development of Sex Differences.* Stanford, CA: Stanford University Press.

Maccoby, Eleanor E., & Jacklin, Carol Nagy. (1974). *The Psychology of Sex Differences* (Vols. 1 & 2). Stanford, CA: Stanford University Press.

MacNamara, D., & Sagarin, E. (1977). *Sex, Crime and the Law.* New York: Free Press.

Madigan, F. C. (1957). Are Sex Mortality Differentials Biologically Causal? *Milbank Memorial Fund Quarterly, 35,* 202–223.

Magid, K., & McKelvey, C. A. (1987). *High Risk: Children Without a Conscience.* New York: Bantam Books.

Mahler, Margaret S. (1952). On Child Psychosis and Schizophrenia: Autistic and Symbiotic Infantile Psychosis. *The Psychoanalytic Study of the Child, 7,* 286–305.

———. (1963). Thoughts about Development and Individuation. *The Psychoanalytic Study of the Child, 18,* 307–324.

———. (1965). On Early Infantile Psychosis: The Symbiotic and Autistic Syndromes. *Journal of the American Academy of Child Psychiatry, 4,* 554–568.

———. (1967). On Human Symbiosis and the Vicissitudes of Individuation. *Journal of the American Psychoanalytic Association, 15,* 740–763.

———. (1968). *On Human Symbiosis and the Vicissitudes of Individuation.* New York: International Universities Press.

———. (1972). Rapprochement Subphase of the Separation-Individuation Process. *Psychoanalytic Quarterly, 41,* 487–506.

Mahler, Margaret S., & Furer, M. (1960). Observations on Research Regarding the "Symbiotic Syndrome" of Infantile Psychosis. *Psychoanalytic Quarterly, 29,* 317–327.

Mahler, Margaret S., Pine, F., & Bergman, Anni. (1975). *The Psychological Birth of the Human Infant.* New York: Basic Books.

Main, M., & Goldwyn, R. (1984). Predicting Rejection of Her Infant from Mother's Representation of Her Own Experience: Implications for the Abused-Abusing Intergenerational Cycle. *Child Abuse and Neglect, 8,* 203–217.

Main, M.; Kaplan, N.; & Cassidy, J. (1985). Security in Infancy, Childhood, and Adulthood: A Move to the Level of Representation. *Monographs of the Society for Research in Child Development, 50,* 66–104.

Malinowski, B. (1927/1961). *Sex and Repression in Savage Society.* Cleveland, OH: World.

Markides, K. S. (1990). Risk Factors, Gender, & Health. *Generations, 14* (3), 17–21.

Markus, Hazel, & Kunda, Z. (1986). Stability and Malleability of the Self-Concept. *Journal of Personality and Social Psychology, 51,* 858–866.

Markus, Hazel, & Wurf, Elissa. (1987). The Dynamic Self-Concept: A Social Psychological Perspective. In M. R. Rosenzweig & L. W. Porter (Eds.), *Annual Review of Psychology* (Vol. 38, pp. 299–338). Palo Alto, CA: Annual Reviews.

Marshall, H. R. (Ed.). (1961). Relations Between Home Experiences and Children's Use of Language in Play Interactions with Peers. *Psychological Monograph, 75.* (Whole No. 509)

Martin, B. (1975). Parent-Child Relations. In Frances D. Horowitz (Ed.), *Review of Child Development Research* (Vol. 4, pp. 463–540). Chicago: University of Chicago Press.

Martin, H. P., & Beezley, P. (1977). Behavioral Observations of Abused Children. *Developmental Medicine and Child Neurology, 19,* 373–387.

May, R. (1986). Concerning a Psychoanalytic View of Maleness. *Psychoanalytic Review, 73,* 579–605.

McEwen, B. S. (1991). Sex Differences in the Brain: What They Are and How They Arise. In M. T. Notman & Carol C. Nadelson (Eds.), *Women and Men: New Perspectives on Gender Differences* (pp. 35–41). Washington, DC: American Psychiatric Association.

McGuinnes, Diane. (1985). Sensorimotor Biases in Cognitive Development. In Roberta L. Hall, Patricia Draper, Margaret E. Hamilton, Diane McGuinness, Charlotte M. Otten, & E. A. Roth (Eds.), *Male-Female Differences: A Bio-Cultural Perspective* (pp. 57–126). New York: Praeger.

————. (1987). Introduction. In Mary Anne Baker (Ed.), *Sex Differences in Human Performance* (pp. 1–4). Chichester, England: John Wiley.

McKenry, P. C., & Price, Sharon J. (1990). Divorce: Are Men at Risk? In D. Moore & F. Leafgren (Eds.), *Men in Conflict* (pp. 95–112). Alexandria, VA: American Association for Counseling and Development.

Mead, G. H. (1934). *Mind, Self, and Society.* Chicago: University of Chicago Press.

Mead, Margaret. (1935). *Sex and Temperament in Three Primitive Societies.* New York: Morrow.

————. (1949). *Male and Female.* New York: Morrow.

Medinnus, G. R. (1965). Delinquents' Perceptions of Their Parents. *Journal of Consulting Psychology, 29* (6), 592–593.

Meltzer, B. N. (1972). Mead's Social Psychology. In J. G. Manis & B. N. Meltzer (Eds.), *Symbolic Interaction. A Reader in Social Psychology* (2nd. ed., pp. 4–22). Boston: Allyn and Bacon.

Meth, R. L. (1990). The Road to Masculinity. In R. L. Meth & R. S. Pasick (Eds.), *Men in Therapy: The Challenge of Change* (pp. 3–34). New York: Guilford Press.

Meth, R. L., & Pasick, R. S. (Eds.). (1990). *Men in Therapy: The Challenge of Change.* New York: Guilford Press.

Milardo, R. M. (1987). Changes in Social Networks of Women and Men Following Divorce. *Journal of Family Issues, 8,* 78–96.

Miller, Alice. (1981). *The Drama of the Gifted Child.* New York: Basic Books.

Miller, N. E., & Dollard, J. (1941). *Social Learning and Imitation.* New Haven: Yale University Press.

Miller, Susan L., & Simpson, Sally S. (1991). Courtship Violence and Social Control: Does Gender Matter? *Law and Society Review, 25* (2), 335–365.

Miller, W. B. (1958). Lower Class Culture as a Generating Milieu of Gang Delinquency. *Journal of Social Issues, 14* (3), 5–19.

Mischel, W. (1966). A Social-Learning View of Sex Differences in Behavior. In Eleanor Maccoby (Ed.), *The Development of Sex Differences* (pp. 56–81). Stanford, CA: Stanford University Press.

Mitchell, G. (1981). *Human Sex Differences: A Primatologist's Perspective*. New York: Van Nostrand Reinhold.

Monahan, J. (1992). Mental Disorder and Violent Behavior: Perceptions and Evidence. *American Psychologist, 47* (4), 511–521.

Money, J. (1961). Sex Hormones and Other Variables in Human Eroticism. In W. C. Young (Ed.), *Sex and Internal Secretions* (pp. 1383–1400). Baltimore, MD: Williams and Williams.

Money, J., & Ehrhardt, A. (1972). *Man & Woman, Boy & Girl*. Baltimore, MD: Johns Hopkins University Press.

Montagu, A. (1940). Anti-Feminism and Race Prejudice. *Psychiatry, 3,* 601–608.

———. (1957). *The Natural Superiority of Women*. New York: Macmillan.

———. (1959). *Human Heredity*. Cleveland, OH: World.

———. (1961). *Man in Process*. Cleveland, OH: World.

———. (1974a). The Origin and Significance of Neonatal and Infant Immaturity in Man. In A. Montagu (Ed.), *Culture and Human Development* (pp. 29–33). Englewood Cliffs, NJ: Prentice-Hall.

———. (1974b). Sex Status, Gender, and Cultural Conditioning. In A. Montagu (Ed.), *Culture and Human Development* (pp. 139–157). Englewood Cliffs, NJ: Prentice-Hall.

Morgan, Elaine. (1972). *The Descent of Women*. New York: Stein & Day.

Morris, D. (1967). *The Naked Ape*. New York: McGraw-Hill.

Moss, H. A. (1967). Sex, Age, and State and Determinants of Mother-Infant Interaction. *Merrill-Palmer Quarterly, 13,* 19–36.

———. (1974). Early Sex Differences and Mother-Infant Interaction. In R. C. Friedman, R. M. Richard, & R. L. Vander Wiele (Eds.), *Sex Differences in Behavior* (pp. 149–163). New York: John Wiley.

Mott, F. L. (1991). Developmental Effects of Infant Care: The Mediating Role of Gender and Health. *Journal of Social Issues, 47* (2), 139–158.

Mueller, C. W. (1983). Environmental Stressors and Aggressive Behavior. In R. G. Gein & E. I. Donnerstein (Eds.), *Aggression: Theoretical and Empirical Reviews* (Vol. 2, pp. 51–76). New York: Academic Press.

Mullahy, P. (1948). *Oedipus. Myth and Complex*. New York: Hermitage Press.

Munroe, R. L., Munroe, Ruth H., & Whiting, J.W.M. (1981). Male Sex-role Resolutions. In Ruth Munroe, R. L. Munroe, & Beatrice Whiting (Eds.), *Handbook of Cross-Cultural Human Development* (pp. 611–632). New York: Garland STPM Press.

Munroe, Ruth H., Munroe, R. L., & Whiting, Beatrice B. (Eds.). (1981). *Handbook of Cross-Cultural Human Development*. New York: Garland STPM Press.

Murdock, G. P. (1945). The Common Denominator of Cultures. In R. Linton (Ed.), *The Science of Man in the World Crisis* (pp. 123–142). New York: Columbia University Press.

———. (1975). *Outline of World Cultures* (5th ed.). New Haven: Human Relations Area Files.

Murstein, B. L. (1974). *Love, Sex and Marriage Through the Ages*. New York: Springer.

Mussen, P. H., Conger, J. J., & Kagan, H. (1969). *Child Development and Personality*. New York: Harper and Row.

Mussen, P. H., & Distler, L. (1961). Child-Rearing Antecedents of Masculine Identification in Kindergarten Boys. *Child Development, 31*, 89–100.

Myers, M. F. (1989). *Men and Divorce.* New York: Guilford.

Nadler, A., Maler, S., & Friedman, A. (1984). Effects of Helper's Sex, Subject's Androgeny, and Self-Evaluation on Males' and Females' Willingness to Seek and Receive Help. *Sex Roles, 10*, 327–339.

Nash, J. (1965). The Father in Contemporary Culture and Current Psychological Literature. *Child Development, 36* (1), 216–297.

National Center for Health Statistics. (1970). *Mortality from Selected Causes by Marital Status.* Washington, DC: Public Health Service.

Neubauer, P. B., & Neubauer, A. (1990). *Nature's Thumbprint: The New Genetics of Personality.* Reading, MA: Addison-Wesley.

Neumann, E. (1963). *The Great Mother.* Princeton, NJ: Princeton University Press.

Newson, J., & Newson, E. (1986). Family and Sex Roles in Middle Childhood. In D. J. Hargreaves & Ann M. Colley (Eds.), *The Psychology of Sex Roles.* London: Harper & Row.

Nicholson, J. (1984). *Men and Women.* New York: Oxford University Press.

Nolen-Hoeksema, Susan. (1990). *Sex Differences in Depression.* Stanford, CA: Stanford University Press.

Notman, M. T., & Nadelson, Carol C. (1991). A Review of Gender Differences in Brain and Behavior. In M. T. Notman & Carol C. Nadelson (Eds.), *Women and Men: New Perspectives on Gender Differences* (pp. 23–34). Washington, DC: American Psychiatric Press.

Nyquist, L., Spence, Janet T., & Helmrich, R. L. (1985). Household Responsibilities in Middle-Class Couples: The Contribution of Demographic and Personality Variables. *Sex Roles, 12*, 15–34.

Oakley, Ann. (1972). *Sex, Gender and Society.* New York: Harper.

Okun, L. (1986). *Woman Abuse: Facts Replaying Myths.* Albany, NY: State University of New York Press.

Olesker, Wendy. (1984). Sex Differences in 2- and 3-Year-Olds: Mother-Child Relations, Peer Relations and Peer Play. *Psychoanalytic Psychology, 1*, 269–288.

———. (1990). Sex Differences During the Early Separation-Individuation Process: Implications for Gender Identity Formation. *Journal of the American Psychoanalytic Association, 38*, 325–346.

O'Neil, J. M. (1990). Assessing Men's Gender Role Conflict. In D. Moore & F. Leafgren (Eds.), *Men in Conflict* (pp. 23–38). Alexandria, VA: American Association for Counseling and Development.

Osherson, S. (1986). *Finding Our Fathers.* New York: Fawcett.

Osherson, S., & Krugman, S. (1990). Men, Shame, and Psychotherapy. *Psychotherapy, 27*, 327–339.

Ounsted, C., & Taylor, D. C. (1972). The Y Chromosome Message: A Point of View. In C. Ounsted & D. C. Taylor (Eds.), *Gender Differences: Their Ontogeny and Significance* (pp. 241–262). Edinburgh, Scotland: Churchill Livingston.

Ounsted, Margaret. (1972). Gender and Intrauterine Growth with a Note on the Use of the Sex Proband as a Research Tool. In C. Ounsted & D. C. Taylor (Eds.), *Gender Differences: Their Ontogeny and Significance* (pp. 177–201). Edinburgh, Scotland: Churchill Livingston.

Parson, T., & Bales, R. E. (1955). *Family Socialization and Interaction Process*. Glencoe, IL: Free Press.

Pedersen, F. A., & Bell, R. Q. (1970). Sex Differences in Preschool Children without Histories of Complications of Pregnancy and Delivery. *Development Psychology, 3*, 10–15.

Peplau, L. (1983). Roles and Gender. In H. Kelly, Ellen Berscheid, A. Christensen, J. Harvey, T. Huston, G. Levinger, E. McClintock, L. Peplau, & D. Peterson (Eds.), *Close Relationships* (pp. 220–264). New York: Freeman.

Phillipson, H. (1955). *The Object Relations Technique*. London: Tavistock.

Piaget, J. (1970). *Science of Education and the Psychology of the Child*. New York: Orion. (Original in French)

Pickens, R. W., Svikis, D. S., McGue, M., Lykken, D. T., Heston, L. L., & Clayton, Paula J. (1991). Heterogeneity in the Inheritance of Alcoholism. *Archives of General Psychiatry, 48*, 19–28.

Plato. (c. 500 B.C./1971). "Symposium," *Dialogues of Plato* (R. M. Hutchins, Ed., and B. Jowett, Trans.). Great Books of the Western World. Chicago: Encyclopedia Brittanica.

Pleck, Elizabeth. (1987). *Domestic Tyranny: The Making of Social Policy Against Family Violence from Colonial Times to the Present*. New York: Oxford University Press.

Pleck, J. H. (1981). *The Myth of Masculinity*. Cambridge, MA: MIT Press.

Pledge, Deanna S. (1992). Marital Separation/Divorce: A Review of Individual Responses to a Major Life Stressor. *Journal of Divorce and Remarriage, 17*, 151–181.

Polani, P. E. (1972). Errors of Sex Determinance and Sex Chromosome Anomalies. In C. Ousted & D. C. Taylor (Eds.), *Gender Differences: Their Ontogeny and Significance* (pp. 13–40). Edinburgh, Scotland: Churchill Livingstone.

Ponzetti, J. J., & Cate, R. M. (1986). The Development Course of Conflict in the Marital Dissolution Process. *Journal of Divorce, 10* (1-2), 1–15.

Pope, B. (1953). Socio-Economic Contrasts in Children's Peer Culture Prestige Values. *Genetic Psychology Monographs, 48*, 157–220.

Popplewell, J. F., & Sheikh, A. A. (1979). The Role of the Father in Child Development: A Review of the Literature. *The International Journal of Social Psychiatry, 25* (4), 267–284.

Potts, D. M. (1970). Which is the Weaker Sex? *Journal of Bio-Social Science Supplement, 2*, 147–157.

Pratt, K. C. (1934). Specificity and Generalization of Behavior in New-Born Infants: A Critique. *Psychological Review, 41*, 265–284.

Preyer, W. (1882/1908). *Die Seele des Kindes* (7th. ed.). Leipzig: Grieben's Verlag.

Price, Sharon J., & McKenry, P. C. (1988). *Divorce*. Newbury Park: Sage.

Pritchard, C. (1990). Suicide, Unemployment and Gender Variations in the Western World 1964–1986. *Social Psychiatry and Psychiatric Epidemiology, 25*, 73–80.

Pruett, K. D. (1987). *The Nurturing Father*. New York: Warner.

Rachman, S. J. (1990). *Fear and Courage* (2nd ed.). New York: W. H. Freeman.

Radloff, Lenore. (1975). Sex Differences in Depression. *Sex Roles, 1* (3), 249–265.

Rank. O. (1908/1952). *The Myth of the Birth of the Hero*. New York: Brummer. (Original in German)

———. (1924/1929). *The Trauma of Birth*. New York: Harcourt Brace. (Original in German)

Ratliff-Crain, J., & Baum, A. (1990). Individual Differences and Health: Gender, Coping and Stress. In. H. S. Friedman (Ed.), *Personality and Disease* (pp. 226–253). New York: John Wiley.

Redl, F., & Wineman, D. (1952). *Controls from Within*. New York: Free Press.

Reinisch, June M., Rosenblum, L. A., Rubin, D. B., & Schulsinger, M. F. (1991). Sex Differences in Developmental Milestones During the First Year of Life. *Journal of Psychology and Human Sexuality, 4* (2), 19–36.

Reuter, M., & Biller, H. (1973). Perceived Paternal Nurturance-Availability and Personality Adjustment Among College Males. *Journal of Consulting and Clinical Psychology, 40* (3), 339–342.

Revenson, Tracy, & Majerovity, Deborah. (1990). Spouses Support Provision to Chronically Ill Patients. *Journal of Social and Personal Relationships, 7* (4), 575–586.

Rheingold, J. C. (1964). *The Fear of Being a Woman*. New York: Grune & Stratton.

Rhyne, Darla. (1981). Bases of Marital Satisfaction Among Men and Women. *Journal of Marriage and the Family, 43*, 941–955.

Richman, N., Stevenson, J., & Graham, P. J. (1982). *Pre-School to School: A Behavioural Study*. London: Academic Press.

Riessman, Catherine K., & Gerstel, Naomi, (1985). Marital Dissolution and Health: Do Males or Females Have Greater Risk? *Social Science Medicine, 20* (6), 627–635.

Robertson, J., & Bowlby, J. (1952). Responses of Young Children to Separation from Their Mothers. *Courrier du Centre International de l' Enfance, 2*, 131–142.

Robertson, J., & Robertson, J. (1971). Young Children in Brief Separation. *The Psychoanalytic Study of the Child, 26*, 264–325.

Robertson, M. F. (1988). Differential Use by Male and Female Students of the Counseling Service of an Australian Tertiary College: Implications for Service Design and Counseling Models. *International Journal for the Advancement of Counseling, 11*, 231–240.

Rode, S. S., Chang, P. N., Fisch, R. D., & Sroufe, L. A. (1981). Attachment Patterns of Infants Separated at Birth. *Developmental Psychology, 17*, 188–191.

Rosenkrantz, P., Vogel, Susan, Bee, H., Broverman, Inge, & Broverman, D. (1968). Sex Role Stereotypes and Self-Concepts in College Students. *Journal of Consulting and Clinical Psychology, 32* (3), 287–295.

Rosenthal, M. K. (1967). The Generalization of Dependency Behavior from Mother to Child. *Journal of Child Psychology and Psychiatry, 8*, 117–123.

Ross, A. D. (1992). *The Sense of Self: Research and Theory*. New York: Springer.

Rubin, J. S., Provenzano, F. J., & Luria, Z. (1974). The Eye of the Beholder: Parents' Views on the Sex of Newborns. *American Journal of Orthopsychiatry, 44*, 512–519.

Rudolf, Mary C., & Hochberg, Z. (1990). Are Boys More Vulnerable to Psychosocial Growth Retardation? *Developmental Medicine and Child Neurology, 32*, 1022–1025.

Russo, Nancy F., & Sobel, S. B. (1981). Sex Differences in the Utilization of Mental Health Facilities. *Professional Psychology, 21*, 7–19.

Scarr, Sandra, & Eisenberg, Marlene. (1993). Child Care Research: Issues, Perspectives and Results. In L. W. Porter & M. R. Rosenzweig (Eds.), *Annual Review of Psychology* (pp. 613–644). Palo Alto, CA: Annual Reviews.

Scarr, Sandra, & Weinberg, R. A. (1976). I.Q. Test Performance of Black Children Adopted by White Families. *American Psychologist, 31*, 726–739.

Schaffer, H. R., & Emerson, Peggy E. (Eds.). (1964). *The Development of Social Attachments in Infancy. Monographs of the Society for Research in Child Development, 29* (3).

Scheier, M. F., & Carver, C. S. (1983). Two Sides of the Self: One for You and One for Me. In J. Jols & A. G. Greenwold (Eds.), *Psychological Perspectives on the Self* (Vol. 2, pp. 123–157). Hillsdale, NJ: Erlbaum.

Scher, M. (1979). On Counseling Men. *Personnel and Guidance Journal, 57*, 252–254.

Sears, R. R., Maccoby, Eleanor, & Levin, H. (1957). *Patterns of Child Rearing*. New York: Harper & Row.

Settlage, C. F. (1971). On the Libidinal Aspect of Early Psychic Development and the Genesis of Infantile Neurosis. In J. B. McDevitt & C. F. Settlage (Eds.), *Separation-Individuation: Essays in Honor of Margaret S. Mahler* (pp. 131–154). Madison, CT: International Universities Press.

Shapiro, R. (1991). *The Human Blueprint*. New York: St. Martin's Press.

Shields, Stephanie A. (1975). Functionalism, Darwinism, and the Psychology of Women: A Study in Social Myth. *American Psychologist, 30* (7), 739–754.

Silverman, M. A. (1986). The Male Superego. *The Psychoanalytic Review, 73*, 427–444.

Singh, J. A., & Zingg, R. N. (1942). *Wolf-Children and Feral Man*. New York: Harper.

Smith, M. B. (1978). Perspectives on Selfhood. *American Psychologist, 33*, 1053–1063.

Smith, S. M., Hanson, R., & Nobel, S. (1973). Parents of Battered Babies: A Controlled Study. *British Medical Journal, 4*, 388–391.

Snyder, M., & Ickes, W. (1985). Personality and Social Behavior. In G. Lindzey & E. Aronson (Eds.), *Handbook of Social Psychology* (3rd ed., Vol. 2, pp. 883–948). New York: Random House.

Spanier, G. B., & Thompson, L. (1983). Relief and Distress After Marital Separation. *Journal of Divorce, 7*, 31–49.

Spieler, Susan. (1986). The Gendered Self: A Lost Maternal Legacy. In Judith L. Albert (Ed.), *Psychoanalysis and Women: Contemporary Reappraisal* (pp. 33–56). New York: Analytic Press.

Spiro, M. (1982). *Oedipus in the Trobriands*. Chicago: University of Chicago Press.

Spitz, R. A. (1945). Hospitalism: An Inquiry into the Genesis of Psychiatric Conditions in Early Childhood. *Courrier du Centre International de l'Enfance, 2*, 131–142.

Spitz, R. A., & Wolf, Kathe M. (1946). Anaclitic Depression. *The Psychoanalytic Study of the Child, 2*, 313–342.

Sroufe, L. A., & Rutter, M. (1984). The Domain of Developmental Psychology. *Child Development, 55*, 17–29.

St. Clair, M. (1986). *Object Relations and Self Psychology*. Monterey, CA: Brooks/Cole.

Stack, S. (1980). The Effects of Marital Dissolution on Suicide. *Journal of Marriage and the Family, 42*, 83–92.

Stendler, Celia B. (1950). Sixty Years of Child Training Practices. *Journal of Pediatrics, 36*, 122–134.

Stern, D. N. (1985). *The Interpersonal World of the Infant*. New York: Basic Books.

Stevens, Gwendolyn, & Gardner, S. (1982). *The Women of Psychology* (Vols. 1 & 2). Cambridge, MA: Schenkman.

Stevens, Gwendolyn, Gardner, S., & Barton, Elizabeth. (1984). Factor Analyses of Two "Attitude Toward Gender Role" Questionnaires. *Journal of Personality Assessment*, *48* (3), 312–316.

Stevenson, J., Richman, N., & Graham, P. (1986). Behavioural Problems and Language Abilities at Three Years and Behavioural Deviance at Eight Years. *Journal of Child Psychology and Psychiatry*, *26*, 215–230.

Stoller, R. J., & Herdt, G. H. (1982). The Development of Masculinity: A Cross-Cultural Contribution. *Journal of the American Psychoanalytic Association*, *30*, 29–59.

Strauss, M., Gelles, R., & Steinmetz, S. K. (1980). *Behind Closed Doors: Violence in the American Family.* Garden City, NY: Anchor.

Strum, Shirley C. (1987). *Almost Human. A Journey into the World of Baboons.* New York: Random House.

Tavris, Carol. (1992). *The Mismeasure of Woman.* New York: Simon & Schuster.

Taylor, D. C., & Ounsted, C. (1972). The Nature of Gender Differences Explored Through Ontogenetic Analyses of Sex Ratios in Disease. In C. Ounsted & D. C. Taylor (Eds.), *Gender Differences: Their Ontogeny and Significance* (pp. 215–240). Edinburgh, Scotland: Churchill Livingstone.

Thomas, A., & Chess, Stella. (1977). *Temperament and Development.* New York: Brunner/Mazel.

————. (1980). *The Dynamics of Psychological Development.* New York: Brunner/Mazel.

Thomas, A., Chess, Stella, & Birch, H. G. (1968). *Temperament and Behavior Disorders in Children.* New York: New York University Press.

————. (1970). The Origin of Personality. *Scientific American*, *223*, 102–109.

Thompson, Clara. (1964). Cultural Pressures in the Psychology of Women. In M. R. Green (Ed.), *Interpersonal Psychoanalysis: The Selected Papers of Clara Thompson* (pp. 217–228). New York: Basic Books.

Thompson, W. I. (1981). *The Time Falling Bodies Take to Light.* New York: St. Martin's Press.

Thrasher, F. M. (1927). *The Gang.* Chicago: University of Chicago Press.

Tinbergen, N. (1951). *The Study of Instincts.* Oxford, England: Clarendon Press.

Tobach, Ethel, & Rosoff, Betty (Eds.). (1978). *Genes and Gender.* New York: Gordian Press.

Toch, H. (1992). *Violent Men.* Washington, DC.: American Psychological Association.

Tolson, A. (1977). *The Limits of Masculinity.* London: Tavistock.

Tooby, J., & Cosmides, Leda. (1992). The Psychological Foundations of Culture. In J. H. Barkow, Leda Cosmides, & J. Tooby (Eds.), *The Adapted Mind: Evolutionary Psychology and the Generation of Culture* (pp. 19–136). New York: Oxford University Press.

Trad, P. V. (1987). *Infant and Childhood Depression.* New York: John Wiley.

Trunnell, L. (1968). The Absent Father's Children's Emotional Disturbances. *Archives of General Psychiatry*, *19* (2), 180–188.

Tuddenham, R. D. (Ed.). (1952). Studies in Reputation: I: Sex and Grade Differences in School Children's Evaluation of Their Peers. II: The Diagnosis of Social Adjustment. *Psychological Monographs*, *66* (1). (Whole No. 333)

Turnbull, C. M. (1972). *The Mountain People.* New York: Simon & Schuster.

Tyler, Leona E. (1965). *The Psychology of Human Differences.* New York: Appleton-Century-Crofts.

Ullian, Dorothy Z. (1981). Why Boys Will be Boys: A Structural Perspective. *American Journal of Orthopsychiatry*, *5* (3), 493–501.

U.S. Bureau of the Census. (1992). *Statistical Abstract of the United States* (112th ed.). Washington, DC.

U.S. Children's Bureau (1914). *Infant Care*. Washington, DC: U.S. Children's Bureau.

———. (1921). *Infant Care*. Washington, DC: U.S. Children's Bureau.

———. (1951). *Infant Care*. Washington, DC: U.S. Children's Bureau.

U.S. Department of Justice. (1980). *Bureau of Justice Statistics (1980) Intimate Victims: A Study of Violence Among Friends and Relatives*. Washington, DC: Government Printing Office.

U.S. Federal Bureau of Investigation. (1990). *Crime in the United States*. Washington, DC: Government Printing Office.

Vaillant, G. E. (1977). *Adaptation to Life*. Boston: Little, Brown.

Vallacher, R. R. (1980). An Introduction to Self Theory. In D. M. Wegner & R. R. Vallacher (Eds.), *The Self in Social Psychology* (pp. 3–30). New York: Oxford University Press.

van Lawick-Goodall, Jane. (1967). *My Friends the Wild Chimpanzees*. Washington, DC: National Geographic Society.

———. (1971). *In the Shadow of Man*. Boston: Houghton Mifflin.

Vincent, C. E. (1951). Trends in Infant Care Ideas. *Child Development*, *22*, 199–209.

Wainrib, Barbara. (1974). Beyond Women's Liberation. *Journal of Humanistic Psychology*, *14* (3), 35–38.

Wälder, R. (1933). The Psychoanalytic Theory of Play. *Psychoanalytic Quarterly*, *2*, 208–224.

Waldron, Ingrid. (1991). Effects of Labor Force Participation on Sex Differences in Mortality and Morbidity. In *Women, Work, and Health* (pp. 17–38). New York: Plenum.

Walker, Lenore E. (1979). *The Battered Woman*. New York: Harper & Row.

Waller, W. (1951). *The Family: A Dynamic Interpretation*. New York: Dryden.

Wallerstein, Judith S., & Blakeslee, Sandra. (1990). *Second Chances: Men, Women, and Children a Decade After Divorce*. New York: Ticknor & Fields.

Ward, L. (1916). *Pure Sociology*. New York: Macmillan.

Warner, Marina. (1976). *Alone of All of Her Sex*. New York: Knopf.

Washburn, S. (Ed.). (1963). *Social Life of Early Man*. New York: Wenner-Green Foundation.

Watson, J. B. (1925). *Behaviorism*. New York: Norton.

Weiner, N. A., & Wolfgang, M. E. (Eds.). (1989). *Pathways to Criminal Violence*. Newbury Park, CA: Sage.

Weingarten, H. (1985). Marital Status and Well-Being: A National Study Comparing First-Married, Currently Divorced, and Remarried Adults. *Journal of Marriage and the Family*, *47*, 653–660.

Weiss, R. S. (1975). *Marital Separation*. New York: Basic Books.

———. (1979). The Emotional Impact of Marital Separation. In G. Levinger & O. C. Moles (Eds.), *Divorce and Separation: Context, Cause, and Consequences* (pp. 201–210). New York: Basic Books.

Wellman, H. M., & Gelman, S. A. (1992). Cognitive Development: Foundational Theories of Core Domains. *Annual Review of Psychology*, *43*, 337–375.

White, Jacquelyn Weygandt. (1983). Sex and Gender Issues in Aggression Research. In R. G. Gein & E. I. Donnerstein (Eds.), *Aggression: Theoretical and Empirical Reviews* (Vol. 2, pp. 1–26). New York: Academic Press.

White, R. (1959). Motivation Reconsidered: The Concept of Competence. *Psychological Review, 66*, 297–333.

Whiting, Beatrice B. (1965). Sex Identity Conflict and Physical Violence: A Comparative Study. *American Anthropologist, 67* (2), 123–140.

Whiting, Beatrice B., & Edwards, C. P. (1988). *Children of Different Worlds. The Formation of Social Behavior.* Cambridge, MA: Harvard University Press.

Whiting, J.W.M., & Child, I. L. (1953). *Child Training and Personality.* New Haven: Yale University Press.

Whyte, W. H. (1956). *The Organization Man.* New York: Simon & Schuster.

Wilcox, D. W., & Forrest, Linda. (1992). The Problems of Men and Counseling: Gender Bias or Gender Truth. *Journal of Mental Health Counseling, 14*, 291–304.

Williams, J. E., & Best, D. L. (1982). *Measuring Sex Stereotypes: A Thirty Nation Study.* Beverly Hills, CA: Sage.

Williams, Jennifer, & Giles, H. (1978). The Changing Status of Women in Society: An Intergroup Perspective. In H. Tajfel (Ed.), *Differentiation Between Social Groups: Studies in the Social Psychology of Intergroup Relations* (pp. 431–446). London: Academic Press.

Williams, R. C., & Myer, R. A. (1992). The Men's Movement: An Adjunct to Traditional Counseling Approaches. *Journal of Mental Health Counseling, 14*, 393–404.

Wilson, E. O. (1975). *Sociobiology: The New Synthesis.* Cambridge, MA: Harvard University Press.

———. (1982). *On Human Nature.* New York: Bantam.

Wilson, Margo, & Daly, M. (1992). The Man Who Mistook His Wife for a Chattel. In J. H. Barkow, Leda Cosmides, & J. Tooby (Eds.), *The Adapted Mind: Evolutionary Psychology and the Generation of Culture* (pp. 289–326). New York: Oxford University Press.

Winch, R. (1950). Some Data Bearing on the Oedipal Hypothesis. *Journal of Abnormal Social Psychology, 45*, 481–489.

Winnicott, D. W. (1960). The Theory of the Parent-Infant Relationship. In D. W. Winnicott (Ed.), *Maturational Processes and the Facilitating Environment* (pp. 140–152). New York: International Universities Press.

———. (1963). From Dependence to Independence in the Development of the Individual. In D. W. Winnicott (Ed.), *Maturational Processes and the Facilitating Environment* (pp. 83–99). New York: International Universities Press.

Wolfenstein, Martha. (1951). The Emergence of Fun Morality. *Journal of Social Issues, 7*, 15–25.

Woolley, Helen T. (1910). Psychological Literature: A Review of the Recent Literature on the Psychology of Sex. *Psychological Bulletin, 7*, 335–342.

Wylie, P. (1961). *Generation of Vipers.* New York: Pocket Books.

Young, Kathryn T. (1990). American Conceptions of Infant Development from 1955 to 1984: What the Experts Are Telling Parents. *Child Development, 61*, 17–28.

Zammuner, Vanda Lucia. (1988). Children's Sex-Role Stereotypes: A Cross-Cultural Analysis. In P. Shaver & C. Hedrick (Eds.), *Sex and Gender* (pp. 272–293). Newbury Park, CA: Sage.

Zilboorg, G. (1944). Masculine and Feminine: Some Biological and Cultural Aspects. *Psychiatry, 7,* 257–296.

Zussman, J. U. (1978). Relationship of Demographic Factors to Parental Discipline Techniques. *Developmental Psychology, 14* (6), 685–686.

Index

About the Authors

GWENDOLYN STEVENS is Professor of Psychology and the Director of Academic Resources at the U.S. Coast Guard Academy in New London, Connecticut.

SHELDON GARDNER is a clinical psychologist in private practice. Together, Stevens and Gardner have presented papers to both professional and civic groups, have written numerous articles for professional journals, and have authored four books: *Women of Psychology, Vol. I: Pioneers and Innovators* (1981), *Women of Psychology, Vol. II: Expansion and Refinement* (1982), *The Care and Cultivation of Parents* (1970), and *Red Vienna and the Golden Age of Psychology, 1918–1938* (1992).

DATE DUE

DATE DUE			
NOV 2 1 1995			
MAR 1 8 1996			
DEC 4 1996			
4-18-97			
NOV 2 2 1997			
MAY 0 2 1998			
MAY 2 1998			
MAY 0 4 2000			
FEB 2 0 2002			
MAR 2 3 2003			
GAYLORD			PRINTED IN U.S.A.